STRUZIKOWNA
Johann

The Stolen Children of Poland

Published in cooperation with

Michał Drzonek, Tomasz Majta,
Ewelina Karpińska-Morek, Monika Sieradzka,
Agnieszka Waś-Turecka, and Artur Wróblewski

The Stolen Children of Poland

Preface by Dr. John Radzilowski

Translated by David McQuaid

Updated Edition

HISTRIA
PERSPECTIVES

Histria Perspectives

Las Vegas ♦ London ♦ New York ♦ Palm Beach

Published in the United States of America by
Histria Books

7181 N. Hualapai Way, Ste. 130-86
Las Vegas, NV 89166 U.S.A

HistriaBooks.com

Translated from the Polish edition *Teraz Jestescie Niemcami.*
Published by Wydawnictwo M

interia

Library of Congress Control Number: 2025947137

ISBN 978-1-59211-662-1 (hardcover)
ISBN 978-1-59211-657-7 (softbound)
ISBN 978-1-59211-658-4 (eBook)

Contents

Recovery

Identity

Preface

In 1939, at the start of World War II, Poland was an impoverished, agrarian nation of nearly 32 million people. Having regained independence only 21 years before, the country struggled to build a viable democracy and overcome deep ethnic and social divisions and poverty. Under other circumstances and given time Poland might have overcome its problems, but in 1939 that time ceased when it was attacked by two of the most murderous totalitarian regimes in human history, Nazi Germany and the Soviet Union. In a manner unprecedented in human history, both sought to destroy Poland and its people—physically, culturally, and socially—to achieve their ideological and political goals. The crimes committed by these regimes are beyond the imagining of many people today, especially generations born in the English-speaking world well after the end of the war. The crimes of the Holocaust against the Jewish people of Poland and the rest of Europe are known and taught in schools at least in broad outlines. Yet, many of the details remain obscure and the mass murder of Polish gentiles in the years 1939-1945 is largely unknown outside of Poland. *The Stolen Children of Poland* seeks to chronicle one of many missing parts of this picture—the German effort to steal Polish children and turn them into Germans or destroy them in the effort. The story is uniquely horrible as any such offenses against the most defenseless members of the human family must be.

Yet, the story of Poland it not merely one of horror, nor is the story contained in these pages. This struggling nation, despite its weaknesses and the immense power unleashed against its people did not collapse or disappear. It resisted and it refused to die, even when abandoned by the rest of the free world. And it survived, outlasting its tormentors and living through 45 years of totalitarian repression before re-emerging as a free nation.

The Polish children whose stories are told in this book followed the same road. What can one say of a 13-year-old girl who has lost her family, alone, abused by strangers demanding she conform to a Nazi ideal of Germanness, who walks into a room with a large picture of Adolf Hitler and rips it down in front of her tormentors knowing that she will be severely punished or even killed for doing so?

Although many of the children taken by the German authorities disappeared or died, the ones who tell their stories here survived. The stories of their survival and courage make this book an essential contribution to the history of World War II.

***

Following the Russian invasion of Ukraine in February 2022, Ukrainian and international observers reported Russian authorities forcibly taking Ukrainian children from parts of occupied Ukraine, sending them to Russia, and offering them to Russian families for adoption. The children were deliberately separated from their relatives and their personal records destroyed or altered to make them difficult to trace. In cases where family members were able to locate their children, Russian authorities blocked or obstructed efforts to reunite them. Russian authorities claimed that the removals were a humanitarian effort for the children's well being. Nevertheless, the efforts to hide the children's identities and to rapidly place them with Russian families with a view toward permanent adoption demonstrated the essentially coercive nature of the program. Additionally, the children effected by this program were deliberately "re-educated" to reject Ukrainian culture and language with the goal of attacking their identity not only as members of their original family but as future citizens of Ukraine.

As of early 2025, between 19,000 and 35,000 children have been taken to Russia from Ukraine.[1] Although the 2022 invasion brought increased international attention to this issue, the Russian program of coercive transfer of children from Ukraine began on a smaller scale in 2014 after the Russian seizure of Crimea. This was a part of a systematic and premediated effort that was a component of Russia's plan to invade, subjugate, and ultimately liquidate Ukraine as a nation. It was not a reaction to the humanitarian conditions caused by Russia's own invasion of its neighbor. Just prior to the Russian attack in 2022, state authorities in the Russian-controlled oblasts of eastern Ukraine began removing children from homes and

---

[1] Karolina Hird, "Putin is Still Stealing Ukrainian Children," Institute for the Study of War Special Report, March 25, 2025, accessed at https://understandingwar.org/backgrounder/putin-still-stealing-ukrainian-children

institutions to Russia proper, under the pretext of protecting them from a Ukrainian invasion.[2]

Russia's campaign against Ukrainian children is the historical foreground of the subject of this important and long overdue book on Nazi Germany's effort to steal Polish children and to try to remake them into Germans during World War II. The parallels cannot be ignored. In both cases, state authorities targeted particular groups of children, often ones in the most vulnerable circumstances—such as those in orphanages or in foster care. Additionally, they targeted children whose parents were in the military they were fighting.[3] During World War II, this meant children of Poles who were involved in the Polish underground, Armia Krajowa or Home Army. In other words, the children selected for this systematic kidnapping already suffered some level of trauma, loss, or separation in their most important human relationship. In both cases, the goal was to radically alter the identity of children, to erase their previous identity and supplant it with a new identity with new families, language, loyalties, and legal status. A crucial component of this re-education was inculcating in the children a hatred of their previous identity.[4] Finally, the methodology for these programs drew heavily on state-sponsored medical, educational, and welfare institutions which while theoretically designed for the good of children and other vulnerable populations, are always and everywhere instruments of state policy and easily turned toward any purpose deemed vital to the state.[5]

It would be wrong to claim that Vladimir Putin's Russia and Adolf Hitler's Germany are somehow the same or that the former is modeled on the latter. *Reductio ad Hitlerum* hinders our ability to understand the unique evils of Nazi Germany between 1933 and 1945 and, equally, the danger presented by Putin's Russia today. Both regimes, however, are totalitarian. That is, the state and those that control it seek to exercise complete and total control over all aspects of society and

---

[2] Nathaniel A. Raymond, et al., "Russia's Systematic Program of Coerced Adoption and Fostering of Ukraine's Children." 3 December 2024. Humanitarian Research Lab at Yale School of Public Health: New Haven, accessed at https://medicine.yale.edu/lab/khoshnood/publications/reports/

[3] Ibid., 21-25.

[4] Ibid., 27-28.

[5] A similar but less well documented campaign has been waged in China against the Uyghur minority by Chinese state authorities. See "Hearts and Lives Broken: The Nightmare of Uyghur Families Separated by Repression," Amnesty International, March 19, 2021, accessed at https://www.amnesty.org/en/documents/asa17/3798/2021/en/

to use that control to impose a particular ideological program. Since the emergence of the first modern totalitarian state in Russia following the Bolshevik Revolution in 1918, totalitarians have sought to control and indeed disrupt the most intimate and powerful of all human bonds, those between husbands and wives and those between parents and children. It was no coincidence that one of the oldest and most enduring myths of Soviet communism was that of Pavlik Morozov, a 13-year-old boy who allegedly informed on his own father for "anti-state" activities. A cult of heroism that included books and statues was created around Morozov as an example for both children and their parents that loyalty to the state and the leader superseded all other loyalties. Whether in Soviet Russia, Nazi Germany, or Communist China, children belonged to the state as future workers or soldiers. Bonds between parents and children, between siblings, with other relatives, or between husbands and wives, were permitted only insofar as they did not conflict with the demands of the state. The state reserved to itself the ability to intervene in or terminate any of these relationships at any time for any reason. Education, recreation, medicine, food, clothing, and shelter for children were neither a basic right nor were treated as loving gifts of parents who worked hard to provide for their offspring. Instead, all these things were provided by the beneficent state and its leader. As recounted in these pages, Polish children who were sent to German institutions ate communal meals under large pictures of Adolf Hitler as the symbolic "father" who provide their daily bread.

Crimes against children, including systematic kidnapping and "re-education" were especially common in Poland during World War II when Nazi Germany forcibly took perhaps as many as 200,000 Polish children from their families and homes as candidates for possible Germanization.[6] Smaller numbers of children were also taken from other occupied countries in central and eastern Europe. This book, previously published in Polish and German, is one of the few efforts to document this corner of World War II and Holocaust history.[7] Although nearly aspect of the war and Nazi genocide has generated academic and popular literature—sometimes in great profusion—this aspect remains unknown to most people.

[6] Various estimates for the number of children taken range from a low of 20,000 to a high of 200,000 which most estimates coming in at the higher end of the range. The reasons for this lack of any certainty about the size and scope of this crime is discussed below.

[7] See Ewelina Karpińska-Morek et al., Teraz jestescie Niemcami: Wstrząsające losy zrabowanych polskich dzieci (Cracow: M, 2018), Als wäre ich allein auf der Welt. Der nationalsozialistische Kinderraub in Polen (Freiburg: Herder, 2020).

Although there are many memoirs of people who experienced the German occupation and genocide in occupied Poland as children, there is only limited literature on the fate of children and even less on the subject of German's campaign to kidnap Polish children.[8]

Why did Nazi Germany target Polish children so intensively? During the occupation of Poland, German authorities could act without any constraints. While the German occupation in western Europe, Scandinavia, or Bohemia was often be harsh, the occupation of Poland was many degrees worse with the Germans envisioning the complete elimination of the nation and its citizens. Jews were to be the first target of extermination with the much larger ethnic Polish population slated for more gradual killing through enslavement, starvation, and targeted murder. Poland's population in the 1930s was quite young with a quarter of the population under the age of 10 in 1931.[9] This meant that am especially large population of young people fell into the shadow of German control.

Poles in the view of the German occupiers were racially inferior. Although Jews were viewed as more racially "corrupt" and thus a greater racial threat to "Aryan" Germans, Poles were also racially tainted. Poles also posed a political threat to German hegemony due to their tradition of resistance to foreign rule, their attachment to the cause of national independence, and their physical presence in lands the Nazi regime considered vital "living space" for the future of the German people. Nazi racial views are a slippery subject due to different pronouncements of leaders and party theorists. Policies implemented by the Third Reich in its various jurisdictions within the Reich and its various conquered lands were based on Nazi racial ideas but often varied in their application and were at times altered especially under the increasing pressure of wartime demands for labor. The result is a fragmented and often contradictory history. While seeing Poles as racially inferior, German racial theory took into account a long history of German Polish intermarriage and centuries of German settlement in historically Polish lands. Thus, a certain proportion of Poles had "German blood" which according to the belief could

---

[8] See Richard C. Lukas, *Did the Children Cry? Hitler's War against Jewish and Polish Children, 1939-45* (New York: Hippocrene Books, 1994), Roman Z. Hrabar, *Hitlerowski Rabunek Dzieci Polskich, 1939-1945* (Katowice: Śląsk, 1960); Roman Z. Hrabar, Zofia Tokarz, and Jacek Wilczur, *The Fate of Polish Children during the Last War* (Warsaw, Interpress, 1981); Czesław Pilichowski, ed., *Zbrodnie Hitlerowskie na Dzieci i Młodzież Polskiej* (Warsaw: Rada Ochrony Pamięci Walk i Męczeństwa, 1972); Idem, *Dzieci i Młodzież w latach Drugiej Wojny Światowej* (Warsaw, PWN, 1982).

[9] *Concise Statistical Year Book of Poland*, 1936 (Warsaw: GUS, 1936), 19-20.

somehow be recovered.[10] Traits like blonde hair or blue eyes among Poles were seen as signs of "German blood" though not all Polish children taken by German authorities had such traits. Another odd twist was that the notion among some Germans that Poles involved in the resistance movement against German rule were suspected of German ancestry. Nazi racial theory was inchoate enough that any potentially favorable characteristic a German might observe in Poles could be taken as a sign of some hidden quantity of Germanness.[11]

Polish adults with potential traits of Germanness were viewed as a potentially serious threat, but children were seen as malleable. German authorities with their implicit faith in science believed with the right program they could turn Polish children with German traits into good Germans. They deliberately targeted children who had already suffered trauma or displacement. The children were in foster care, orphans, or those whose parents were in prison or were slave laborers.[12] Many of the children were young enough that with sufficient brainwashing began to adapt to a new identity and forget parts of their former life, including the ability to speak Polish. This was reinforced by draconian punishment for those caught speaking Polish or exhibiting "non-German" traits. Although being selected for potential admittance to the "master race" might be viewed as an advantage, for those children whose behavior did not meet the standards of German welfare authorities and teachers or who sought to retain their identities, the fate was often death. While older children might be sent to labor camps, younger children could be sent to death camps. In spite of the danger, many children resisted, usually

---

[10] For the sake of brevity, I will omit a discussion of the strange notions of biology, heredity, and culture held by many leading German scientists, doctors, and thinkers of the time. These ideas were not, however, exclusive to Germany nor did they necessarily all originate there. The so-called science of race and eugenics were widely supported among the educated classes in Europe and North America.

[11] See also Lukas, *Did the Children Cry?* 112-116.

[12] On the children of slave laborers and German's children's homes, see Annette Schäfer with Stephan M. Janker, *Zwangsarbeiter in der Diözese Rottenburg 1939–1945. Herausgegeben von der Kommission zur Klärung der Fragen nach der Beschäftigung von Fremd- bzw. Zwangsarbeitern in kirchlichen Einrichtungen in der Diözese Rottenburg-Stuttgart* (Stuttgart, Akademie der Diözese Rottenburg-Stuttgart, 2002), 112-120. German companies using slave labor tried to force the children of these women into German children's homes to avoid the burden of caring for them and to coerce more labor from their slaves. The homes resisted taking in those considered non-German but did accept those who evinced German characteristics who were potentially fostered in German families. In some instances, separate facilities for children of slave laborers existed such as the infamous "welfare department" of Volkswagen, where Polish and Ukrainian children of slave laborers were taken from their mothers and deliberately starved to death.

passively but sometimes actively. In one children's home, for example, older children woke their younger counterparts at night to secretly practice speaking Polish.[13]

The Germans were particularly efficient in altering and destroying records related to stolen children. By definition, the young have a small imprint on public records, and Nazi authorities made a particular effort to hide their kidnapping of Polish children and their placement in German foster families. The situation in post-war Germany also discouraged attempts to document what happened and to recover the kidnapped children. In some cases, children and their foster parents had developed strong bonds and did not want to be separated. This was especially the case with the youngest victims. In post war Germany a deliberate amnesia developed about many aspects of the war and citizens mentally distanced themselves from the country's war time crimes.[14] On the Polish side, the authorities of the new Soviet-dominated government failed to aggressively investigate the cases of stolen children, a subject that deserves further research as well. Compared to other crimes of Nazi Germany, the stealing of Polish children and the fates of the victims remains largely unknown, so that even the estimated number of children who fell victim varies by a factor of ten.

While postwar Germany got high marks for coming to terms with Nazi crimes against Jews and even made efforts to come to terms with its atrocities against the peoples of Soviet Union, the Germans undertook no such reckoning with the genocidal savagery they inflicted on non-Jewish Poles. During the war, Germans broadly viewed Poles as aggressors who oppressed ethnic Germans, a sentiment that drew on a deep well of anti-Polish prejudice that existed for over a century. To be sure, such sentiments were not universal and Prussian and German Imperial policies toward Poles prior to 1918 varied from harsh repression to patronizing tolerance.[15] However, after the 1945 the wartime crimes against Poles were largely

---

[13] S. Sawicka, "Zbrodnia Niemiecka nad Dzieckiem Polskim," *Przegląd Zachodni*, no. 9 (1947), 736, quoted in Lukas, *Did the Children Cry?* 118.

[14] See Nicholas Stargardt, *The German War: A Nation under Arms, 1939-1945* (London: Bodley Head, 2015).

[15] A similar range of German attitudes toward Jews prior to 1918 also existed. It remains fairly common for German and western historians writing about these topics to discuss German attitudes toward Poles through administrative documents with little reference to the mass killing that took place from the first day of the war which was planned prior to start of the campaign against Poland. One important corrective is Alexander B. Rossino, *Hitler Strikes Poland: Blitzkrieg, Ideology, and Atrocity* (Lawrence: University of Kansas Press, 2003).

ignored in a more general context and it became quite common for German authorities to delay or ignore efforts to investigate and prosecute even high ranking Nazi criminals often using the pretext of old age or ill health. If there was little appetite to bring high-ranking SS and Gestapo officials known to have murdered tens of thousands of people in Poland to justice, there was no interest at all in uncovering the story of Poland's stolen children.

The Stolen Children of Poland is a candle lit against the darkness of this topic and the ignorance of what happened that continues to this day. It is also a warning for the present that we cannot postpone or delay uncovering, preventing, and prosecuting systematic kidnapping or other crimes against children by totalitarian regimes in the twenty-first century. The stories of the children in this volume have waited 80 years to be told. We have an obligation to ensure that children who suffer similar wrongs in Ukraine or elsewhere do not need to wait so long.

John Radzilowski, Ph.D.
Orchard Lake, Michigan, USA

"Joey, We Don't Have Parents Anymore"

Janina is seven years old, Irena 12. They are running with their mother. Mom's hair is in long, dark braids. German soldiers are shooting at them from the outbuildings of the Sowa family's burning farm.

Gene, Joey, and Pete are being held in the farmyard. The boys can see their mother and sisters running across the fields. The Germans keep firing and missing.

Their father's beaten and bloody body lies beside the barn.

Had the weather been slightly colder, rising water vapor would have betrayed the ventilation duct only a dozen yards away in the field, where six people being hidden by the Sowas crouched in an underground bunker. It's them the Germans are looking for.

The date is September 1, 1943.

***

"When was the last time you spoke to your sister Janina?"

"Half an hour ago."

***

We drive down a long gravel road leading to what was once the Sowa family farm.

"It looks just the way Dad left it," Józef says. We're listening to a cassette tape made by Janina's husband Rolf, Józef's brother-in-law. He's playing German folk songs.

We approach Wierzchowisko, a village near Częstochowa. Józef waves at a neighbor, Lucyna Kalisz, who inherited the farm from her in-laws. Her backyard still contains the root cellar where Józef's mother and sisters hid.

From here you can see the Sowas' farmland, all 12 acres of it. The millet crop failed this year. But there are cornflowers galore, great bright-blue splotches of them. A miracle.

Wierzchowisko. A grave and cross mark where the Sowa farm once stood.

Right in the middle of this wonder is the lime pit, now marked by a tombstone. The pit into which Józef's mother and father were tossed by the Germans, along with bodies of the five Jews the Sowa family were hiding and of Zyskowski, the resistance fighter.

"All we heard were splashes, one after the other. They spared one Jew to help dispose of the bodies."

– "Did he survive the war?"

– "No. The Gestapo tortured him to death."

Today the pit is covered by a terrazzo and marble slab. The plaque is inscribed: "We ask for a sigh to God." Nearby stands a tall wooden cross. Every so often the two brothers – Gene and Józef – repaint it. It's not an easy job. You need to bring a long ladder and climb to the very top.

Often, the brothers bring along their children and grandchildren. So they can remember.

***

We stand ankle-deep in cornflowers. Farms and patches of woods are visible in the distance. The border between the *Generalgouvernement*, as occupied Poland was then called, and the German *Reich* used to run through here. Now it's a picture of tranquility.

Józef's gaze is directed inward, towards his vanished home. He invites us to join him.

Striding across the empty field, he paces off the distances and gestures. "The house was here, the fruit trees over there as a windbreak." He points in succession to where the cowshed, workshop, and barn stood. "That's where we stabled the horse."

Underneath the manger there was a secret entry, leading to the underground bunker a dozen yards from the house. The ventilation duct was no more than a foot high, while the bunker itself no more than a man's height, maybe less; you had to stoop a little. A seven-by ten-foot rectangle.

"For two years, that was the whole world for these Jews. They used to come out for walks in the evenings, to catch a little fresh air. They ate what we did – mostly sorrel soup, sometimes with a few potatoes if we were lucky."

"Already, they had become our Jewish friends. After all, we were living together, entertaining ourselves and telling stories. When my parents were at work, the Jews used to sneak out to babysit us."

***

"It was the fall of 1941. When we got up in the morning, we saw people burrowed into the straw in the yard. It was a quiet night, but I could see Dad was frightened. What was interesting was that our dog didn't bark, the overnight visitors must have given him something to keep him quiet. They were freezing cold and asked for food and water. Father woke up Mom. Frannie, Frannie, come and see, there are people in the yard," he said.

– "Mom and Dad fed them, but they didn't want to leave. You have to remember, there were informers everywhere, just waiting to snitch to the Germans about Jews walking around the Sowa farm. After talking it over with Mom and the kids – Mom was having none of it, but Dad insisted – we agreed to take them in for three months. They ended up staying for two years."

There were five children in the Sowa household.

"The whole time, Mom was worrying herself sick that one of us kids would blab about hiding Jews. Those nerves literally gave her a stomachache."

***

"At that time, a partisan group was operating in the area, attacking outposts and killing sentries. Right over there, by that row of trees, was the border of the Reich. We had the bad luck that one of those partisans asked us for shelter. That was on September 1, 1943. I remember he was a big, hulking guy, the whole Zyskowski family was on the large side. What was Father supposed to do? He let him stay in the bunker, shut everything down, and went to sleep. At half past four, we woke to the sounds of motors and barking dogs. At first, the Germans went to the wrong house, to our neighbor, Jakub Sączek. Then they came here. Four trucks drive up, they immediately let the dogs loose and set up machine guns in the corners."

"The weather was already getting cool, with occasional frost. We went to the front door. Father was first out of the house. He was immediately struck with a rifle butt. A second German kicked him in the face and Dad fell to the ground, covered in blood. They dragged him beside the barn and started kicking Mom."

"At a certain point Mom came to and started screaming at Father, 'Józek, tell them, because they're going to shoot us all!' but Dad was already too far gone to understand or even speak. He had a broken head and was bleeding from his abdomen."

"They threw all the children into the yard and searched the entire house, barn and root cellar. They stuck riding crops and pitchforks into the straw. They looked down the well, checking its depth and whether there were any other outlets where Jews could hide."

They didn't find anything.

The Germans went into a rage and set fire to the farm.

"They grabbed the youngest, Pete, by the legs and went to crack his head against the wall and throw him on the fire. Meanwhile they're saying to Gene: 'Tell us where it is.' Gene looks at me, I look at him, gripping each other's hands. Not a peep… then my brother gets down on his knees and begs the Kraut not to burn Pete, to give him back."

Józef Sowa shows the location of the bunker entrance on his parents' farm.

"When the Germans found out that there were rabbits and chickens upstairs, they ordered Joey to go inside the burning house and fetch them. When he came out, his trousers were burning. For an instant, they seemed to take pity on us."

"We were stripped half naked, they'd taken our shoes, and our shirts had gotten lost somewhere. It was freezing cold. They kept demanding we confess where the Polish bandits and Jews were hiding. None of us said anything. They yanked our youngest brother away from Gene and threw him on the ground. He was crying and screaming. They were stomping him into the ground with their boots. Meanwhile, I was being kicked and beaten, they even dragged a rifle butt over my rib cage to scare me into saying where the Jews were."

"Not one of us gave them away, nobody said anything."

"Then the Germans took pitchforks and went to the barn."

"One of them was jabbing and shouting that he'd found something. *Komm hier,* everybody! They cleared away the manure and saw the entrance to the bunker where the Jews were hiding. The Germans were shouting: "*Alles raus*!"

"In the bunker, our five Jews were sitting with the Polish partisan, who in a few moments would shoot himself."

"Suddenly, there was a violent detonation, a really big explosion. Everything was on fire, and we were tossed aside by the blast. One of the Germans had thrown a grenade into the house."

The women came out of the bunker first.

"I remember it like today. These were teachers from the Jewish junior high school in Częstochowa – respectable, good-looking women. The Germans grabbed them by the hair and threw them into the fire, because the house was already burning. They threw Zyskowski in, too, but quickly pulled him out because the smell of his burning flesh bothered them."

Then the men came out – Stan, Henny and Leon.

"They were immediately beaten senseless. And when I say beaten, I mean the Germans were pounding them like they were threshing grain: with pitchforks, flails, and potato hoes. The three were already lying there unconscious, and the Germans still walked over their bodies and beat them."

"Mom grabbed Irena and Janina by the hand and started running – across the stubble of the mown grain and potato fields. And the Germans were shooting at them non-stop."

"At a certain moment, Mom went down. One sister fell, then the other. Gene said: 'They're dead now, Joey.' But then they all got up and kept running. It was only 200 yards from our outbuildings to the nearest neighbor, Józef Kalisz.

"They ducked into a root cellar – the same one you can see today in the neighbors' yard. From there they certainly would have been able to see the house burning and the Jews being beaten to death. The neighbors saw and were terrified – they cleared out and hid in the forest."

Mom told the girls to run away. "I can't take another step; I have a heart condition. I'm going to die here."

"Irena and Janina managed to make it to the woods. Today it's a forest, but back then it was mostly scrub and bushes. The dogs found Mom."

"I remember she had long, black braids. The Germans dragged her by that hair over the stubble. They dragged her like a corpse from the gas chamber. They threw her in on top of the others. Mom was pregnant. Family and neighbors said she must have been in the sixth or seventh month at least. They used a pitchfork. Not clubs, not wood, but a pitchfork. They drove metal tines into her belly. The same belly that ached with fear for us. By then she had stopped talking."

"Nobody was talking."

Root cellar where Józef Sowa's mother and sister hid from the Germans.

***

"The Germans collected us, bound our hands and took us to a car. They strapped us tightly to the seats so we wouldn't run home to our parents. But there was no one to run home to, because our parents were nearly dead..."

"They dragged everyone into the orchard. That's when they started shooting at Mom and Dad, lying there broken under the fruit trees, while the kids were in the car. The boys could see everything through the side window. Gene said: 'Joey, we don't have parents anymore'."

"They always shot twice – the second time to finish them off. My brother and I remembered this. After they'd killed everyone, the Jew they'd spared to give them a hand, Henny Cukrowski, dragged the bodies away with the Germans. Since they didn't want to foul the water in the well, the Germans decided to dispose of the corpses by dumping them into the lime pit twenty yards away that Dad had dug to prepare for building a new house."

"My parents had been wanting a new house since the one we were living in was half-timbered, half masonry. That didn't suit my father, who was a qualified carpenter and wheelwright. He said a family with growing children needs a new house. He never got to build it, but the lime was there."

"We could hear the splashes and see the smoke rising, since lime burns easily. Especially because some of the people were already undressed."

***

Józef shows a photo.

"That's my older brother, Eugeniusz, who became a father to us after our parents died. That's me, that's Irena, who died last year, and here's Piotr the youngest, and Janina. The Germanized one…"

Józef Sowa and his siblings (From left: Eugeniusz, Józef, Irena, Janina, Piotr)

Selection

“I had blue eyes”

It almost seems as if nature wanted to protect Łaziska, near Lublin, from history’s merciless steamroller. To the north and east, the village is cloaked by forests stretching beyond the Vistula River’s eastern bank, their foliage enclosing it snugly like earmuffs on a fur cap. To the south, it is enfolded by a series of gently undulating ridges. And to the west, the majestic Vistula cuts through its valley like a giant moat.

Łaziska’s inhabitants themselves took care to seek protection from higher powers to ward off evil. At a crossroads that marks the village center, beneath a spreading maple tree, stands a small roadside shrine. To its bleached cross with a crucified figure of Jesus, a small niche has been attached with an image of the Virgin Mary, today hidden behind bouquets of flowers. But back then, neither nature nor Providence could save the village from the onrushing cataclysm. Łaziska’s coat of arms bears an image of the early medieval hero Piotrowin of hagiographic legend, resurrected by Saint Stanisław of Szczepanów to testify before an ecclesiastical court in a land inheritance case. Piotrowin is silent, however, about what happened to Łaziska in 1942. What little we know of the truth comes from survivor testimony.

Among the village residents that year were the family of Julian Grudzień. They ran a shop and did reasonably well. For baby Julian, born in 1938, the world was an uncomplicated place. His mother made sure he lacked for nothing. Soon the family would grow as Julian’s mom had another child on the way. But history begrudged Julek an idyllic childhood and gave him September 1939 instead.

At first, the shouted commands in German and Russian, the crackle of gunfire, the detonations and screams of the dying were not clearly audible in Łaziska. Horror stories about the Nazi and Soviet invaders came mainly via hearsay and rumor. “In 1939, we had no direct experience of the war. Living where we did, the fighting just passed us by,” Julian acknowledges years later.

Why Zamość?

However, this period of relative peace did not last long. War soon reached out to the Zamość region and Łaziska. And it came in the most brutal form, as the Nazi German war machine mercilessly crashed into a completely defenseless civilian population. The Zamość region had been selected as the testing ground for a special German racial experiment, or *Sonderlaboratorium*. What sort of experiment did the mastermind of this genocidal scheme, *Reichsführer-SS* Heinrich Himmler, have in mind?

Julian Grudzień

"The experiment was German colonization of the Zamość region," explains historian Agnieszka Jaczyńska, who is also Julian Grudzień's daughter. "It resulted from *Generalplan Ost* [Master Plan East], a blueprint for conquered territories that Himmler had commissioned from German officials in charge of settlement and ethnic policy. *Generalplan Ost* assumed that within 20 years, anywhere from 30 to 50 million people would be displaced from Central and Eastern Europe, including Poland. In various stages of the plan's evolution, the expelled population was to be sent beyond the Urals and dispersed or – in the final version – dispatched to special camps, which was tantamount to physical extermination through overwork, starvation, and generally debilitating conditions. The space vacated by deportees was to be filled by several million so-called *Volksdeutsche*, or ethnic Germans. Originally, these were supposed to be Germans from the Third Reich, but also people of German descent from foreign countries who were classified as "recovered German blood". *Generalplan Ost* designated the Zamość region as the first so-called "settlement area" in the General Government.

This genocidal scheme was set into motion immediately after combat operations in Poland ceased in October 1939. The Germans worked closely on demarcating occupation zones in Poland with the Soviets, who were implementing their own barbaric policies of ethnic cleansing and displacement of the Polish population. Discussions between the two invaders went far beyond the question of borders. The Germans also obtained Soviet consent to repatriate ethnic Germans scattered by the winds of history across the former territories of the Russian empire. This "recovered German blood" was to be transfused, among other places, into the Zamość region, one of the areas intended to give Germans *Lebensraum* and make the Third Reich racially pure as well as economically and agriculturally self-sufficient.

The Nazis had not intended to stop at the Polish territories awarded to them under the Molotov-Ribbentrop Pact. Their apocalyptic project for world conquest encompassed the defeat of the Soviet Union and colonization of European Russia as well. After easily overrunning French and British forces on the Western front, the *Wehrmacht* turned against the Soviets on June 22, 1941. Despite initial successes, Operation Barbarossa soon bogged down in Russia's endless space. Colonization plans were predicated on a quick victory, yet the war dragged on. Himmler was increasingly less disposed to wait.

Demarcation of Soviet and Nazi German zones of interest in Poland, Sept. 28, 1939

"Why was Zamość chosen? Geography was certainly a factor, but not the only one," Jaczyńska says. "Himmler wanted to create both a bridgehead and a bastion for the German national idea. Various concepts of how this would work are revealed by the correspondence between German bureaucrats. The geographical area discussed was a belt of territory stretching from today's Baltic states to Transylvania in western Romania, with Zamość situated almost exactly in the middle. It was a very fertile agricultural region, which at the time was an unusually important economic consideration. Moreover, Zamość and its immediate vicinity had already experienced colonization in the late 18th century, when Habsburg policies brought in settlers from Alsace-Lorraine. In 1941, the Germans dispatched a research team to Zamość to determine whether these settlers' progeny had maintained ties with German language and culture. Their findings were negative. The descendants identified as Poles and were entirely ignorant of their German heritage."

Market In Zamość, 1941

In a report prepared for Odilo Globocnik, the SS commander of the Lublin district, it was explicitly stated that the team had only incidental success in finding "Germans". This was unquestionably a huge disappointment to the Nazis, who were fond of cloaking their genocidal activities with pseudoscientific motives. In soon-to-be Germanized Zamość, a key element was missing – there were no Germans. Globocnik could not afford to risk Himmler's displeasure by leaving the matter at that. He therefore ordered a new census of the region's population, which was then used to select 8,000 residents deemed by the Nazi bureaucracy to be descendants of ethnic German settlers. However, the "Germanness" of these people was too flimsy to escape notice. Therefore, Globocnik ordered them to undergo re-indoctrination as Germans.

In July 1941, Himmler visited Zamość as part of an inspection trip to the Lublin district. It was decided to make Zamość an "experimental area" for field-testing broader plans for population displacements and colonization. The city itself, built in the 16th century by magnate Jan Zamoyski according to Italian Renaissance ideals of urban design (*la città ideale*), made a favorable impression in Himmler. The Reichsführer thought it the perfect place for his SS elite, whose personnel would constitute most of its new inhabitants. A complete urban renewal scheme was planned, including restoration of its partially demolished defensive walls that had turned back 17th century Swedish invaders. Himmler's ambitions for Zamość went farther, however, as he wanted the city to be renamed *Himmlerstadt*. Ultimately, the name was never changed. Reportedly, Himmler was advised that if the Führer Adolf Hitler did not have a city named after him, then surely the Reichsführer-SS would not merit such a distinction. The rest of Himmler's plans, however, got the green light.

"From this moment, the preparations started," Jaczyńska said. "In November 1941, the Germans conducted what they called a pilot resettlement in the Zamość region. The displacements involved several villages adjacent to Zamość and affected about 1,000 Poles in all. The Germans had no idea what to do with these people. For a time, they were held in makeshift detention centers, after which they were released and basically left to fend for themselves. However, the deportees had no right to return to their homes, which in the meantime had been occupied by ethnic Germans. More pilot resettlements the following year showed the Germans how to fine-tune the displacement apparatus. In the meantime, a camp for displaced persons was organized on the site of a former Soviet POW camp in Zamość, located on what is today the corner of Piłsudski and Okrzeja Streets. At the same time, it was decided that responsibility for resettlement operations would be shared between various German formations, including the gendarmerie, police, and Wehrmacht, along with units of the Ukrainian auxiliary police.

"I can still hear him shouting: *Weg! Weg! Weg!*"

Actual displacement of the population began on the night of November 27, 1942, when the Germans launched *Aktion Zamość*. The first operation was targeted at the village of Skierbieszów and nearby settlements. Evictions continued steadily through the end of December. A second phase, which ran from mid-January through mid-March 1943, focused mainly on the Hrubieszów district (*powiat*). Finally, a third phase, lasting from June 24 until mid-August 1943, concentrated on removing villagers from the Biłgoraj district. It is estimated that these evictions took as many as 60,000 Poles from their homes.

For each of these deportees, resettlement was a terrifying experience. Shocking stories began to circulate about removals from Zamość.

"The village got tense as people grew increasingly anxious about the possibility of eviction," said Julian Grudzień. "As a young boy at the time, I don't remember much, but I do recall family members talking about the whole situation later, after the war. They'd been expecting to be deported. The resettlement operation for the Skierbieszów district, including our village of Łaziska, had been planned for November 27, 1942. My mother's family lived only eight kilometers away in Wysokie, a village exempted from resettlement, so my parents asked for a cart to take our things. One of my uncles was coming to fetch us when the Germans blocked the roads. He couldn't get through and we didn't get away."

"The resettlements took villages by surprise, especially in the first phase, when nobody really knew what was happening," said Agnieszka Jaczyńska. "Their first warning was when German units cordoned off the village, and after that the net tightened as a squad entered every household. We know quite a lot about how this went from eyewitness accounts. There was a lot of shouting and screaming. People were given 20 minutes to pack a single piece of hand luggage." Jaczyńska's grandparents were given that amount of time to gather a few valuables and household necessities. All the rest, the fruits of a lifetime's labor, was lost in a single instant."

When resettlement came for Agnieszka's father Julian, he was just four years old. The shock and horror of these events fixed details in Julian's mind for the rest of his life.

"I remember a few things. For example, a German dressed in a green uniform shooing chickens through the door. I can still hear him shouting: "*Weg! Weg! Weg!*" ("Out! Out! Out!"). I remember a skirmish line of Germans approaching the house from the garden side. The "chicken" guy and a *Volksdeutsch* dressed in civilian clothes walked up to us. I may not remember everything, but even now I can see those helmets and pistols. For a very long time I used to dream about it, but now that's stopped," Julian says with evident relief.

"When the Germans entered the house, as a small child I was standing somewhere off to the side," he recalls. "Mother packed a lot of things, including her best china. I can still see the whole bundle with an alarm clock sitting on top, one of those round ones on metal legs. And a German came along, smashed it with his rifle butt and swept the fragments onto the floor. I don't know what happened later to all that stuff. Mom packed another bundle. You could take 20 kilograms, but who's going to weigh it?" Julian recalls how his clever mother wrapped him in her own sheepskin jacket. "On her it was rather short, but for me it was a floor-length coat that would keep me warm through the entire occupation," he says with the ghost of a smile.

According to deportee accounts, the German and Ukrainian auxiliary police were often drunk as they brutally evicted Polish families from their homes. "If anyone protested or tried to escape, soldiers had the right to use firearms and shoot Polish civilians, which they did," Jaczyńska stressed. "Everything went by a certain procedure. Men were separated from the women and children, which was a simple way to keep them from resisting or offering support. After being evicted from their homes, the deportees were rounded up at a collection point and loaded on carts or lorries to be driven away."

Julian was still too young to fully grasp the gravity of the situation. "We were being driven to the edge of the village, along a road with ditches on both sides. The water in those ditches was frozen, so I kept trotting and sliding on that ice, just like a little kid," he says, almost apologetic for having fun during an atrocity.

Polish farmers displaced from the Zamość region, winter 1942/1943

After the impromptu skating, perhaps his last taste of childhood innocence, the boy found a freezing, dirty resettlement barracks waiting for him in Zamość. But first, there was the pseudo-scientific racial inspection and selection that would decide how the four-year-old from Łaziska would spend the rest of his life. "People already knew we were headed to a camp," says Julian Grudzień, his words sounding ominous even today.

"I remember they transported us in a lorry covered with a tarp. The road was iced over and slippery so we drove over the side, but it was an off-road vehicle and could handle the rough ground. That's how we reached Zamość," Julian said.

"The Zamość camp is a perfect example of the terrible fate awaiting displaced Poles," his daughter adds.

Four Categories

Secret guidelines issued by Obersturmbannführer Hermann Krumey for classifying inmates at the Zamość resettlement camp separated displaced persons into four categories. The document stipulated that "Polish people delivered to the transit camp by requisitioned transport or lorries" would be sorted "by criteria".

The document goes on: "Poles assigned to Groups I and II will be dispatched (...) after processing by the camp unit of the Race and Settlement Main Office in Łódź (...) to the Reich with the aim of re-Germanification. Families and individuals in Group III classified as capable of work (excluding unfit family members) will be sent by special train to work in Berlin, after sufficient labor is allocated to essential projects in the Zamość district. Hardworking families of good reputation are to be kept apart for assignment to newly consolidated farms. Those unfit for work in Group III, along with all children through age 14 in Groups III and IV and all persons over the age of 60, will be sent by special trains to so-called "retirement villages" (*Rentendörfer*).[16] Families and people classified for racial reasons to Group IV will be transferred as forced labor to Brzezinka."

[16] *Translator's note*: These villages, often emptied of their Jewish former residents, were earmarked by the Nazi authorities in the Garwolin, Sieldce, and Mińsk Mazowiecki districts for the use of deportees. According to historian Agnieszka Jaczyńska, the Germans took little interest in their subsequent fate and left the deportees to the mercy of their new neighbours and the Central Welfare Council (*Rada Główna Opiekuńcza*, or RGO), the main charitable organization allowed in the Nazi-occupied General Government. See Maciej Foks, "Zamość: próba generalna. Rozmowa z Agnieszką Jaczyńską, autorką albumu *.Sonderlaboratorium SS. Zamojszczyzna –'pierwszy obszar osiedleńczy w Generalnym Gubernatorstwie'*" Instytut Pamięci Narodowej, https://ipn.gov.pl/pl/publikacje/nie-tylko-o-ksiazkach/168116,Zamosc-proba-generalna.html

This dry bureaucratic terminology masked some of the worst German crimes of World War II: child kidnapping, forced labor, death by overwork and starvation, and mass extermination in Auschwitz.

The deportees were supposed to be segregated into these four categories during physical examinations at the Zamość camp by a special medical commission. The camp's first commandant, Obersturmbannführer Krumey, assigned a man named Riel to oversee the racial selections and gave him the courtesy title of "Doctor". Riel was assisted in this procedure by a particularly sadistic guard named Grunert. Known as "Canary", this man, along with later camp commandant Artur Schütz, would be remembered as the most brutal German at Zamość. For inmates, the horror began even before the humiliating physical examinations.

"The first selection, separating children from women, took place just inside the camp gates. According to eyewitness accounts there were heart-rending scenes," says Agnieszka Jaczyńska. "Mothers and caregivers didn't want to give up their kids. If the men were nearby, they came rushing to protect their families. It always ended with intervention by the guards and very brutal scenes. Everything happened to the sounds of sobbing, shrieking children. For the young ones, this was more trauma. Children cast into a ruthless killing machine were also forced to watch their helpless and despairing parents.

Another tragedy awaited displaced families at the camp administration building, where the medical board made decisions on life and death. Its rulings were denoted by laconic abbreviations: WE meant transfer for re-Germanization, AA – forced labor in the Reich, RD – resettlement to a "retirement village", AG – work assignment in the General Government, and KL – deportation to Auschwitz-Birkenau.

The physicians had one more task, however.

"During the physical examination, they were instructed to look for kids with Nordic racial characteristics. The children were judged by external appearance, cranial dimensions, the spacing of eye sockets, and hair and eye color. Those of the appropriate age were classified as suitable for Germanification. Such children had wooden badges hung around their necks with the inscription "Ki" (*Kinderaktion*) and were also given identification numbers. They were ruthlessly torn away from their parents and usually taken in an unknown direction," says Agnieszka Jaczyńska.

Zamość camp barracks for displaced Poles

By some miracle, her father was not one of them.

"They hung a sign on me – suitable for Germanification"

"I was standing with my mother before the medical board," says Julian Grudzień. "There were two doctors: a German and a Pole. I was undressed, my eyes were checked, I had to raise my arms, and they examined my hair. It turned out that I was suitable for dispatch to the Reich to be Germanized. My hair was blond, and my eyes were blue, so they put a plaque around my neck."

Little Julian was saved from deportation and Germanification by his mother, then six months pregnant. "Mom began to cry and begged them to let her keep me at least since Father had already been separated from us. After the war, Mom said she was able to persuade the Polish doctor and they let me go," says Julian, who never saw his father again. As a suspected member of the Home Army (*Armia Krajowa*, or AK), he was designated for transport to Auschwitz, where he was murdered. Julian and his family only found out after the war that his father had belonged to the resistance movement and what happened to him. For his family's safety, he never revealed his AK membership.

But for now, avoiding deportation did not mean the end of Julian Grudzień's problems. Together with his mother, he landed in one of the Zamość camp barracks. Conditions there were indescribable. The wooden frame huts were unheated, water streamed through their leaky roofs, and bunk beds made from rough wooden planks were a luxury – in some barracks children slept on mud floors. Disease was rampant, sanitation nonexistent, doctors nowhere to be found, and every day the corpses of people who died in the night had to be carried out of the wooden huts.

"The barracks I was assigned to with my mother had tiers of bunk beds on each side. They were lined with straw, cut up into little pieces like chaff," Julian recalls. "That's how we camped out – lying down most of the time. Conditions were horrible – everything filthy, no toilets. The latrine was outside, suspended on wooden pegs. The whole thing was iced over and sometimes children slipped through and drowned, so my mother always went with me. We got lice from the filth and crowding. I remember they ate me alive along the underarm seam of my shirt. Mom told me to take the shirt off and she started to crush them with her fingernails. That's how I learned to de-louse myself," Julian says. He was not quite five years old.

Sickness and lice weren't the only worry. Hunger gripped the whole camp. Feeding prisoners was not something the Germans cared about.

"On the left side of the barracks entrance was a huge kettle. From that they used to feed us a soup made from horse hooves. I can still remember a leg with a hoof on it sticking out of the pot. For bunkmates, we had neighbors from Łaziska, the Galan family – just the mother and two sons, Gene and Marian, because their father and older brother had been sent on forced labor to Germany. The boys were older than me. They had meat because they'd smuggled a rabbit into the camp. They used it to cook some broth and let me have some. It wasn't much, but Mom said we should be perpetually grateful, because thanks to them, I survived. To this day, it chokes me up," Julian says, wiping tears from his eyes for the first and last time in our conversation. "Anyhow, we managed to live through it. On December 10, 1942, they loaded us into freight cars and off we went into the unknown," he says after a moment.

The journey was a nightmare. "The boxcar had no toilet, so someone knocked a hole in the floor until it froze over. That was no fun," he pauses in thought. "From the trip I remember some railway workers at the Rejowiec station who passed us some hot drinks through the window. I was lucky enough to be wearing my mother's sheepskin coat. Finally, we got to Piława station near Warsaw, and they told us to get off.

Monument honoring child victims of pacification and deportation operations at the Peowiaków Street cemetery In Zamość

"On the far side of the tracks there was a meadow where the locals were waiting to collect us. My mother and I happened on a fellow who lived in Śniadków Górny. He took us home. I remember a frozen pond and ducks. You had to climb some steps to get into the house, and once inside, I could smell a cake baking in the oven. When I saw it there, I was so overcome with hunger that I started to cry. But they wouldn't give me any cake because it was scalding hot, and they were afraid I'd hurt myself. That's the first time I remember getting spanked by my mother. Mom knew the man's surname was Adler, although I can't say for certain whether he was German. He lived alone with his sister and was keen on marrying my mother, who was an attractive woman. Mom had no time for that, since she was still counting on my father coming back from Auschwitz. I think my mother had managed to keep a little money. I don't know whether she gave it to Adler, but he bought us a train ticket to Miączyn, which is just east of Zamość on the way to Hrubieszów. That's where my grandfather, Mom's father, lived. When we got there, they took us to his house by sleigh. The village where my grandfather lived wasn't subject to resettlement. Mother became very depressed. Apparently, I was terrified by the whole situation and wouldn't calm down. That's where we were when the war ended."

Not everyone was so lucky.

What happened to the children of Zamość?

What happened to all those Zamość kids suitable for deportation to the Third Reich for – as they said in the camp – "racial" purposes?

"The fact is, we don't know," admits Agnes Jaczyńska. "Neither I nor any other historian, as far as I know, has found any documentary evidence that would allow us to state with confidence how many children were abducted from the Zamość region for Germanization. There are, however, indirect sources – for example, situation reports from local resistance units, entries by railway workers who monitored transport movements for the Home Army, or eyewitness accounts of civilians who encountered such transports. From these sources, we know that trainloads of Zamość children were directed to Warsaw and beyond into territory absorbed by the Third Reich, e.g. Pomerania. Information on these transports can be found in the underground "Information Bulletin" [*Biuletyn Informacyjny*] published by the Home Army.

Jaczyńska points to some circumstantial evidence suggesting what happened to the children. "Fragmentary information survives about a group of children from the Zamość district entrusted to the care of a special facility on Szporna Street in Łódź, and at another site just outside the city," Jaczyńska said. "We're talking here about several hundred children. Another figure appearing in the literature is a list of 4,455 children compiled by a female employee of the Lublin Central Welfare Council. This concerned resettlement transports from Zamość that were routed through Majdanek in August 1943 and then expedited into the Third Reich. The children were aged two to fourteen. From indirect sources, we know that at least some were abducted for Germanization."

The German decision to abduct the very young was premeditated, because they would take more easily to being Germanized. Infants not yet able to speak were adopted *ad hoc* by eager German families, who often failed to realize their children came from Poland. Older kids, on the other hand, were sent to transitional facilities where they were strictly forbidden to speak Polish and everything possible was done to expunge memories of their previous lives. Only after this brutal process was complete would these Polish children – now given new first and last names and falsified birth certificates, isolated from their siblings and even children from the same locality – be sent to German families for adoption. Great care was taken to cover their tracks.

After the war, the communist Ministry of Labor and Social Affairs created a special office dedicated to recovering Polish children abducted by the Germans. A barrister, Roman Hrabar, was put in charge of the unit. From 1947-1950, Hrabar conducted searches throughout occupied Germany but found no children from the Zamość area. Most had probably already been Germanized, their memories erased, and all traces of their past lives expunged. Any documentation of this criminal procedure was also most likely "purged" at this stage.

Asked whether any documents preserved in the archives shed light on these stolen children, Jaczyński replies: "None. I haven't found a shred of evidence about children who were sent to Germany for Germanization purposes and later returned home." Her father, Julian Grudzień, who miraculously avoided that fate, is one of the last eyewitnesses to this mass kidnapping. "After the war, my dad became a history teacher, and the subject always interested me. I always knew what had happened to my family," Jaczyńska says.

Trauma: Kinderlager Pogrzebin

When the Germans came, my father wasn't home. They took me, my sister, and Mom. They came for him later at the mine.

We were all taken down to Mysłowice, to a processing camp.

The next day they tore my sister and me away from Mom. We were packed into huge lorries and sent to Pogrzebień. I was six.

— Anna Szafraniec

***

They herded us to the edge of the forest. We were loaded into trucks and driven to Mysłowice. Me, my mother, and two siblings – three and eight years old. Not father. He had time to hide. He was in the resistance.

At Mysłowice, they split us up. I tried to fight – I grabbed Mom by the neck and wrapped my legs around her – but it did no good. They put us back on the trucks. I was five years old then.

— Józefa Posch-Kotyrba

***

They came at night. They loaded us into the back and drove us to Mysłowice. Father was taken away immediately with the other men. I spent the first night with Mom, then they separated us. I was put in a group of older kids. One of the women tossed me her two-year-old son and begged: "Take care of Wiesiek!"

The lorries with women turned left, towards Auschwitz. The ones with children turned right, towards Katowice. That's when they were taking us to Pogrzebień. I was 12.

— Halina Skalbmierska

***

We pass the gate and turn down a broad drive leading up to a stately palace. The broad leaves of a chestnut tree are tinged with rich-hued colors from the autumn sun. Across its trunk, about a dozen feet up, there is an elongated scar. It marks where the barbed wire that used to encircle the *Kinderlager*, or children's camp, was once strung. We drive onto a small plaza in front of the building. This is where starving children were forced to do calisthenics every morning. Behind the palace is a garden where the Polish kids worked for 12 or so hours every day. The weaker ones were buried there.

The Palace in Pogrzebień

The palace itself is lovely, built in an early 19th-century neo-Renaissance style. First the country seat of an aristocratic family, it later became a seminary. During World War II, it served the Germans as a detention camp, first for Polish civilians as *Polenlager Nr. 82* and later as a special camp for children – *Kinderlager*. Today it is a home for the Roman Catholic order of Salesian Sisters.

Karina Noga is already waiting for us. She's a smiling, energetic blonde and a local social activist. She knows everybody and has contacts everywhere.

Anna Szafraniec, Halina Skalbmierska, Karina Noga and Józefa Posch-Kotyrba on the palace staircase in Pogrzebień

We are in Pogrzebień thanks to her. A month earlier, she sent an e-mailed tip to the Interia.pl website's editorial offices: "Hi, I have some information about children abducted from Silesia. Please contact me. Karina."

The story she tells is one of horror. "The nuns said that as recently as the 1970s they could hear children moaning and the patter of little feet at night. They were so frightened that they used to go to the toilet in pairs," Karina told me in one phone call.

On the palace steps we are greeted by Sister Superior Teresa Czekała. She's short and round, with a kindly face. "The first Salesian Sisters arrived here in 1946. The palace was badly damaged and bore traces of tragedy. There were bloodstains on the walls, metal hooks in the ceilings," Sister Teresa says.

She leads us to the second floor. Up sweep the monumental marble stairs – an absolute must-see according to the local tour guides. These stairs also appear in the stories of children who survived the *Kinderlager*, but not due to their architectural merit.

On the landing hangs a large painting of the Madonna and Child gazing benignly on passers-by.

***

I remember those beautiful marble stairs. And me sitting on the last step, waiting for my sister.

I was lucky to have her. She was eight years older. My caregiver, really. We slept together on one bunk.

There's not much I remember. But I can recall perfectly those screaming, crying, dirty, smelly kids. We suffered together, starved together, and at night wet our beds together.

I was too young to work. The days I spent crouching terrified on these stairs or hiding in some corner. That's what all the little kids did. And we called out: "Mommy, Daddy!"

But there were just SS men – shouting, giving orders, mocking us.

— Anna Szafraniec

Palace staircase in Pogrzebień

***

In the middle room, cake is waiting for us, baked by the sisters. Karina leaves to make coffee. She obviously feels at home here. Sister Teresa shows us around the place. Here's the room where the children slept crowded into double deck bunks. And there's where the racial board probably held session. Above us are lavish ceilings, studded with ornamental plaster and cornices. Everything carefully sculpted and painted. They've witnessed not just the aristocratic past but the horrors of war. The floors creak. Some of the boards have been replaced, but others were trodden upon by the original camp commander, Kratky, and those hungry kids.

***

> *I remember a big hall and two-story beds with straw pallets. In the morning, we got a cup of black coffee and a slice of bread. Then calisthenics on the drive out front, the girls jumping rope, the boys doing chin-ups.*
>
> *The day I spent working in the garden. We grew beets, rutabaga, and potatoes. Afterwards we tried to cook something from that, but mostly we went hungry. Our stomachs hurt. There was a family of four brothers and sisters in the camp, one of the boys was only six months old. He died shortly after arrival.*
>
> *They said my Wiesiek wasn't going to make it, either. We slept together in a bunk by the window. Even though it was August, the nights were freezing. Wiesiek cried "zhoo-zhoo, zhoo-zhoo", meaning he was cold. I poked a hole in the pallet and stuck his legs inside the straw, then covered us both with a blanket. And that's how we cried and slept.*
>
> — Halina Skalbmierska

***

We go down to the basement where children were abused. Today it's a laundry. The walls are covered with white tiles. Any bloodstains have long been covered over with epoxy glue.

Basement at the palace in Pogrzebień

Józefa Posch-Kotyrba

***

I was very frightened at Pogrzebień. There was a room in the basement with a small box you could see through the window. A child's body was inside. They

> *used to threaten us that if we misbehaved, they would lock us in there for the night.*
>
> — Józefa Posch-Kotyrba

***

Joining us for coffee is Beno Benczew, a historian with the Institute of National Remembrance in Katowice. He's reserved, but with a slight glint in his eye and mussed hair. Before we've finished the first slice of cake, he's added some context to the stories told by Karina and the Sister Superior.

The so-called *Polenlager* system comprised a series of camps for Polish civilians in Upper Silesia. People displaced to make room for German settlers or sent for forced labor to Germany spent time there, along with those suspected of being hostile to the German occupation. The principle of collective responsibility meant that whole families were sometimes sent to the camps.

"The Pogrzebień camp was established in 1942. Initially it was used for deportees from the Żywiec region. Then, after some police and repression operations in 1943, people from the Zagłębie and Małopolska regions were brought there. The idea of creating a *Kinderlager* may have appeared after Operation Oderberg, which detained about 750 people, including many children. Some were sent to Pogrzebień and most likely on 11 September it was decided to set up a special children's camp here," says Benczew.

"The parents of these children were killed, for the most part. They were sent to the death camp at Auschwitz, and some, especially the men, were condemned and executed during their initial detention," he said.

"We have eyewitness accounts from both children and adult *Polenlager* inmates that racial boards were active in all the camps. We don't know what percentage of the children in the *Kinderlager* were Germanized. What we do know is that there was such a procedure, because after the war people from Germany and Austria started showing up and stating they spent time here as children. They were raised as Germans or Austrians but said they knew where they came from. Either they remembered this place, or else their adoptive parents told them the truth," said Benczew.

***

There was an oval room on the second floor. People in white coats were sitting behind a table. Everybody else was naked. I remember feeling ashamed, because there were expectant women and older boys. It was all very embarrassing. Then we were weighed, measured, tabulated and interrogated.

I was classified as Group I – suitable for Germanization – because of my fair hair. My cousin, who was also at Pogrzebień, was assigned to a different group. We cried because first they separated us from our parents, and now they separated us. But in the end, they didn't Germanize me. I don't know why.

— Halina Skalbmierska

***

For unclear reasons Germany the Germans quickly gave up the idea of a special *Kinderlager* and in October 1943 dispersed the children to nearby camps.

"Probably it had to do with insufficient water and sanitation," Benczew says. "We don't know how many of the children sent here survived the war. A few names have turned up, but we're still investigating."

That such research could even begin is largely thanks to Karina Noga. She examined some old papers brought by a man who lived next to the convent. He found them while renovating a building that used to house the *Polenlager* camp offices. The sisters showed the documents to Noga, and she recognized them as a registry of underage prisoners. The names, addresses, birth dates and sometimes dates of death of 220 children who went through hell on earth in the Pogrzebień *Kinderlager.*

Karina handed over the documents to the museum Wodzisław Śląski. She also notified the Institute of National Remembrance.

***

Now we're in the garden, where autumn has settled in. Karina shows where the documents were found. We stroll through the garden and Karina talks. "It was a list of deportees from the Subcarpathian, Dąbrowa Basin and Żywiec districts. Altogether, 220 children through the age of 16, including 12 infants, and a pregnant woman. There were also regulations on food rationing and punishments. For example, the daily allowance for one child was 600 calories, including a half liter of milk and boiled semolina for lunch and dinner."

"We know for certain that eight children died at the camp. They were buried at the local cemetery and their names were entered into the Pogrzebień parish register. But we also have eyewitness accounts that other dead children were buried inside the camp.

Karina Noga is not the idle sort, so instead of waiting for the state administration to react, she took matters into her own hands.

"We did a preliminary survey with ground-penetrating radar and found three places in garden with a 99 percent probability of buried bodies. But only more research will tell us whether they were children," she says, showing the possible locations of the grave sites.

"I began to look for whether any of the former *Kinderlager* prisoners were still alive." Karina says. "I wanted to confirm whether it was indeed possible for children that young to be sent here. I'm a mother myself. I've raised eight kids. I simply can't imagine someone breaking into my house and stealing my children. So that I'd never see them again..."

Working from the wartime addresses given for the deported children, Karina was able to locate Józefa Posch-Kotyrba, Halina Skalbmierska (née Kasprzyk) and Anna Szafraniec (née Szczupider). We have an appointment to see them at the Racibórz Cultural Center, where they will appear in a documentary film to be shown about the Pogrzebień *Kinderlager*.

Palace in Pogrzebień seen from the garden

Thus, we say goodbye to the hospitable Salesian Sisters. As a party gift, we receive a jar of homemade zucchini jam.

***

Anna Szafraniec

The ladies are waiting at the Culture Center. Arriving at the café, we find them sitting together at a table, sipping coffee and nibbling cookies. The conversation is animated and they burst out laughing. It all seems dramatically different from what we will be talking about in a moment.

We get started with few preliminaries. They want to get it over as soon as possible.

They're not eager to relive wartime memories. During the conversation, their eyes are often wet with tears. They pause sometimes to catch their breath. And when they finish, it's with evident relief.

***

Later I was sent to other camps, but Pogrzebień was the worst. It was the first after losing my parents. It takes time to adjust.

After the war, it turned out that my parents were dead. My father had belonged to the "White Eagle" underground group. My mother was sent to Barracks 15 in Auschwitz. By February 1944, she was already dead.

Grandmother took care of us after the war. How did my life go? I'd rather not dwell on it. The memories of a postwar orphan aren't pleasant. For a while I received a pension, but then they determined that my father wasn't fighting for communism, so they cancelled it. We lived hand to mouth.

I feel a sense of rage building inside me about everything that happened. Why me? Why did I have to go through that?

— Anna Szafraniec

The main staircase at the palace in Pogrzebień.

***

Grandmother took us in after the war. Father was shot during a roundup, and Mom died at Auschwitz.

When grandmother died, I was 14. I was devastated. They sent me to a juvenile facility in Krzeszowice, where I finished high school. Later I studied math. My husband was geologist from the Science and Technology University in Kraków. We bought some land in Jaworzno and built a house. Today I have two kids and a pair of grandchildren.

As a small child, the war didn't really register with me. We lived out of town, where you hardly ever saw a German soldier. The horror of what I went through only dawned on me when I became a mother. What it means to have a child taken away from you, when you don't know what's become of him...

—Józefa Posch-Kotyrba

***

Not many people were able to lead normal lives after wartime experiences like ours. After the war, I was rushing to catch up at school. I got married early. I thought I'd make something of myself, but it didn't work out. I had two kids, but I had to file for a divorce because my husband drank.

Now I'm a great-grandmother already. I have six grandchildren.

People often ask about what happened to Wiesiek. After Pogrzebień I looked after him at the other camps they sent us to. We went through a lot together. Somehow, we made it through to the end of the war, and we still see each other today.

—Halina Skalbmierska

Halina Skalbmierska

Łódź: Hell For Polish Children

In 1944 I received a summons to appear in court on August 8, here in Łódź on. Dąbrowski Square. I don't speak German and didn't know what it was all about. Then I got an official document, and someone explained to me that I was losing custody of my children because I was educating them to be Polish. After a few days, some policewomen came and took all three children away.

— Janina Matych[1]

***

When Janina Matych's children were taken away, her German husband was already deceased. After his death, the occupation authorities appointed a "guardian" for the three siblings. It was he who applied for a court hearing and a judgment separating the children from their Polish mother.

Matych's account is one of thousands concerning the Germanization of young Poles in Łódź – or Litzmannstadt, as it was called by the German authorities. The city was a key center of Germanisation on occupied Polish territory.

Łódź was absorbed into the so-called *Wartheland* after being annexed to the Third Reich. Selection of children deemed suitable for Germanization started right away. The search for "valuable blood" began with orphanages, foster homes and families of mixed nationality. "Racially suitable" children were then separated from their less acceptable parents.

***

According to Artur Ossowski, head of the Institute of National Remembrance (IPN) Educational Office in Łódź, the first goal was to "recover every drop of Germanic blood." That is why during the war's early years the racial program mainly targeted children of German descent or belonging to German-acculturated families.

---

[1] Institute of National Remembrance Archive [hereafter: IPN Archive], GK 164/566/8.

After 1941, due to growing casualties on the Eastern front, it was decided that children should also be harvested from conquered nations. It was explained that any "valuable" child should be raised as a German or at least come from German stock.

"By order of the Führer, this city is called Litzmannstadt" – a sign posted in 1940 on Łódź's Deutschlandplatz (formerly "Freedom Square" in Polish).

Research aimed at demonstrating the "Aryan" character of certain nations had already been underway in Germany before the war. This work was continued later in the occupied countries. For example, in 1940, Polish residents of Poznań were subjected to screening which determined that no more than 15-18% of the population met the criteria for classification as Nordic. Later it was estimated the figure could be as high as 20-25%. Hitler of course ordered the estimates to be classified, but they indicated the existence of a pool of Polish children to draw from.

***

Stanisława Kalowska adopted a baby from an orphanage in 1931. In the summer of 1940, the girl was subjected to racial testing. At the time, she was allowed to go home.

On 6 November 1941, while I was out of the house, the German official showed up again and forcibly took the child away, even though she was screaming and tearing herself free. My sister was there at the time and was told she would be arrested if she didn't give up the girl.

—Stanisława Kalowska[2]

***

German efforts to obtain children from the former Polish Republic went through several stages, says Artur Ossowski. The first selections were carried out in areas annexed to the Third Reich, including the Gdańsk region in eastern Pomerania, Upper Silesia and the new *Reichsgau Wartheland*, comprising the former Polish provinces of Kujawy, Greater Poland and Łódź.

Pomerania and Upper Silesia were accorded special status as regions that enjoyed closer cultural and historical ties with Germany than with Poland. Thus, Upper Silesians were automatically given German citizenship. Most were entered in the second and third categories of the so-called *Volksliste*. Category I was reserved for people who had actively campaigned for the Nazis during the prewar period. If parents were registered on the *Volkliste*, their children were left alone.

It required considerable courage to apply to a German bureaucrat to give up German citizenship, because that would initiate a procedure to punish the offending family. Most often, the parents ended up in resettlement camps, the so-called *Polenlager*, or were sometimes even sent to concentration camps or prison. The children were generally removed to Germanization centers or strict regime labor camps.

One of those children's camps, with certain features of a concentration camp, was located on Przemysłowa Street in Łódź. About 30 percent of its prisoners came from Upper Silesia.

Pomerania, on the other hand, had both Polish and Kashubian populations. Germans regarded the Kashubians as a separate nationality and accorded them German citizenship, Poles who had settled in the region after 1920 were subject to mass deportations. Those who remained were required to apply for registry on the *Volksliste*.

---

[2] Roman Hrabar, Norbert Szuman, *Germanizacja dzieci polskich w świetle dokumen- tów*, IPN Archive, GK 162/1277.

Headquarters of the Central Resettlement Office in northeast Łódź, Litzmannstadt, Adolf-Hitler Straße 133 (now Piotrkowska 133)

In the *Warthegau*, the procedure for granting German citizenship was similar and lasted anywhere from several months to two years.

In the General Government, which was occupied but never incorporated into the German state, Germanization in its brutal form did not start until resettlement began in the Zamość region. Mass deportations and pacification operations started in autumn 1942, mostly under the supervision of the Central Resettlement Office in Łódź, now officially renamed Litzmannstadt.

The location of this office (*Einwandererzentralstelle*, or EWZ in German) was a sign of the city's growing importance. From 1940 the Łódż Office began a dramatic expansion under the leadership of SS-Obersturmbannführer Hermann Krumey from its headquarters at Piotrkowska St. 133. It quickly became independent from the Poznań head office and took the lead in resettlement operations in Łódź and Zamość.

It's worth noting that the SS Race and Resettlement Main Office in Łódź was nearby at Piotrkowska 113, which allowed close coordination and free exchange of information.

Łódź was also the site of several important resettlement camps, including the textile patterns plant at Łakowa 4, the men's hostel at Kopernika 53/55, the cotton wool factory on Leszno Street (now Żeligowskiego 41/43), and the women's hostel at the 28th Kaniowski Light Infantry Regiment Street 32. Tens of thousands of people were crammed into these large, factory-sized buildings, including 60,000 local residents.

These were far from the only resettlement facilities, however, Outside Łódź, a camp in Konstantynów Łódzkie specialized in resettlement until 1941. Many deportees from the Zamość region also passed through camps at Zwierzyniec, Budzyń, Zamość and Lublin. Some were immediately sent on to concentration camps.

Piotrkowska Street, Łódź, in 1939

***

In 1940 I was deported from Polesie district, where I lived with my husband, and placed in the camp on Łąkowa Street. Initially, I was supposed to transported to the General Government, but they kept me there as a hospital nurse (...) The deportation train I was on must have contained several thousand people. This whole group was held at the Łąkowa camp for six weeks. Conditions were very bad. The building had no running water, few toilets, and was in terrible shape. Food was brought in from town; it was wintertime and everything arrived cold. If you wanted to wash myself, you had to do it outside, in the snow. There were no bunks, straw was supplied after we'd already been there 10 days. It was so overcrowded that we had to sleep in shifts. (...)

While racial screening was being conducted at Łąkowa in 1940, I often heard whole groups of people being told they would get better living conditions in Germany if they volunteered for the examination, that they would be full-fledged human beings (...) various tricks were used to mislead people, for example, telling them the rest of the family or their husbands had already applied.[3]

— Julia Makowska

***

Arthur Ossowski: "Children from displaced families did not always undergo racial selection. That would have exceeded the capacity of the German administration. However, this should not obscure the fact that displacement was a crucial element in the Germanization policy.

At that time, transports from Kujawy and Greater Poland were being routed through Łódź – mostly from Gniezno, Poznań and Kalisz. We are talking about very large numbers of people.

The Germans quickly realized that deporting, for example, Łódź residents to the General Government would waste an opportunity to exploit these people. From 1941 on, local families increasingly are being split up, with the adults being sent to forced labor deep inside the Reich.

This raises the question: what to do with the kids? The Germans decided they needed to set up screening tests to find out how many of these children were suitable for Germanization. By 1940, they had already built a special racial camp at 73 Sporna Street (now Blessed Aloysius Pankiewicz 15) at the former Bernardine monastery. Children and sometimes whole families were sent there, because we know that adults, too, were investigated for 'racial value'."

Sporna Street were somewhat better than in the displacement camps – less crowding, more food, and at least minimal washing and laundry facilities. But the conditions were still an affront to human dignity.

Racial screening itself was extremely stressful, because people were treated like objects. Craniums and eye sockets were measured, dental work examined, and a medical interview conducted, including determination of blood type and hair

[3] IPN Archive, GK 164/310/2.

color. Everything possible was done to confirm the sick racial theory that we were dealing with sub-humans.

Plaque on Piotrkowska Street, Łódź, commemorating children who were racially selected for Germanization

Reproductive capacities were also investigated. Body shape was evaluated, especially pelvic width. Occasionally there were even gynecological examinations, but these were mostly for older girls. A Home Army intelligence report refers to a "racial and reproductive camp" run by the Nazi Lebensborn ("Fount of Life") organization, which in mid-1941 moved into the prewar "Fabianka" Jewish orphanage in Helenowo (today, Krajowa Street 15). According to Captain Zygmunt Janke, pseudonym "Walter", who ran Łódż intelligence operations for the underground Union of Armed Struggle (renamed the Home Army in 1942), about 500 young people were placed here for procreative purposes. But this is only hearsay. We lack incontrovertible evidence.

We also don't know exactly how many people passed through Sporna. Many researchers, including Roman Hrabar, believe the camp may have processed as many as 50,000 people by the time its activity peaked in 1943. If that assumption is true, then at least 10,000 or 15,000 were given the putative classification of "racially valuable."

***

Urszula Jachowicz was abducted when she was 14 years old:

> *I was caught at home during a roundup and taken to the camp in Łódź on Sporna Street. This was in 1941. They did a medical exam in front of the entire commission, and I was photographed as well. Before we were packed onto a transport, a German official gave us a little speech in Polish. He said we were going to Germany and that we would be Germans there. He extended his best wishes that we would have a lot of children, perhaps even a dozen. I was put on a transport to Kessel and placed at the home of an SS doctor.* [4]

***

Arthur Ossowski: Besides deportees, some Sporna inmates were transferred from the "Security Police Preventive Detention Camp for Young Poles", which today is sometimes called "a concentration camp for kids".

[4] IPN Archive, GK 164/310/2.

Roll call at the Security Police Preventive Detention Camp for Young Poles in Łódź

Girls' barracks at the German work camp for Polish children on Przemysłowa Street, Łódź. Visible at the back is supervisor Genowefa Pohl (aka Eugenia Pol after 1945), who was sentenced to 25 years in prison by a Łódź court in 1974.

Children screened at the Przemysłowa Street Camp were first transferred to special sub-camp in the women's section, where they received slightly preferential treatment – i.e., they weren't beaten, didn't have to work and got higher-calorie rations. From there, they were dispatched to different camps, with the older ones going to Sporna or Bruczkowa, where a Germanization center was operating until 1941, or else to Kalisz. The youngest – aged two at most – went to Ludwikowo or Puszczykowo.

Only after this stage was a child considered to be sufficiently isolated from his prior life to be "suitable" for German society.

SS Doctor Herbert Grohmann, commandant of the Sporna Street camp, regularly visited the children at Przemysłowa.

***

I was born on June 15, 1929 into a working class family from Gdańsk-Wrzeszcz. In 1940, I was deported with my parents to the General Government. A year later my mother died, and my father was arrested, so I was given (I don't know by whom) to a foster family to be Germanized. That's when they gave me the surname Pillersdorf. Because I refused to be Germanized, they threw me into a work camp for children and teenagers on Przemysłowa Street in Łódź, where I stayed from 1942 to 1945. (...) During that time, I was repeatedly injected with kerosene and other substances. (...) After the injections I remember running a fever and having headaches so bad I blacked out; one time I ended up in hospital. The injections were given at the camp infirmary by making the kids count off and selecting every tenth.[5]

— Kazimierz Dybowski

***

In 1943 I was living with my mother at 13 Pagonowski Street. I was nine years old. A playmate of mine, a German girl, called me a "Polish swine" and I hit her for it. Her father served in the German police. The next day the police came and took me to the Bureau of Investigations and then to the children's camp on Przemysłowa.[6]

— Włodzimierz Jabłoński

***

Kids were taken from their homes for the most trivial offenses. (...) The mother of an eight-year-old told me her son was taken away for having matches. A German farmer wrote a denunciation saying he might try to commit arson.[7]

Henry Sierankowski, a driver who delivered food to the Prezmysłowa Street camp

***

Arthur Ossowski: Germanization of children in Litzmannstadt was also overseen by three branches of the city administration: the Social Welfare Office, the Youth Office and the Health Office. The Health Office had two departments: heredity and racial welfare, the latter headed by Dr. Grohmann in 1940-1943.

This SS physician had already earned a reputation for ruthlessness in the T4 Operation, which in 1940 led to the deaths of about 1,500 mental patients from the Kochanówka Psychiatric Hospital at 159 Aleksandrowska Street in Łódź and a similar facility in Warta. The operation was resumed in 1941, when another 200 people were murdered. They were perfectly healthy ex-patients who had been discharged from the hospitals but still figured in their medical files.

---

[5] Hrabar, Szuman, *Germanizacja dzieci polskich*, GK 162/1277.

[6] IPN Archive, Ki 53/1058.

[7] IPN Archive, GK 177/61.

Grohmann worked closely with Lebensborn, which probably operated as many as four nurseries and kindergartens in Łódź on Karolewska, Lokatorska, Kopernika and Przędzalniana Streets.

***

As I recall, it was in 1941 when my German neighbor denounced me for not being employed. My daughter was seven months old. They demanded that I volunteer for work, and because I tried to refuse since I needed to care for my daughter, they took her away and placed her in the nursery on Karolewska Street. I managed to get her back and even had her baptized, but the police tracked us down and discovered where we were hiding. I was beaten and my daughter was placed back in Karolewska, but this time they refused to let me see her. After a few months, after I repeatedly pleaded with them, the nursery informed me that the child had been taken to Hamburg. She was a year old then. No matter what office I went to (...), nobody wanted to give me any more information about what had happened to my daughter.[8]

— Feliksa Dzigińska

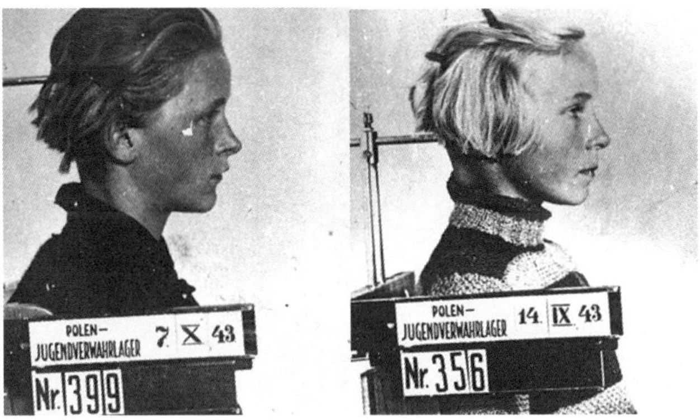

Unidentified girls held at the Security Police Preventive Detention Camp for Young Poles

***

My grandmother received a summons in 1942 to report with me to the Health Department on Piotrkowska Street, where she was photographed and given a

[8] IPN Archive, GK 177/61.

thorough medical examination. The next day I was told to report there again and was immediately detained and sent to the children's facility on 36 Kopernika Street. There were very many Polish children there at the time. After weeks, I was deported to Bruckau [Bruczków – note ed.][9]

— Helena Bukowiecka, detained when she was eight

***

When I was eight, a German neighbor reported to the Social Welfare Office that Mommy was sick and they sent me to Kopernika Street. From there I was taken for a medical examination to Piotrkowska, where I was photographed (...) At Kopernika they taught me German and made sure I didn't speak Polish. After this I was deported to Kalisz.[10]

— Bogumiła Roztocka

***

During the German occupation, maybe 1943 or 1944, I don't recall exactly, I was transported to the facility on 85 Brzeźna Street. (...) The food they gave us was awful –rotten potatoes, for example. When we showed up hungry in the kitchen, they kicked us out and told us to look in the garbage. They drove us to work and made us speak German only.[11]

— Eugenia Szarc, aged about nine or 10

***

Artur Ossowski: Perhaps the most terrible aspect of Germanization was that it targeted families involved in the anti-German resistance. To put it simply, the children of people murdered by the Germans were used as raw material. An example is the family of Dr. Franciszek Witaszek, a physician who was one of the leaders of the Home Army's sabotage and diversion operations in Poznań. The Germans executed him for refusing to cooperate after his arrest, while his wife was sent to Ravensbrück. Of the Witaszek family's five children, three were hidden by

---

9 Hrabar, Szuman, *Germanizacja dzieci polskich*, GK 162/1277.

10 IPN Archive, GK 164/310/3.

11 IPN Archive, GK 164/310/2.

relatives, but two girls were taken away for Germanization. After the war, the mother, who miraculously survived the camp, managed to find her daughters with Roman Hrabar's help.

Candidates for Germanization were also obtained from other sources. For example, of the 105 children who survived the massacre at Lidice, 95 ended up in Łódź. The Czech village was destroyed by the Germans in reprisal for the June 1942 assassination of SS Reich Main Security Office Chief Reinhard Heydrich. To set an example, all adult males in Lidice were murdered and the women sent to concentration camps.

To this day, we don't know what happened to the other 10 children and whether they were Germanized as well.

The Lidice children sent to Łódź were placed in a separate hall at the camp on 41/43 Żeligowski Street, to which Polish medical staff were given access.

From the testimony of nurse Julia Makowska and Dr. Jan Zielina, we know these kids were in very bad physical and psychological shape. Dirty, hungry and scared, they banded together in small groups and shied away from adults. Only after a few days did they start talking to the staff, while the Germans even allowed them to correspond with relatives. Meanwhile, a bureaucratic scuffle over what was to be done with them raged between Łódź and Berlin. By early July, the decision was taken to exterminate them. But by then, seven children had already been selected for Germanization and transferred to the Sporna facility.

***

I remember a group of Czech kids arriving at the camp on Leszno Street in the summer of 1943, there were 88 of them. (…) These children were in a pitiable state, virtually naked after their long journey, so famished they even ate the wrapping paper from the margarine. They stayed only a few weeks until Gestapo cars took them away.[12]

— Julia Makowska

***

Not all children marked for racial evaluation passed through camps in Łódź. There were other Germanization centers. But the city was important, for two

[12] IPN Archive, GK 177/61.

reasons. First, it was a resettlement center, making it convenient to carry out selections for children as well. Second, it had a very charismatic leader in Hermann Krumey.

— Arthur Ossowski

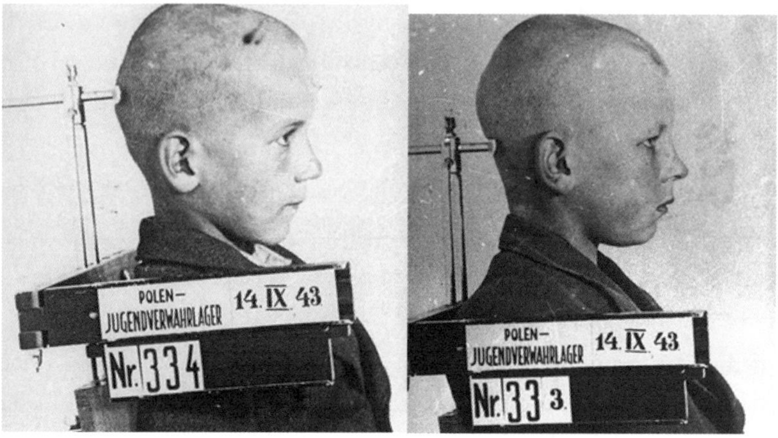

Photo of unidentified boys, prisoners of the "preventive camp for young Poles of the Security Police"

***

What happened to Janina Matych's three children? *After Poland became independent again, I looked for my children through the Social Welfare and the Red Cross. We put announcements on the radio and got tips from listeners. I know from the kids' stories later that they moved around a lot (...) Their names had already been changed in the court order denying me custody. In the Catholic church they had been christened as Halina and Richard, and in the court document they were called Lidia and Berthold. The Germans named my youngest girl Mazga. To this day, I don't know what happened to her. She was only three when they took her away. My older daughter says she was picked out and purchased by a German woman.*[13]

[13] IPN Archive, GK 164/310/2.

14 IPN Archive, GK 164/566/8.

“Abgeschoben” Means “Removed”

Anna, 21, had been more than a year at forced labor in Germany. She worked in a large city in southern Germany, at the home of married university professor. In 1944, she got pregnant with a Pole, who would later become her husband.

Just as Anna entered her eighth month of pregnancy, the professor’s wife denounced her. The Polish woman was taken to the hospital, where she gave birth to twins. Boys? Girls? One of each? The only thing they told her is that the children were stillborn. They were immediately taken away and Anna was too exhausted from the childbirth to protest.

However, a Russian woman working at the hospital, another forced laborer, told Anna the children were born alive. When she started demanding that the hospital staff show her the twins, the Russian woman vanished, and Anna was sent back to work. She was told to forget about it.

Birth and Forget

That year, Nazi racial policy was at its strictest. By late 1942 and early 1943, the authorities realized that children of forced laborers made good German stock. Their first decision was to halt repatriation of expectant women, while at the same time trying to limit the number of “racially undesirable” births.

Under the Third Reich, Germany’s criminal code punished abortion with prison. However, this penalty was waived for *Ostarbeiterin*, or foreign slave workers from the East, while a scheme was approved to set up special facilities for their children. In addition, separate facilities were established for children fathered by Germans and deemed to be of “racial value.” These centers were to be run by the National Socialist People’s Welfare (*Nationalsozialistische Volkswohlfahrt*, or NSV).

The war’s rising toll, however, forced a change in this policy. By Reichsführer Heinrich Himmler’s special decree of July 27, 1943, the definition of valuable paternal material was widened to include nationalities “racially kindred” to Germans. Infants judged to be “racially unsuitable” were to be sent to special nurseries for foreign children.

However, these measures still produced an insufficient flow of children abducted for the benefit of the German nation. Consequently, the Nazis began to consider Polish mothers. A Nazi party circular on January 20, 1944, singles out Polish women among foreign slave workers, stating that if they make a "good racial impression", abortions are not permitted. The nationality of the father in such cases no longer mattered.

***

Anna evidently made a "good racial impression". Her twins were taken away based on a document which probably read as follows:

"The Polish woman A.B. (…) is expecting twins (eighth month) by the father C.D., a Pole (…). Since racially valuable progeny can be anticipated, the mother's application to terminate pregnancy is rejected. After birth it is requested that the children be entrusted to the care of the NSV. Authorized by: [signature illegible] SS-Hauptsturmführer"[1]

A German publicity photo purporting to show how well children born to slave workers were treated at special care centers.

[1] Based on the wording of guidelines issued by the Reich Commissioner for the Strengthening of Germandom in Nuremburg to the People's Welfare Office in Würzburg, 15 April 1944, IPN Archive, GK 162/1277.

2 Hrabar, Szuman, *Germanizacja dzieci polskich*, IPN Archive, GK 162/1277.

By Nazi law, the twins would become wards of the local child welfare office (*Jugendamt*). Custody decisions were made administratively, with no need for court proceedings in cases involving stateless persons such as slave workers. The children were subject to the same social welfare provisions that applied to German children. All these measures served to maximize the difficulty of any future attempt to establish the child's true parentage. They were certainly effective, since Anna never saw her children again.

***

Children destined for Germanization were not restricted to those born in Germany. The abduction victims also included children who had been deported to the Reich with their parents. The Central Welfare Council archives in Lublin contain letters of families deported from Volhynia acknowledging aid packages and requesting help in locating their children.

"Dear Polish Welfare, when they took us from Lublin and we arrived in Ludwigshafen and went straight to work at the factory making gauze bandages, not that it matters, but they took our boy to the hospital and didn't return him. Please ask in Berlin because he hasn't come back. Please help us, Polish Welfare! Little Dyzio Łogowski, 2 years old. Dear Welfare, please, we beg you."

Most often the children were taken to make their parents work harder.

Janina K., testifying in 2003:

"I was born in Wrocław [Breslau] on 28 March 1944 and just a short time later the daughter of the farmer for whom my parents worked – I can't remember the name – took me to Wąsosz. I know this was done against my parents' wishes, it was done so they would work instead of caring for a child."[3]

Undesirables – removed

The "Wąsosz" to which Janina K. refers is a foundling and retirement home on St. Joseph Street in Wąsosz, near Rawicz, which at the time was one of the facilities taking in the "racially worthless" progeny of foreign slave laborers. Children who did not pass racial screening were classed as "unwanted population growth" and

[3] IPN investigation files on the extermination activities of German staff at the children's facility in Wąsocz, near Rawicz, in 1943-1945, S.5/00/Zn.

were dealt with under a completely different scheme than their "racially suitable" peers.

The fate of both groups – racially "valuable" and "worthless" children – was regulated by Himmler's decree of July 27, 1943:

"Because the presence of foreign nationals incapable of work is a serious burden on the state administration and increases the risk of national-political activity among these foreigners, all foreign mothers of children of undesirable race should be deported as soon as they can be easily replaced at work."[4]

Other translations of this document render the key verb as "removed" instead of "deported", which better reflects the true situation. For in reality, Himmler's decree was a death sentence for Polish infants and other foreign children.

What were these "care facilities for foreign children" like? Perhaps the best description is by the German local historian Joachim Woock, who in a work about the Verden district in Lower Saxony writes that these infants were "nursed to death."

Newborns were kept in conditions calculated to induce slow death by starvation, while at the same time enduring extra suffering imposed by the need to keep their mothers quiet. It was decided that simply disposing of the infants risked unpredictable reactions from their mothers, hurting their motivation and productivity at work. Various maladies were therefore invented to help explain infant deaths. Most often, the death certificates cite something called "hospitalism," an illness supposedly caused by poor sanitary conditions. Debility and gastric disorders are also listed. All were an obvious smokescreen. The real cause of death was starvation.

In practice, what emerges from testimony gathered by the Central Commission for the Investigation of German Crimes on the extermination practiced by German personnel at the Wąsosz children's facility in 1943-1945 is a horrifying picture of children's suffering:

---

[4] July 27, 1943 decree of Reichsführer SS and German Police Chief Heinrich Himmler on the treatment of pregnant foreign workers (translated in the IPN investigation files on murders committed by German Nazi personnel in 1943-1945 of Polish children born to slave workers in the Third Reich), S.58/03/Zn.

Two large rooms, their floors strewn with tightly bunched straw pallets on which children sat or lay down. The kids ranged from newborns to five-year-olds. All are exhausted, too weak to move.

Cemetery in Braunschweig dedicated to the memory of infant victims

The children don't speak. Some are unable; the rest are frightened. Speaking Polish is punishable by beatings. Only German is permitted.

The children are dressed in rags and their heads are shaved bald. They are filthy. Through holes in their tattered clothing, open sores are visible, and sometimes wounds going straight to the bone. The rooms aren't heated, so in winter they freeze.

The kids are frightened, especially of light and of loud noises. But mainly they're hungry. The daily ration for infants is a half liter of milk and a single sugar cube. Older children are fed boiled carrots and turnips from a wooden trough.

Deaths are frequent. When that happens, the corpses are often left lying for hours alongside those still living. Bodies are collected once a day. They are packed into wooden crates and taken by wheelbarrow to the cemetery. Then the empty crates are wheeled back.

The facility is supervised by Lutheran sisters. Their mother superior is Marta "Borgia" Götzler.

***

The Wąsosz center took children of slave workers from Lower Silesia, then part of the Third Reich. The facility was founded in June 1943. By April 1945, it had taken in at least 485 Polish children. Of these, 39 survived.

The facility accepted children born in Germany but also those deported with their families for forced labor. Most likely due to the presence of this second group, racial screening was also conducted at the Wąsosz nursery.

Walentyna H., an employee at the Wąsosz Children's Home, testified in 1994: "I was told by Józefa Zacharewicz, since deceased, who had worked as a cleaning lady at the Home during the German occupation, that the personnel there were killing children. They gave the children injections, after which the kids died. They'd be buried in the evening at the cemetery in Wąsosz or at Góra Śląska. Children with blond hair and blue eyes were left alone. The ones with black hair and dark eyes were killed. (…) From Zofia Mocha, also deceased, I heard that children at the center were screened and those unsuitable for Germanization were killed."[5]

Jan B., born in January 1940, the oldest of 39 Wąsosz survivors, testifying in 1997: "I remember sleeping on a wooden floor, one right next to another. I don't recall having anything to cover ourselves. I felt hungry. They were always doing selections. (…) Some adults would show up and take the kids away."[6]

Calculated Cruelty

A similarly terrifying picture emerges from the testimony of Ernst Wirtz, an employee at one of the Krupp factories. This leading Nazi armaments group was operating 57 forced labor camps by mid-1943. During the 10th Nuremberg Trial, Wirtz described what he had seen at one of these camps – in Dinslaken, near Essen. The work camp there had a special facility for children of foreign slave workers.

"Q: What did the witness see in the barracks where children were housed?

A: The children were malnourished. I didn't see one child whose arm or forearm was thicker than my thumb.

Q: How old were the children?

---

[5] IPN investigation files on the extermination activities of German staff …

[6] IPN investigation files on the extermination activities of German staff …

A: From newborns to two years.

Q: Under what conditions were the children being kept when the witness saw them at the Voerde camp?

A: They were lying on prison-type bunks. The beds had rubber sheets and the children were completely naked.

Q: Did the women slave laborers tell the witness how many children died each day?

A: Yes, they said 50 or 60 children died each day and about the same number were born, since there was a steady supply of new women workers and their children from the East.

Q: What happened to the children of those Eastern workers? Did they say what happened with the children who died?

A: I requested the translator to ask them why so many children were dying and whether they were buried; the translator answered that their bodies were cremated inside the camp."[7]

Wirtz's testimony was confirmed by Lorenz Schneider, the director of the work camp at Voerde West. Schneider said he was horrified by the high child mortality rate. He was allegedly informed by the camp doctor that the cause was malnutrition, especially insufficient milk and fats. Krupp management knew how many children were dying, yet no inquiries were made. That led Schneider to suspect that the deaths were intentional.

[7] Roman Hrabar, *Rabunek dzieci w celach germanizacji i zagłada polskich niemowląt w III Rzeszy*, IPN Archive, Gd 637/33/DVD.

A sobbing Polish woman tells US soldiers about her experiences as a slave worker in Augsburg, April 1945

***

The extermination of "racially worthless" children was carried out at places like Wąsosz and Voerde. Mothers were compelled to give up their children. Newborns were taken from their mothers immediately after birth, while the women were forced to return to work. Slave workers often had their wages docked to finance the operations of these children's "death mills." A letter survives from the mayor of Verden advising one of the companies to deduct "1 Reichsmark from the November earnings of every Eastern worker in the Verden district, rising to 2 Reichsmarks from December 1, 1943" in order to "equip and maintain" children's facilities. In addition, local firms deducted 40 percent from the wages of parents whose children remained with them on site.[8]

[8] Joachim Woock, *Przymusowa praca zagranicznych robotników na terenie regionu Verden nad Aller (1939–1945);* IPN investigation files on murders committed by German Nazi personnel, S. 58/03/Zn.

In most cases, parents were not allowed to see their children at all. Permissions to visit were exceedingly rare.

Helena O., born in November 1920, deported for forced labor to the Trzebnica area, testifying in 1993: "On Feb. 12, 1942, a slave worker just like myself gave me a lift on his cart, which was carrying manure, to the hospital at Trzebnica. There I was placed in a lavatory. On the morning of Feb. 13, 1942, I gave birth to my daughter Dorota. A nun by the name of Maria took care of me, who was the mother superior of the other nurses. (…) I stayed there for nine days. On the tenth, an SS man arrived with a nun from an orphanage or children's home. They took my daughter without saying anything. I was sent back to the farmer."[9]

Helena O. belonged to a rather small group of Polish women who were allowed to visit their children: "Until August 1942, I was allowed one visit a month. There were 100 or perhaps many more children at the orphanage, newborns and several months old. I don't know what nationality. In these small rooms there were wicker baskets shaped like little bathtubs, supported on bars or shelves. In the baskets were children. Some were wrapped in rags. The children were emaciated and malnourished, if truth be told. I was allowed to view my daughter for half an hour, but I wasn't allowed to hold her in my arms."[10]

Helena O.'s daughter ended up at Wąsosz. She was allowed to visit on three occasions – the last in October 1944. "My daughter was in a bad way. She was malnourished." Later the Germans transported Helena O. to Czechoslovakia, where she lived to see the end of the war. It wasn't until 1952 that she managed to find her daughter in Rawicz. The court battle to regain custody from her foster parents lasted until 1954.

Janina K.'s mother visited her four times at Wąsosz, on average once a month.

K.: "The first time she saw me in August 1944, I know she was only allowed to hold me when a guard was present. I know I was thin and that mother wasn't allowed to put me in a diaper or take me outside. Mom could hear crying children. When she asked the sister why I was so skinny, the sister replied: 'You're slender, too.'"[11]

---

[9] IPN investigation files on murders committed by German Nazi personnel…

[10] IPN investigation files on murders committed by German Nazi personnel…

[11] IPN investigation files on murders committed by German Nazi personnel…

***

The cruelty involved in gradually starving children to death was evident even to the Nazi dignitaries who occasionally inspected facilities for the "racially worthless." Among other evidence, there is a letter to Himmler dated Aug. 11, 1943, from SS-Grupenführer Erich Hilgenfeldt, written after his visit to a facility at Spital am Phyrn in Austria: "During the inspection I determined that all the infants in the facility were malnourished, owing to a decision by the local rationing office, as I was informed by SS-Oberführer Langoth, to allocate only a half liter of whole milk and one and a half sugar cubes per child per day. On such rations, infants must surely die of malnutrition after several months."[12]

From this extermination of babies, Hilgenfeldt drew a terrifyingly cold conclusion. "There are only two possibilities. Either there is an unwillingness to keep these children alive – in which case they should not be killed by diverting large quantities of milk from the general food supply, since there are other ways to accomplish this without pain and torment. Or else the intention is to raise these children for exploitation as a labor resource – in which case, they should be fed sufficiently to ensure they will be fully fit to work".[13]

It is unclear whether and how Himmler responded. What we do know is that extermination in this form continued until the end of the war.

A crime of unknown scale

The true scale of the operation to Germanize or exterminate Polish infants born in the Third Reich remains unknown to this day. The Allied occupation authorities failed to take up the cases in the immediate postwar period, when they would still have been possible to investigate. We don't even know how many children were born in Germany and Austria to Polish women sent there as forced laborers.

Roman Hrabar, who was the first researcher to describe the extermination of slave workers' children, says only that on the instructions of the military governments in the British and American occupation zones, about 40,000 birth certificates were located for such children. We don't know how many of these were live

[12] Hrabar, Szuman, *Germanizacja dzieci…*

[13] Hrabar, Szuman, *Germanizacja dzieci…*

births. We do know, however, that not all births were registered and not every document was submitted.

We also don't know the exact number of facilities engaged in the killing of slave workers' children. According to some sources, the total could be as high as 400.

Some idea of the scale of these crimes against Polish children can be gleaned from the archives of various centers which the Nazis failed to destroy before they were seized in the Allied advance. For example, of the 800 children who passed through the Braunschweig maternity center for Polish women and other Eastern workers after May 1943, approximately 400 died. Almost 60 percent of the children born at Laberweinting were exterminated, more than 40 percent at Voerde-West, and roughly half of the children at Indersdorf near Dachau. The infant death toll was 152 at Burgkirchen/Alz, between 250 and 350 at Rühen, and 132 in the Verden district (which included separate facilities at Cluvenhagen, Armsen, Beppen, Otterstedt, Eitze and Dörverden). Hundreds of children were born at a special camp for pregnant women at Pfaffenwald. Their fate is unknown.

Researchers estimate that death rate was about 50 percent at the facilities for which we have any data, while in some places it approached 90 percent.

Files from the murder investigation into the deaths of slave workers' children include an entry concerning a "storage unit for Poles" in Cluvenhagen. The facility was located in a former pigsty. Of its 37 inmates, 23 died, including 21 Polish children.

Marian Ś., just 13 months old, arrived at Cluvenhage in February 1945. One night, his father sneaked into the pigsty.

As Marian Ś. described in a letter to Joachim Woock in 2001: "When my father entered the pigsty, he was stunned by what he saw. It was 11 p.m. Some of the children were asleep, others were crying, and I was the only one standing up and hanging on to the side of my crib. I was crying, too, and rocking back and forth. My crib was at the end of the row on the left-hand side. The exterior wall was about six feet away from my bed, and beyond that the orphanage staff was holding a loud party (...) The place wasn't heated at all, and partly due to the cold draft from the door, I had caught pneumonia."

Soon afterwards, thanks to the intercession of their German employer, Marian's parents were able to collect him.

Kazimiera J. was 20 years old when she gave birth to a daughter in June 1944 and was assigned menial duties at Cluvenhagen: "Life there was poor and sad.

Rations were thin and meagre, just a half liter of skim milk per infant (...), almost no diapers or blouses for the kids. A lot of them died from food poisoning. There was no pediatric care – Dr Kohlschuetter said he couldn't abide Polish kids. Mothers could come visit their children for two hours on Sundays. The kids slept in beds or cradles."

Memorial plaque at Velpke cemetery to murdered Polish and Russian infants

There is also information about a facility at Velpke where at least 84 children died from May to December 1944. Among them was eight-month-old Bruno, whom his mother had tried to save by entrusting him to Emma Hoppe, a German woman. Hoppe lived on Velpke's main street and often watched the slave workers visiting their "racially worthless" children at the nursery. She never said a word until Weronika Plutkacy – a Polish woman ordered to give up her baby son – turned to her as a last resort. Completely desperate, Plutkacy knocked on Hoppe's door and asked her to take the child. The German woman agreed. But after three days the police appeared and threatened Hoppe with punishment unless she handed over the boy.

Testifying at the Eighth Nuremberg trail, Hoppe stated that she went the next day to visit Bruno.

Q: "When you brought the child to the nursery on Sunday, did you leave food for him?

A: Yes, I left a bottle of milk.

Q: What did you see when you arrived Monday?

A: The same milk in the bottle, but it had gone sour.

Q: You said you visited again on Wednesday.

A: Yes.

Q: Can you describe to the Court the conditions in that nursery?

A: When I entered, the first thing I noticed was that it was filthy.

Q: Could you provide more detail?

A: Right by the entrance was a kitchen, where it was much too hot, and beyond that a large room, which because of the weather was also stifling. I saw the child lying there naked and dirty. He was lying in a crate – all the children were in crates. The pallets and covers were soiled and very dirty.

Q: Do you mean to say that every child had its own crate?

A: Yes.

Q: And the children were lying there on mattresses?

A: No, they were on straw pallets.

Q: What was the children's condition?

A: From what I could tell, there were completely famished and neglected.

Q: Were there any visible signs on the children that would indicate neglect?

A: They were stick-thin and had faces like old people."[14]

Emma Hoppe saw Bruno just once more, some three weeks later. She went to the nursery with Weronika after hearing the boy was ill. They weren't allowed inside. Bruno was brought to the window for a moment so they could see him. Two weeks later, he was dead. Bruno's mother wasn't notified. Only after her son was buried did she learn about his death from Emma.

Nobody is Guilty

The children from Wąsosz who survived until liberation owe their lives to Pastor Paul Tillman. He was the one who stopped the Germans from blowing up the building together with all the children. He remained to care for them until the first Soviet patrols appeared. The soldiers turned over 39 kids to the sisters of St. Elizabeth in Rawicz. They were severely emaciated and stunted in their physical and mental development. One was too far gone to save.

Just nine of the kids were restored to their families. The rest were put up for adoption.

Many years later, in 1993, their cases were taken up by the Institute for National Remembrance, which started an investigation into the mass murders committed by German personnel at the Wąsosz children's home. The investigation lasted until 2006.

As Prosecutor Sylwester Napieralski said in his summation: "Our inquiry led to the unambiguous conclusion that the Wąsosz facility staff treated their charges in inhuman fashion, starving and beating them, keeping them in unheated rooms, forcing them to sleep on straw pallets, and depriving them of medical care. The evidence confirms that these children were systematically and ruthlessly subjected to extermination."[15]

---

[14] Case files (copies) on Trial nr 8 ["The RuSHA trial" or "The United States of America v. Ulrich Greifelt etc."] against members of the SS Main Race and Settlement Office, IPN Archive GK 151/607.

[15] IPN investigation files on the extermination activities of German staff...

Defendants at the Eighth Nuremberg Trial reading their indictments.

Even so, it proved impossible to establish who was directly responsible for creating this hell on earth. With no suspects having been identified, prosecutors were forced to discontinue the case.

For the most part, those directly involved in the campaign to Germanize or exterminate children never answered for their crimes. Certainly not the heads of companies and manufacturers who exploited slave labor. It is difficult to believe that industrialists like Krupp did not realize the scale of this tragedy.

Some perpetrators were punished for crimes against the children of slave workers, however. The Eighth Nuremberg Trial delivered guilty verdicts against 13 of 14 members of Nazi organizations responsible for racial programs. Four of those convicted were released immediately after the trial for time already served, while the others were given prison sentences ranging from 10 to 25 years.

Anna's family did not agree to the publication of her full name and personal data.

Phenol Shots For "Undesirables"

While the children targeted by the criminal Germanization procedure suffered cruelly, their fate was often incomparably better than that of those deemed unsuitable. Children relegated to the category of "undesirable population increase" were dispatched to Germany for forced labor, sent to death camps, or simply executed on the spot.

It is estimated that more than 2 million Polish children died during the Second World War. About 200,000 were abducted and sent for Germanization to the Reich, while 700,000 more were deported as slave workers. Close to 1.5 million children who survived the war were orphaned of one or both parents.

The wartime experiences of these youngest victims, as the historian Norman Davies[1] has observed, shatter the traditional view of war as an armed conflict composed of campaigns and battles. The Zamość children overturn this perspective. Their symbol is Czesława Kwoka, a village girl from Wółka Złojecka, killed at Auschwitz by a phenol injection to her heart. Thousands of children in occupied Poland met similar deaths.

***

In late 1942 and early 1943, as selection for racial and labor fitness continued among Poles held at the Zamość resettlement camp, the Germans sent three trainloads of about 1,500 people to Auschwitz. Among them were at least 150 children and teenagers. These were individuals whom the German classification system had officially rated as superfluous to economic needs (*Unerwünschter Bevölkerungzuwachstum*, or "undesirable population growth).

Each of the cattle cars carrying these Zamość area residents through the bitter winter cold to Auschwitz had two small, barred windows. We don't know if the Germans simply tossed the youngest and smallest children onto the heads and shoulders of other prisoners in the tightly packed cars. This is what was done in

---

[1] Norman Davies, wstęp do: Wiesław Adamczyk, *Kiedy Bóg odwrócił wzrok. Odyseja wojenna, wygnanie i wybawienie*, Poznań 2011.

Radom during the German liquidation operations of its two ghettoes. What we do know is that the car doors which slammed shut in Zamość were only opened three days later, when the trains reached the unloading ramp at Auschwitz. More than a dozen prisoners died during the first transport, and a similar number of deaths seems to have occurred on subsequent ones. The main causes were cold, lack of food and water, no toilet facilities, and diseases contracted in the Zamość camp.

At the Auschwitz rail platform, SS guards brutally separated the men and women, sending them to separate camp sectors. Initially, the children were allowed to stay with one of their parents. But later that changed, as shown by the testimony of Auschwitz prisoner Czesława Węcławika:

"In our transport (…) besides adults there were about 200 children of between eight and 10 years of age. These kids stayed with the adults for about two months; then the Germans took them away and they vanished without a trace. Not one of these children came home. There were many kids from Skierbieszów on our train who didn't come back. (…) The Germans must have killed about 100 of them at Auschwitz,"[2] recalled one man whose wife and newborn child were both killed by phenol injections.

Another witness, Stanisław Głowa, told investigators of German war crimes in 1946 about what happened to the Zamość children:

"They picked 90 or more boys from transport aged eight to 14 (…) and took them to Block 20, where they were given fatal injections by Scharpe, an N.C.O. medic."[3].

***

Horrifying as it sounds, the phenol injection may have been a release for some children. Some of the Zamość boys were placed with a group subjected to pseudo-scientific medical experiments. Most died in unimaginable torment. Children were injected with pathogens (for example, typhus) and then left in the barracks with no medical care. Their death agonies often lasted for days. Such suffering was regarded as beneath notice by the Germans because Nazi ideology had decreed only

---

[2] Helena Kubica, *Zagłada w KL Auschwitz Polaków wysiedlonych z Zamojszczyzny w latach 1942–1943*, Warszawa 2004.

[3] Kubica, *Zagłada w KL Auschwitz…*

two uses for enemies of the state – forced labor or death by scientific experiment. Accordingly, children were treated like inanimate objects.

"During and after the experiments, staff behaved with a total lack of human sympathy and utter brutality, treating [children] purely as research subjects," writes Agnieszka Fedorowicz[4].

"Simply living in a concentration camp was a huge trauma for children, physically and psychologically exhausting. This made the impact of medical experiments even more devastating, since children were subjected not just to indescribable physical pain but also bore the psychological burden of suffering alone and isolated from their loved ones. (…) For most of them, the experiment ended with death," writes Fedorowicz.[5]

Pseudo-scientific experiments on abducted, "undesirable" Polish children were conducted in at least two locations in occupied Poland: at the Lubliniec Children's Hospital in Upper Silesia, and at 37 Frydecka Street in Cieszyń. Helpless children were dosed with psychoactive drugs such as the barbiturates Luminal and Veronal to test their pharmaceutical reactions and resistance. Children who failed to die immediately were considered interesting cases by these pseudo-physicians.

Those who survived these barbaric drug tests could not count on having their lives spared. Of the 235 inmates of the *Medizinische Kinderheilanstalt* in Lubliniec, 221 died.[6]

***

Czesława Kwoka was not experimented on. The 14-year-old arrived with her mother at Auschwitz on Dec. 13, 1942 with the first Zamość transport. Three months later, she was dead, by a phenol shot to the heart.

Her story is symbolic not just of the Zamość children but of all those who experienced a German concentration camp.

---

[4] Agnieszka Fedorowicz, *Skutki eksperymentów medycznych przeprowadzanych na ko- bietach i dzieciach w niemieckich obozach koncentracyjnych*, Lublin 2010.

[5] Fedorowicz, *Skutki eksperymentów medycznych…*

[6] Kamila Uzarczyk, *Podstawy ideologiczne higieny ras i ich realizacja na przykładzie Śląska w latach 1924–1944*, Toruń 2003.

Czesława's fate was brought to light by camp photographer Wilhelm Brasse, who remembered her face from the crowd of more than 40,000 prisoners whose identity pictures he took.

"I remember the girl's photograph particularly well, because she looked so disarmingly young and innocent in that prisoner's outfit. When they called out the ID numbers in German, the girl didn't understand, which got her whipped by an SS woman guard. They hit her face, too," Brasse recalled in "The Portraitist," a 2006 Polish TV documentary about him.[7]

In Czesława's identity photo, welts from the beatings are clearly visible on her face and split lip. But the little girl's terrified eyes are hardest to ignore. On March 12, 1942, they must have appeared even more frightened, when the executioner plunged the phenol-loaded needle into her chest.

***

Not all Zamość children were sent to Auschwitz. "The estimate is that about 30,000 children were deported from the Zamość area, of whom about 10,000 died either during the initial pacification operations, in transit, or at the camps. A total of about 1,900 children under the age of 10, taken during the deportation's first and second phases, ended up at the so-called *Rentendörfer* in the Garwolin, Siedlce and Mińsk Mazowiecki districts near Warsaw. These "retirement villages" were designated relocation sites, usually selected from localities where the Jewish population had been deported. The Germans expected the children and old people sent to these villages to fend for themselves," says historian Agnieszka Jaczyńska, author of the album *Sonderlaboratorium SS: Zamojszczyzna* [Zamość: A Special SS Testing Laboratory].

"Children deported in the third phase, in January 1943, went to the Majdanek concentration camp. The conditions prevailing there caused them to die quickly. Even during a relatively short stay of several weeks, the death rate was over 10 percent. And while hard frosts during the winter of 1942-1943 decimated deportees, the effects of a hot summer in 1943 were even worse.

Eyewitness accounts from Majdanek prisoners are graphic.

---

[7] Ireneusz Dobrowolski, *Portrecista*, documentary film about the work of Auschwitz camp photographer Wilhelm Brasse, 2005.

"There was a fenced-off area in an open field where they took the dead and severely ill. I saw relatives carrying dying children, they had to leave them there while they were still alive and often conscious. People ask me if they cried. Nobody was crying. Not the ones left in the fields, not the ones who left them there," remembers Janina Buczek-Różańska, deported from the village of Bidaczów Nowy.[8]

In August 1943, some of the prisoners were released from the camp. Sick children were treated in Lublin and nearby hospitals. Most were in critical condition by then and past saving. At the St. John of God Hospital in Lublin, for example, the death toll was 155 out of 299 children. Most were under the age of 12.

---

[8] Ludwik Staszyński, *Przemoc, poniżenie, poniewierka. Wspomnienia z przymusowych robót rolnych 1939–1945*, Warszawa 1967.

Lebensborn –
Heinrich Himmler's Megalomania

Only 15-20 percent of Polish children abducted during the German occupation were returned after the war to the care of their relatives or foster parents in Poland. Those who remained in Germany often don't know of their Polish parentage, says Dr. Dorothee Schmitz-Köster, a scholar and journalist who has written several books on the topic.

Tomasz Majta: You've earned degrees in German literature and philosophy but have chosen to spend 25 years studying the Germanization of children. Might I ask why?

Dr Dorothee Schmitz-Köster: It has something to do with my having lived in Bremen, where I just happened to find out that a facility nearby had belonged to Lebensborn, the organization responsible for helping pregnant women of German nationality or deemed racially valuable [*editor's note: by Nazi criteria*]. I realized nobody was working on the topic and very little was known about it. At that time, I was fascinated by the Nazi period and Lebensborn, especially because I was deeply involved in women's history. All those strands were tied together by this research topic. The stories of women, women and children, were ones I could relate to. And then there was Lebensborn – uncharted territory and the chance to break new ground.

How was the subject of Lebensborn dealt with in Germany after the war? Did people discuss it, or was it taboo?

I wouldn't say it was a taboo. There was no scholarly work on Lebensborn, but there were the Nuremberg trials, a separate trial before the Munich court, and media discussions of the topic. It also came up in the Bundestag.

On the other hand, there was an almost universal expectation in postwar society that a thick line should be drawn to set the Nazi period apart from the postwar era. And if that were so, there was really nothing to discuss. The first serious academic study of Lebensborn was only written by George Lilienthal in the 1980s.

After him, more and more researchers began to take a closer look at the organization.

What can you say about the current state of research?

Georg Lilienthal was the pioneer, and his doctoral thesis, published in 1985 as *Der 'Lebensborn e.V.': Ein Instrument Nationalsozialistischer Rassenpolitik* [Lebensborn: An Instrument of Nazi Racial Policy], was the groundbreaking work. My own book, *Deutsche Mutter, bist du bereit: Alltag im Lebensborn* [German Mother, are you ready? Everyday life in Lebensborn, first published in 1997], continues in this vein. I've interviewed Lilienthal and know him rather well. Two scholars who have published more recently are Volker Koop with "*Dem Führer Ein Kind Schenken*": *Die SS-Organisation Lebensborn e.V.* [Give the Führer a Child: The SS Lebensborn Organization, 2007] and Thomas Bryant with *Himmlers Kinder* [Himmler's Children, 2011]. There has also been a dissertation on the Schwartzwald Lebensborn facility. In addition, the Norwegian researcher and archivist Kåre Olsen and his colleague Lars Borgersrud have written about Lebensborn activities in Norway and what happened to these children after the war.

Did Georg Lilienthal know the details of everyday life at a Lebensborn facility? Did he describe Germanization and racial policy, or the issue of punishing the perpetrators?

Georg Lilienthal made an invaluable contribution to exploring the main themes outlined above. But everyday life at a Lebensborn facility was not his topic. That was left to me. My work deals with eyewitnesses, interviewing them and collecting their life histories. That's what I write about.

And today there are three or four historians in Germany who write about the subject?

Exactly. But I should also stress that several autobiographical accounts have been published by the Lebensborn children.

Does this research get any special funding?

I don't know whether Dr. Lilienthal received a grant for his research. Royalties are paid for published book. Personally, I haven't received any additional funding for my research.

So German politicians aren't paying much attention?

Not politicians at the federal level. But the situation looks different at the state or regional level. Various local initiatives are springing up in places where Lebensborn facilities existed. Foundations are at work and exhibits and memorials are being organized. Sometimes they put plaques or historical markers on former Lebensborn sites.

What about documentation? The Nazis tried to destroy the written evidence. Did anything survive?

Much was lost. Some records were destroyed or simply lost. Perhaps they were hidden somewhere. For example, the records for the Lebensborn center near Bremen were buried and later dug up. Some files were burned by local officials, others were confiscated by the US military authorities, who also destroyed some documents. On the other hand, we have the International Red Cross archives, which contain about 400 large folders, each containing roughly 400 files. These were the main sources for Georg Lilienthal's work. Anyone who wants research their family history can get access to this collection. You can file a request for information. If someone knows they were born in a Lebensborn center, they can go to the civil records office and ask. We have complete records for a few facilities. But on the other hand, the Lebensborn children's home in Bad-Polzin, which is now in Poland...

...In Połczyn.

Yes, in Połczyn. That facility has no surviving records. We do have partial documentation for centers in western Germany.

Just the facilities in Germany?

That's right. The Połczyn documentation was probably removed during the evacuation.

Does that mean most Lebensborn children will never know what happened to them?

About three-quarters of the documentation has been preserved, one quarter is lost.

So the bulk of the records survived?

Yes. But this concerns only the register of births. There is a second way to search, through the *Bundesarchiv* [Federal Archives] holdings in Berlin.

What about the children abducted from Poland to Germany. Not the ones born at Lebensborn facilities, but those taken to Germany by force?

It's hard to give a definite answer. I've dealt with this subject and even written a book to be published next year [*editor's note*: Dorothee Schmitz-Köster, *Raubkind: Von der SS nach Deutschland verschleppt*, Verlag Herder, 2018]. Only 15-20% of these children returned to their relatives or foster parents in Poland. The ones who stayed in Germany often don't realize they are of Polish descent.

Do these people identify as Germans?

Yes. Their foster or adoptive parents never told them where they came from. They were raised as little Germans. The kids never realized – and still don't as adults – that they were born Polish. And because they never knew, they aren't trying to find out.

Yet there are some who know about their origins and still can't find any records. What about them?

I encountered one such person – a man who lives in Germany and will be 80 next year. For a long time, he'd felt that something wasn't right about the story his foster parents told him. At his request, I did a search, among other places, of the International Red Cross archives at Bad Arolsen. And his records were there! They gave his Polish and German surnames, along with other personal data. Of course, it was a stroke of luck that they entered both surnames. Usually there's no trace of the Polish name and the children are given a false German one. They were forced to learn German and forget Polish, like that elderly gentleman. He didn't know he was from Poland but sensed that his roots were there.

Volksdeutsche resettlement operation. Heinrich Himmler (fourth from R *in the group of officers) greets new settlers. San River bridge, 1940*

So why was the operation so effective?

I don't think it was effective at all.

Why not?

What Heinrich Himmler had in mind as Reichsführer SS and architect of the Third Reich's racial policy was on a different scale altogether. The raw numbers were quite modest compared with the Nazis' goals and expectations. For Polish society, the results were painful and even devastating for those directly involved, but in Himmler's eyes the operation was ineffective, or at least did not proceed as he had imagined. Everything depends on one's perspective. What is your view?

Well, some estimates put the number of children deported from Poland to Germany at between 50,000 and 200,000. Only a few came back. So that led me to assume that the operation was mostly effective.

From that standpoint, you're quite right! I'd just like to correct the numbers. According to current German research, about 20,000 children were taken from

Poland. The estimates mentioned in postwar discussions—in my opinion and according to the sources—turn out to have been exaggerated. Be that as it may, only about 15-20 percent of those 20,000 people returned home... That's why you asked about the operation's effectiveness in the case of the 18,000 who stayed in Germany. These are people who don't know they're Polish because their identities were changed and they were forced to stop speaking the language. We're talking about small children—of kindergarten or primary school age at most. The older kids often remembered where they came from, but the younger ones forgot. It was brainwashing, pure and simple. The point was to make them forget about their real mother, home and fatherland. Sometimes the children knew that something was wrong, but they didn't know what. They had no reference point to start looking. In that sense, it was effective.

I still want to ask about numbers. Polish researchers from the IPN estimate that about 11,000 children were born at Lebensborn facilities, while at least 50,000 were deported from Poland. The numbers you give are much lower. How did these discrepancies arise?

I think that as we do more research, our numbers become more precise. These are indeed significant discrepancies. We continue to analyze new source documents and compile fresh data. My own estimates are based on data from Prof. Isabel Heinemann's *Rasse, Siedlung, deutsches Blut* [Race, Land, German Blood] and on research by Dr. Ines Hopfer, who described what happened to Germanized children in Austria in her book *Geraubte Identität* [Stolen Identity]. These are both relatively new publications, from 2003 and 2010, respectively.

You mentioned the International Red Cross. I know other groups and associations in Germany speak for the Lebensborn children, especially Lebensspuren e.V. What does that organization do?

Lebensspuren, or "Traces of Life", is an association founded 10 years ago by former Lebensborn children. It's a place where people who went through these facilities can meet. Mostly these are people living in Germany. Originally there were also some attendees from Denmark and Norway, but now they have other organizations in their own countries. Lebensspuren members meet once a year to exchange information about Lebensborn and their own lives. It even has a website with basic information and instructions on how to join: http://www.lebens-spuren–deutschland.eu/. Sadly, the Lebensborn alumni are getting older…

…in their 70s and 80s by now…

…Exactly. In the beginning there were lots of meetings, but now few are willing to travel distances of 500 kilometers or more. It's just too much of an effort for many older people.

Are there any other organizations besides Lebensspuren?

There is a group called "Stolen Children – Forgotten Victims" that focuses on children abducted from Poland, Czechoslovakia, and Ukraine. The organization's most important purpose is to fight for reparations – and thus far it has had no success.

"Everything for a healthy child" – German propaganda photo

Do you think getting reparations is even possible?

Well, judging by the actions of German politicians, I wouldn't expect the Finance Ministry to make it a priority over the next few years. One gets the impression that politicians are simply dragging things out until the interested parties die off. I know a few Lebensborn children in Poland, e.g. Barbara Paciorkiewicz, who told me a lot about the experience of child deportees. What those children went through is very sad and terrifying.

What about the question of social accountability? Do Germans feel responsible for any wrongdoing?

The history of abducted children from Eastern Europe is not well known. Those who do have some knowledge, especially young people, are very interested in finding out more and deeply sympathize with these children. There are also social activists like me. I try to help people looking for their roots. Red Cross and Bundesarchiv employees are very aware and unusually helpful on the topic.

Sometimes families were separated with the sister, for example, being deported and the brother staying in Poland. Later such families stayed divided. Are you familiar with such cases?

Barbara Paciorkiewicz was one. She was living with her grandmother and had a sister who was under the care of her other grandmother. The sister stayed in Poland, while Barbara was abducted. To me this just shows how far Nazi ideology was detached from reality. Race was just a construct built on a false premises. There is not a shred of scientific evidence for the existence of a so-called Aryan race. A self-appointed member of the race police raises his finger and says: "You come with me, and you stay". Even though Basia and her sister were siblings, one with blonde and the other with black hair. The Germans simply took the blonde. An additional factor was that Basia and her grandmother lived in Łódź, which was a center of Nazi activity. They took the children who were at hand. Sometimes it was pure accident.

So the roundups and deportations weren't as carefully organized as people generally believe?

No, they weren't, which is what I had in mind when I spoke earlier about effectiveness. The whole operation began in the so-called *Warthegau* (comprising parts of present-day Łódź, Greater Poland, Lubusz, and Kujawy-Pomerania provinces), in territories that belonged to Germany before the First World War. As a next step, the Nazis wanted to forcibly remove the entire population of Eastern Europe – "shift and sift", as Himmler liked to say. At the same time, he wanted to deliver "good blood" from the conquered territories to Germany. This was simply megalomania!

What about bringing the guilty to justice?

It's linked with the issue of dealing with the legacy of National Socialism in Germany after the war. Heinrich Himmler, the initiator of the whole operation, passed judgment on himself and committed suicide. Those responsible for Germanization were tried by American judges at Nuremberg. Lebensborn was ruled by them to be a charitable organization. That is why the perpetrators were not given prison sentences. However, they were punished for belonging to the SS, which was ruled to be a criminal organization. This was their crime—not Lebensborn. The verdict was later upheld by the Munich court.

We've already established that many children from Lebensborn don't realize they are not of German descent. We also know that the issue of responsibility has not surfaced in public debate. Are young people in Germany aware that some of their fellow citizens were forcibly Germanized?

I give talks all over Germany and can honestly say that Lebensborn is a topic of public interest, especially among young people. There are a lot of questions and stormy discussions during the Q&A sessions. More lectures are being given and student theses written on the subject. However, it's also true that young people are mostly interested in Lebensborn activities in Germany.

Lebensborn as a stud farm?

What do you mean by that?

A place where young women go to give birth and…

…I ask because a lot of people believe Lebensborn was where where young women met SS men to produce offspring within the walls of the facility. Is that what you were thinking?

Well, in a way.

So let me clarify the issue by saying that never happened. Lebensborn centers weren't places where young people could meet to sleep together and beget children. Not at all! It's a very popular myth that has nothing to do with reality. The truth was quite different. Pregnant women went to these facilities to give birth. Some of them were married, but most not. Some were mistresses, others got pregnant from brief flings with servicemen, including members of the SS. Cases vary, but in no circumstances were the Lebensborn facilities breeding centers or brothels. Children were born at Lebensborn, not begotten. But the myth fascinates people, which is why genuine crimes like the abduction of children from Eastern Europe fade into the background.

I wanted to ask about the children who were deemed "racially undesirable". What happened to them? Such children are said to have starved to death after being deliberately deprived of food and care. Is that true?

Yes. Both children and their mothers were checked according to racial criteria, but also very carefully examined from the standpoint of their general health. "Racially undesirable" children were sent away as soon as possible. If they did not suffer from serious disabilities, they were sent to non-Lebensborn facilities. However, if the child had a condition such as Down syndrome, then the whole euthanasia apparatus was engaged. The murder of such children was assigned to special "pediatric detachments". They would be given tranquilizers and put to bed, left to die through neglect and susceptibility to infection. It was a slow, terrible death.

What about children initially classified as "desirable" who later, in Germany, resisted being Germanized?

These children were sent back to Poland. I know several such cases and have seen the documents. Worth stressing is that these children were not sent back to their places of origin. They were not returned to their parents or guardians, but instead sent to other orphanages. In this way, they lost their families.

So the Nazis wanted to uproot even those children deemed unworthy of being considered for Germanization?

That's right. The only question is why they were considered unsuitable. All children at Lebensborn facilities were supposed to meet certain demands. They were expected to obey rules, speak German, and do what they were told, and sometimes a few of the older children refused. They would surreptitiously converse with each other in Polish and tell the younger kids not to forget about where they came from, that they were Poles. A few even tried to run away. They just wouldn't adapt. And this was considered dangerous in terms of racial policy because it showed that children could be strong and defy authority. That's why they were not simply sent back home, because as Himmler kept saying, it was the Polish children "of good blood" who might become the German nation's worst enemies once they grew up. That's why, according to Himmlerian logic, they had to be destroyed.

October 2017 interview with Dorothee Schmitz-Köster conducted by Deutsche Welle and Interia for the "Stolen Children" project.

Turning Polish Children into Germans

"Heinrich Himmer's vow to 'rob and steal German blood' reflected a larger genocidal vision mapped out in Generalplan Ost that also encompassed the ruthless, brutal abduction of children from countries conquered by the Germans."

— Dr. Joanna Lubecka, a historian at Poland's Institute of National Remembrance (IPN).

If we wanted to draw a blueprint of how the entire Germanization apparatus was put together, including the plan to steal children and turn them into Germans, where would we start? With Himmler saying in 1938 that "I really do have the intention to gather Germanic blood from the whole world, to rob it, to steal it wherever I can"?

— Artur Wróblewski

Joanna Lubecka: "I think you can go much farther back than that, to the turn of the century and Chancellor Bernhard von Bülow's 1897 speech in the Reichstag about Germany's 'place in the sun'. From that time onward, and basically from the moment of German unification in 1871, Germany began looking for its 'place in the sun'. Wrapped up in this search were several ideas that would later get fused together and developed by the Nazis. You can see the results of this process in Himmler's speech, and also in certain texts by Adolf Hitler, including a general order issued in 1939, after the attack on Poland, which refers to this issue.

Here we need distinguish several aspects of German policy at the time. Firstly, Germany had begun to feel hemmed in, but this feeling of constraint arose from a sense of entitlement – that Germans deserved more. To be fair, such attitudes were the norm among great powers of the day, but Nazi ideology later magnified them enormously. Secondly, the late 1800s saw the rapid development of "racial philosophy", a trend that would strengthen in the early 20th century. Here Germany took the lead. A distinction began to be made between the Nordic and

Bernhard von Bülow, Germany's chancellor in 1900–1909, who said it was high time for Germany to "demand our place in the sun"

Adoption ceremony for a German family at a Lebensborn facility

Slav races, which would later be exploited and accentuated by the Nazis. A third aspect is the famous German geopolitical concept of *Lebensraum*, or "living space", which also appears in *Mein Kampf*. In Hitler's book, *Lebensraum* is applied to Eastern Europe, with its fertile farmland and inhabitants whom the Germans regarded as racially inferior. All of these concepts had been constructed earlier, but under the Nazis they were systematized, assembled and honed into *Generalplan Ost*.

This plan was an incredibly comprehensive, deliberate and cohesive document that identified specific aims along with the methods and tools necessary to achieve them. Its complexity and precision show that it was drafted by scholars and military professionals. Its objective, in a nutshell, was to create a German racial superstate.

What fate did *Generalplan Ost* foresee for other nations?

Since the superstate was to be inhabited by members of the Germanic race, the question arose of what to do with people of other races living on the territory of the future superstate. In keeping with the philosophy outlined above, *Generalplan Ost* made clear distinctions between races and indicated what should be done with each. Thus, we have the *Herrenvolk*, or "master race", made up not only of Germans but of Austrians and other "desirable elements" that could be "recovered" for the Germanic race. The assumption was that some nations, such as the Scandinavians, were predestined to rejoin the Germanic peoples. The English, originally seen by Hitler as potential partners, were also seen as belonging to the Nordic race. Other peoples, such as the Slavs, were expected to provide only individual "elements". As to the rest, the plan was to deport or exterminate them.

Generalplan Ost called for the liquidation of about 32 million Slavs. Another 14 million were to be allowed to survive, to put it frankly, as slaves. They were to be used as forced laborers on farms run by model German families who were to settle the conquered colonial lands. It's worth stressing that these families were not to be former residents of the Third Reich itself, but rather German stock drawn from the entire world to populate the eastern marches of the new German superstate. The Germanic race was to live in a single vast territory, a concept the Nazis termed *Heim ins Reich*, or "Home to the Reich". All Germans had the right to feel "at home in the Reich", which in practice meant getting rid of the Slavs, either through extermination or, when possible, by extracting "racially desirable elements" from the conquered peoples.

How strongly did Himmler's words about "robbing and stealing" children figure in *Generalplan Ost*?

This was something that emerged as the plan was carried out, which is why it's difficult to state precisely when *Generalplan Ost* became a complete and finished document. For all its precision and comprehensive scope, the plan was envisaged in multiple stages that depended on the changing situation. In its basic outlines, *Generalplan Ost* took shape between mid-1941 and mid-1942. In subsequent years the document went through various iterations and evolutionary stages. The farther east the German advanced on a wave of military victories and territorial expansion, which is the period in which *Generalplan Ost* was taking shape, the faster Himmler reacted. This scheme and the quest to "recover Germanic blood" became an obsession with him. That's why he kept harping upon the point. He pressed ahead by establishing institutions such as the newly merged SS Race and Resettlement Main Office, which gave the policy a more cohesive thrust. What's interesting to note is that toward the end of the war, the Wehrmacht high command started trying to put a stop to the German blood recovery campaign, demanding that its whole apparatus of state officials, bureaucrats, police and military personnel be dismantled because there were more urgent problems to deal with. The army was in full retreat, defeat was staring Germany in the face, and all resources needed to be diverted to the armed forces and the front. Himmler refused. In any case, his race and resettlement offices were already experiencing huge problems finding qualified specialists.

Adolf Hitler and Heinrich Himmler ordered a hunt for "Germanic blood"

When did Lebensborn first appear as an institution tasked with "renewing German blood" and "breeding a race of Nordic supermen"?

The Germans avoided the word "breeding" in this context, perhaps because it revealed too much about the oddly mechanical nature of the whole enterprise. Lebensborn got its start much earlier, in 1935, as what the Eighth Nuremberg Trial with some justification described as a charity care institution. And in the beginning, Lebensborn did have that character. Of course, its ultimate goal was to produce the largest possible number of German children, which didn't succeed. The whole Lebensborn program is estimated to have been responsible for about 11,000 births. Let's be honest, that's a drop in the bucket. But the organization's original function was to care for women. Initially these were married women, because the model German family was composed of a husband, wife, and children. And once the husbands were sent to the front, many single mothers found themselves in trouble. Lebensborn offered help. In time, though this was never a focus, there were also attempts at matchmaking.

A few researchers claim that what amounted to brothels operated under the guise of Lebensborn. Such instances occurred, but they were not widespread, since Lebensborn promoted marriage. But as the program brought failure instead of success, it changed. In 1940, Field Marshall Wilhelm Keitel was already complaining in a letter to Hitler that the Wehrmacht would run short of men unless German women started having more babies. The letter noted that 600,000 abortions were performed in Germany each year. Please compare that figure with Lebensborn's results. So, the program had to evolve. They began to seek "German blood" in mixed Polish-German or Czech-German marriages, or among people with a few German ancestors. These "finds" were of course then subjected to racial screening, as were the women who had participated in earlier Lebensborn programs.

At what point did Lebensborn change from a charity care institution to an organization that abducts children, which was later qualified by the courts as a crime of genocide?

When Germany made its first conquests in the East. The process occurred along several tracks. The first was quite simple: Wehrmacht soldiers received orders and instructions to be on the lookout for Nordic-looking children with blond hair and blue eyes. This especially applied to German officers, who had a responsibility to report such children to the local Lebensborn unit or representatives of the Race and Resettlement Office. That initiated the procedure. The second track was through orphanages. In Germany that matter was straightforward. After a time, orders were issued to institute what the Germans called an annual "sifting" in orphanages. A commission would appear to racially screen the children, and after that cases were decided according to an established procedure. The third path were the *Sonderaktionen*, or "special operations", such as Zamość or Lidice in Czechoslovakia. The Zamość operation was staged in great haste, over the protests of the German military. Time was found to collect the Polish children in one place, summon medical and racial experts to screen them, then select and dispatch suitable candidates to Germanization centers. The focus was on children under the age of 10. These were the three main "recruitment" channels.

Can you describe the typical experience of a stolen child?

The procedures were harsh, clearly defined and strictly followed by the Germans. Himmler was a stickler on all racial matters, so any cheating or bending the rules was out of the question. The child had to be racially pure according to Nazi criteria. The same approach applied in every channel, but there were chronic staffing problems due to the shortage of qualified racial experts. Not only were very few such experts to be found, but the ones who were available were reluctant to exchange their comfortable university offices and laboratories for field duty on the Eastern front. As time went on, vacancies on "expert" commissions were filled by medical students who performed the selections. Age was the decisive factor in determining an abducted child's fate. The Germans preferred infants and very young children who could not yet speak or knew only a few words in Polish. This came out in the initial screening. In Poland, stolen children usually were sent to one of six Lebensborn facilities, including the main center in Łódź, or to what we could call "children's homes", although they were traditional orphanages in name only. The first selection concentrated on physical characteristics—especially nose and cranial measurements. After the physical examination, a child's psychological makeup was evaluated. At this stage, children deemed to be hyperactive were often screened out—for example, colicky infants. Rude or rebellious children were rejected as well. The last stage of screening was reserved for "experts" from Lebensborn or the Race and Resettlement Office, usually physicians. From that point on, the paramount factor was age. The youngest children were usually taken by German families waiting on the adoption list. Older children were rarely put up for adoption, generally being sent instead to boarding schools that specialized in "manufacturing" Germans, if you will forgive the expression. For many, the next stop was the Hitler Youth or the Wehrmacht.

Stolen Polish children often went straight from boarding schools to the Hitler Youth

What happened to the "unsuitable" children?

Their fate varied. In the early stages of the war, children from Poland were often sent home. However, it soon decided that this procedure was too costly and time-consuming. Another consideration was that the German were now trying to cover their tracks and remove evidence of the children, who were often violently abducted from their parents or guardians. This was the main reason why the practice of returning children to their homes was stopped. Especially given the fluid military situation, which made other matters more urgent.

The children can be divided into three categories. Children who had undergone screening and the entire Germanization process ended up with German families. Here the situation also varied. Older children who remembered their Polish parents had it the worst. But it should also be kept in mind that despite the horrifying plight of these abducted children, they were often put under the care of genuinely good people and sometimes had excellent conditions in their German families. Some of these Germans longed for children and loved these adopted Polish kids as their own. At the same time, we can imagine that stolen children also encountered situations that were less benign.

The second category were children who did not make it through the Germanizing process. These would have been children who met the racial criteria but whose character was deemed unsuitable. They were not put up for adoption but stayed in Germany as a source of slave labor, mostly in agriculture. The treatment of these farm workers also varied enormously. There are no precise data on the numbers of these children, but it is estimated that about 50 percent of children taken from Poland went through the entire Germanization process and stayed in Germany, while the rest were rejected. Those deemed "unsuitable" to become Germans had in effect received a death sentence; they were to be exterminated. The older children were often sent to concentration camps, where they were either murdered right away in the gas chambers or died more slowly from hunger and exhaustion. Infants and younger children met a no less horrifying fate. They were sent to pseudo-nurseries that were in fact dying rooms filled with starving, crying children. These infants were left to die in torment in indescribable squalor. Eyewitness descriptions of what happened in these facilities are hideous. The horror was such that children who were given a fatal injection of phenol may be regarded as lucky. I know that sounds horrible, but it's the truth. For them, a quick death was a blessing.

Do German and Polish estimates of the number of stolen children differ greatly? In Poland, as many as 200,000 are mentioned.

The Polish figures do run to about 200,000, but any historian would add the proviso that these are very rough estimates. Here one issue should be stressed. Of these 200,000 children—it's possible the number was greater, and I personally think there were more—only a portion, about one quarter, went through the Lebensborn procedure. Most likely the remainder, the much larger part, were children Germanized into the workforce as cheap labor. They fared very differently. Some German farmers treated them as ordinary farmworkers or hired hands, while others took them into the family and raised them on the farm. Among these 200,000 we should include the children of Polish slave workers in Germany. Abortions were often performed in such cases, but if the Polish mother had a "Germanic" appearance, she was allowed to have the child, which was later examined. Such children of Polish mothers or fathers on forced labor in Germany were then put through the Lebensborn procedure and put up for adoption. It was very rare for a child to be left with its Polish parents. These were isolated instances, usually involving a farmer concealing from the authorities that one of his Polish women workers had given birth. This was often an act of kindness. It's also difficult to estimate the number of children in such cases. After all, there were more than 2 million Polish slave workers in Germany. We can only imagine the estimated number of children born to them.

As for German historians and their estimates, the issue is not self-evident. After the war, the Germans talked about very small numbers. Their estimates ran to about 20,000 children. Now, however, if you look at the historical literature or media publication, you'll find German authors most often citing Polish estimates. The numbers range from 50,000 to 200,000. You can see the change, but it's not attributable to German researchers. They are simply repeating the findings of Polish historians.

It's also worth noting that after the "Stolen Children" campaign, organized by Deutsche Welle and Interia.pl in 2018, there was extensive press coverage in Germany. I follow German media publications closely and there was a noticeable change. Germans are no longer denying that children were abducted or trying to defend the low numbers they mentioned after the war. At the same time, it would be hard to say that German scholars and researchers have seized upon the topic. The exception is those investigating individual cases. As for the total number of children abducted by the Germans, besides Poland, where the procedure was most widespread, there must be included another several tens of thousands of stolen children from Ukraine and Belarus. Elsewhere in Europe, the main examples are from the Slavic countries. In Slovenia approximately 1,000 children may have been taken, and we know there were abductions of Czech children as well. On the other hand, I wouldn't compare this procedure with situations that took place in Western and Northern Europe. Those cases mainly involve mixed couples, for example, a German soldier and a Norwegian or Swedish woman. There aren't children being picked up off the street and ripped away from their parents—which not to say that they are not tragic stories, only different. After the war, for example, Norway refused to accept the offspring of German soldiers.

Were abducted Polish children forcibly Germanized or was it a more natural process?

That's a good question. I've considered it and looked through German publications to see how the process is described and in what context. Terms corresponding to "Germanization" [*Germanisierung*] in a more general sense and the forcibly compelled variety [*Eindeutschung*] are used interchangeably, including by historians. But in contemporary German wartime documents on *Generalplan Ost* or the *Volksliste*, the term referring to a forced process, or *Eindeutschung*, is employed. What difference does that make? *Eindeutschung*, which could perhaps be rendered in English as "Germanification", is almost exclusively used by historians to describe events of the Second World War. Germanization, on the other hand, is a much broader concept, even though for us it certainly carries some negative baggage. The word itself functions similarly to Americanization and describes a much broader process than compulsory Germanification, without necessarily having negative connotations. For example, by any objective measure, Prussian policies in Warmia and Masuria did not exclusively depend on forcible and compulsory Germanification, but also relied on the positive power of attraction. Children who went to German schools could hope for a civil service career. In much the same way, the Germanification of abducted Polish children was part of a bigger, broader Germanizing operation.

Resettlement in Zamość, 1942

After the war, Roman Hrabar tried to locate these Polish children. Can you describe this mission and the resistance it encountered not just from the Germans but also from the Allies?

What Roman Hrabar did was truly exceptional. Especially because this was the effort of a single individual, largely without financial help from the Polish government. Hrabar's memoirs make it clear that he was perpetually short of funds and personnel. To some extent his shoestring operation is understandable given Poland's poor financial condition and internal politics at the time. But this does not detract from Hrabar's achievements. Paradoxically, the chaotic conditions of the immediate postwar period offered the best opportunity to recover Polish children. Their memories of Poland and their parents were still fresh and regaining custody was possible, though it was a thankless and exhausting task.

The Allied authorities' reluctance to help Hrabar is not strange. Please recall that the immediate postwar period coincided with the Nuremberg trials and a general Allied determination to punish Germany. Otherwise, the trials would never have taken place. However, political fissures had already appeared in the wartime coalition and, at least since the Tehran conference in 1943, it was apparent that Poland would be in the Soviet camp. Starting in 1947, when the eighth Nuremberg trial on the SS Race and Resettlement Main Office (RuSHA) took place, the working relationship between representatives of Poland and the Western Allies in various institutions began to deteriorate. The occupation authorities started to make things harder for Poles because our country was then seen as part of a hostile bloc. Whereas it had earlier been possible to extradite German war criminals for trial in Poland, now cooperative ties were severed and assistance dried up. It was not so much a question of lack of faith in Polish courts, because there had been no previous objections to their verdicts, even when these courts operated under the supervision of the local communist or Soviet authorities. In the case of children, however, the attitude was taken not to give them up so they would remain on the right side of the Iron Curtain.

The Allies' negative attitude toward recovering stolen Polish children was just one element of a much bigger picture. It is only honest to admit, despite how brutal it sounds today and how many children were victimized, that at the time the question of returning abducted children to Poland was just one more detail among a mass of contentious issues and problems the Allied powers were trying to untangle, amid a worsening East-West conflict and the complications that brought for Poland's relations with the Western allies. It was a minor issue. For this reason, recovering children dropped lower and lower on the ladder of Polish priorities.

Did this situation affect the RuSHA trial? Even though abducting children was ruled to be a crime of genocide, no defendant got more than a few years in prison.

The Eighth Nuremberg Trial was the moment when the East-West breach became quite evident. At this time the joint commission that administered occupied Germany, the Allied Control Council, broke down and essentially stopped functioning, which undoubtedly influenced the ongoing trials. The RuSHA trial started in late 1947 and ran through 1948, but you can also see a similar shift in other court proceedings, not just at Nuremberg, toward lighter sentences. By 1949, Germans would be allowed to face war crimes charges in their own courts. While Allied jurisprudence remained in place, German judges were handing down the sentences. As you can easily imagine, the severity of punishment significantly decreased.

The punishments handed down in the RuSHA trial were harsh, including one life sentence and several 10- and 15-year terms. The Lebensborn defendants were found innocent, however, which was a disastrous ruling. Even German researchers describe the verdict as a disgraceful miscarriage of justice. One historian went so far as to state that the Allies let themselves be swindled. But perhaps they weren't fooled, and the decision was a deliberate. The facts are that the entire Lebensborn leadership were punished only by pre-trial detention and later exonerated, including the organization's chief. The verdict is even more bizarre because the selection of defendants was very precise, including virtually everyone responsible for *Generalplan Ost* and the whole genocidal apparatus. Among those on trial were scientists, physicians, Lebensborn members, racial experts and RuSHA officials, showing the true breadth of German operations. The problem was that after these people were tried and sentenced, they were very quickly secured early release from prison. This applied to all war criminals, not just those sentenced in the Eighth Nuremberg trial. The wider the East-West breach, the more the Germans felt they had the Western Allies on their side and could feel free to announce amnesties and release war criminals from prison. The RuSHA trial, therefore, should not be seen as an exception but as part of a logical chain of events tied to postwar relations between the great powers.

Hrabar's activities ceased in 1950, which ended any further attempt to recover abducted children. How did German-Polish relations develop in subsequent years, especially given the very complicated international situation?

Poland's communist regime could only conduct a foreign policy aligned with the interests of the Kremlin and the entire Soviet bloc. The USSR called the shots. As for the communist German Democratic Republic, from the very beginning a very simple rule applied of not discussing the Second World War at all, since the GDR was a country inhabited solely by people who opposed Hitler. There was no point in discussing German war crimes with a country that had no war criminals. This wasn't true, of course, but it put an end to any attempt to raise the issue of stolen children. The situation with West Germany was complicated because communist Poland did not initially have full diplomatic relations with the German Federal Republic. But it was not only that.

Official diplomatic relations are one thing, and unofficial relations are another. Warsaw and Bonn did not have even informal dealings with each other save for a few minor exceptions. Due to a lack of official and unofficial channels, it was impossible to pursue the topic of stolen children. In any case, it is unlikely Germany would have seen any reason it should be willing to help Poland with this matter. Besides, there were many more pressing issues to deal with in bilateral relations. Most of all, the whole time there was no German recognition of Poland's western border on the Oder-Neisse line. Once again, the question of children abducted during wartime was just one of a long list of issues to be resolved.

Once full diplomatic relations were restored in 1970, other matters were again prioritized. West German recognition of Poland's Western border was recognized as a success, but issues considered minor from the standpoint of grand diplomacy were not discussed. This was when Poles got reparations, thanks to Chancellor Willy Brandt and his ruling SPD, which had a rather pro-Polish orientation. There was also some movement in West Germany at this time on Nazi war crimes, in part thanks to the Frankfurt trials of Auschwitz camp personnel in 1963-1965. These helped change German attitudes, as did the 1968 student revolt, whose sharp end was directed at the older generation held responsible for Nazism. "You are the Auschwitz generation!" young Germans shouted accusingly at their elders. This created an atmosphere conducive to paying reparations for war losses – small and inadequate, but reparations, nonetheless. And here again the stolen children never came up. For all its horror, their suffering was dwarfed by the enormity of

German crimes elsewhere, whose size and scale reduced the issue to marginal status. Automatically, it was downgraded.

Heinrich Himmler (L) greets Volksdeutsche settlers, 1939/1940

And what about German scholars? You said that they didn't pursue the topic of stolen children.

It just wasn't a hot research topic. There was no grant money. Our idealized view of the academic world assumes a free marketplace of ideas and research methods, but that's not the reality. To a large extent, funding for certain types of research is provided by the state, and the state often suggests topics that further its own interests. After the war—not in the GDR, but in West Germany—large amounts of money were sporadically devoted to studying the mass flight and expulsion of Germans. This was the main research area in German-Polish relations. Little work was done on the war itself, which was considered an unfashionable topic. And who would be doing the research, anyway? A war veteran with front-line experience? The same dilemma applied to the judicial system. Who should be judging war criminals? The same judges who were implicated in the Nazi system. It's a very ticklish question. Meanwhile, Germany was preoccupied by its postwar economic boom and European integration. Germans were told they had made a clean break with the past; everything was starting afresh, and catastrophe was being remade into success. Nobody wanted to talk about the war.

Things changed in the 1970s. First, a German-Polish Textbook Commission was established under UNESCO auspices. While it could not enforce wholesale changes in the content of school textbooks, since that was a prerogative of German state governments, the Commission's work was still important and influential. This is about the time books started to appear that showed German historians writing in a new way. Not coincidentally, they were also forming close friendships with their Polish colleagues, often tinged by feelings of guilt and shared responsibility. But I don't associate the topic of stolen children with this period. If the issue is mentioned at all, it is usually just a passing reference to the existence of such a procedure. The main focus was on concentration camps, life under occupation, lots of publications on purely military topics, and of course the hot topic of post-war German expulsions.

There was another book boom in the 1990s, although German historians writing about war crimes in Poland or against Poles, like Jochen Böhler or Dieter Schenk, complain that they were still having a hard time finding German publishers. That is the situation to this day. You won't be able to find German books about abducted children. There are studies of Lebensborn, which is unquestionably an interesting topic that addresses an important domestic German issue. However, the situation is very different when it comes to journalists dealing with the same subject, and here especially Poland plays a leading role.

Germany's policy on historical studies certainly appears to have been effective in avoiding the topic.

To me, that's entirely understandable. When commenting on German policies towards the past, I refuse to indulge in bizarre conspiracy theories. The German approach is an example of completely rational behavior, even if it is unquestionably often threatening to Poland. Germany is simply pursuing its own interests. There is nothing unusual in that. Besides, no one likes to admit to their own guilt, that's obvious. Poles are also reluctant to talk about uncomfortable topics, even though we have much less to atone for in history than the Germans. We don't like to go back and rake up past sins. Germans find it hard to grapple with their own history and thus avoid certain topics. The politics of history follow a few basic principles.

First, accentuate the positive and discuss matters which bring some tangible gain. Admit to guilt when the admission benefits us.

Historical politics is above all politics; it has very little to do with history. Germany admitted to the Holocaust and to a certain extent has genuinely tried to grapple with its responsibility. But the extermination of European Jews was a crime for which Germany realized it could never evade responsibility. Denial, which was the response they followed well into the 1960s, proved to be entirely counter-productive, while admitting guilt and self-recrimination brought nothing but gains in the international arena. Today Germany is considered a model country for settling accounts with past crimes. Meanwhile, little pressure has been exerted on Germany to account for its crimes against stolen children. Considering the truly large number of articles appearing in the German press as well as published memoirs, however, I see a real chance that the issue of stolen children could gain traction. From the public relations point of view, it's a catchy topic. These are gripping human stories and great photo opportunities, which is probably why they were quickly picked up by German journalists. They aren't thinking in terms of historical politics, they're counting readers and hits. Perhaps in this way the topic of stolen children will leak into the larger political discourse.

I take it that in the immediate post-1989 period, the subject never came up on the government level?

Neither stolen children nor reparations. Of course, it's easy for us to pass judgment after the fact, with the wisdom of hindsight, but today people are talking about how a major opportunity was lost in the 1990s to initiate these kinds of discussions, that we didn't press the Germans hard enough on war-related issues. As I said, it's easy to point out errors with the benefit of hindsight, but at the time we were absorbed by entirely different matters. Not to make excuses, since one can always do better, but it's worth remembering that at the moment of German reunification, Poland still didn't have official confirmation of its western border. This was a fundamental problem. Poland was genuinely frightened, while Germany recognized the border relatively late, in 1990. So, at the time, there were other problems to deal with. Later, Germany became our biggest partner and ally, as well as a strong supporter of our membership in NATO and the EU. Of course they had an interest in shifting NATO's border farther east, but the fact is that Germany was Poland's most powerful advocate. Given the circumstances, the Polish side naturally wasn't anxious to bring up the war. It may sound callous, but foreign policy is always about horse-trading.

Recently the subject of war reparations has been revived, but that probably won't change the situation of abducted children?

I don't think so. The topic is very difficult to investigate or even define. For one thing, how do you locate victims? Very few stolen children are still alive who know their histories and true identities and have the documents to prove it before a court of law. Everything is wrapped up in procedural issues. There are, of course, politically motivated reparations. The German-Israeli reparations agreement involved installment payments to Israel that were then apportioned by the Israel government – all without any documentation or evidence. I don't see any chance of this happening again.

Even the potential payment of reparations to Poland has more to do with politics than law. Could this be an opportunity to revive the topic of stolen children? Since very few people know about this criminal procedure, it would be useful to make it known in an international forum. On the other hand, it might simply become a political football. Most lawyers claim that the possibility of any state-to-state reparations is minimal. Perhaps some damages might be claimed in a civil suit. To me this seems like a good approach, especially due to the publicity that lawsuits would bring in Germany and Poland. Except for the claimants themselves, the eventual settlements would be less important than the legal precedent they would set. The very fact that a trial is taking place, and that brave people are willing to tell their stories in court, would attract media attention, which of course is the ultimate goal of these lawsuits in the first place. After all, we're talking about a token number of cases. It would cost Germany little to make a small gesture of goodwill, though of course there would be worries that one lawsuit would engender others. Governments are always leery of such precedents.

And what are the German media saying now?

Articles on stolen children have appeared in *Der Spiegel* and other magazines. My impression is that German journalists are mainly picking up stories from the Polish media. Much of it is copy-paste, but that also helps. There have also been interviews with Germans who were Lebensborn children. At least the topic is finally being raised, since journalists see stolen children as a gripping human story. Let's see how long it lasts…

Monument at the site of the former Zamość resettlement camp

Germanization

Bruczków: Polish Secret School, Germanizing Center

History can be perverse. Today, the Bruczków palace has a trampoline sitting in front. Bright-colored washing hangs from a clothesline. The plaster is crumbling, and the old cobblestone ramp has seen better days. The formerly spacious front hall is now sectioned off with partition walls. Laundry carts and drying racks stand by the old front doors. The interior walls are covered by wood paneling. At the chapel entrance, local residents and the head of the village council are gathered. On the half-mown lawn, children are playing.

During a period of intense Germanization in the late 19th and early 20th centuries, when Poland was partitioned, the Bruczków palace hosted a clandestine Polish school founded by Wanda Koczorowska. During World War II, the Germans used the same facilities to indoctrinate children abducted from Polish orphanages and children's homes, remolding them into little Germans.

Memory

How many children underwent Germanization at Bruczków?

"A fair number. They always went out for walks twice a day. We weren't permitted to approach those children, and they weren't allowed near us. The ladies who minded them made sure there was no contact between us," says Maria Nowakowska.

How old were they?

"Anywhere from three to 16 years old. For a while there were even younger kids. We wanted to play with them, but it was forbidden. During the war, a few boys from the youth facility at Cerekwica were also staying here. They were older and knew more, they might have said something," Nowakowska adds.

The first group of children, aged 10 to 14, arrived at Bruczków in December 1941 from the orphanage at Wolsztyn, escorted by sister Jadwiga and sister Maria. The nuns were then transported to Kobylin and an unknown fate.

"When I was eight, my aunt got a summons to take me to 113 Piotrkowska Street for a medical examination. They looked us over and took us to Bruczków. We were taught to read and write German. Speaking Polish was not allowed – I was beaten with a stick for that. They were cross with us for not reading German fast enough. At Bruczków, there were children older than me, but also tiny little kids they left lying on pillows."

— Krystyna Mikolajczyk[1]

Starting in March 1942, the decision on whether a Bruczków child had the requisite character traits for Germanization was made by Hildegard Hetzer, held in great esteem by the Nazis.[2]

A Secret Polish School

Perhaps Wanda Koczorowska, née Rotkiewicz, would not have devoted her life to the upbringing and education of Polish orphans and children from poor families had her 11-year-old daughter not died during a trip to Rome, and had she not been widowed herself before giving birth to her first and only child. After these personal tragedies, in 1882, Wanda began applying to the Prussian authorities for a permit to open a school at the palace she owned in Bruczków.

Bismarck's *Kulturkampf* had been in full swing since 1871. The Polish language was banned from use in Prussian schools and offices. Polish teachers were dismissed from the state system, Polish land was transferred to German ownership, and the Polish press had been put under German supervision.

It was precisely at this moment, when Germanization of Polish lands under Prussian control was at its peak, that Wanda Koczorowska was allowed to open an educational institution. This minor miracle was due solely, as one of her later pupils Ludmiła Sługocka explained, to "the unrivalled tact she displayed in handling any administrative matter, along with her boundless energy."[3]

---

[1] Statement by Krystyna Mikołajczyk, 14 May 1946, in Janina Kacperska, "Germanizacja dzieci polskich w okresie okupacji", master's thesis, Łódź University Humanities Department, Social Pedagogy Section, 1946/47 r., Archiwum Akt Nowych [Central Archive of Modern Records, hereafter: AAN], karta nr 95.

[2] Theo Herrmann, *Hildegard Hetzer in Polen*, Mannheim, 2012 citing Ines Hopfer-Pfister, *Geraubte Identität,* Böhlau Verlag, Wiedeń 2010 (p. 111). https://www. dgps.de/fachgruppen/fgge/beitraege/psychgesch-beitr_1-2010.pdf

[3] Ludmiła Sługocka, *Bruczków. Tajna szkoła polska i dom dziecka w byłym zaborze pruskim,* Bogucki Wydawnictwo Naukowe, Poznań 2015, p. 19.

Koczorowska was permitted to open her school in 1884 under the condition that she pay for everything with her own funds, hire qualified staff, teach the Prussian primary school (*Volksschule*) curriculum, and put the single-teacher school under the supervision of the Prussian authorities.

Koczorowska agreed to those terms. She added a new wing to the palace containing classrooms, a dormitory and a chapel. She also employed a German teacher—Franziska Habertsroh.

"Wanda Koczorowska operated a school, but nobody realized it was THAT kind of school. She taught in Polish, although the children also had to learn German," says Maria Nowakowska.

The official classes strictly followed the Prussian curriculum. Pupils received their school certificates in German, while simultaneously attending clandestine Polish language classes.

"Koczorowska lacked professional pedagogical training, but she did possess a good fund of general knowledge. Her lessons cannot be reduced to a fixed methodological template. They somewhat resembled the combined teaching method or project-based learning. Very often, she would use a specially selected dictated text to assemble cognitive elements from varied disciplines, such as geography, history, literature, and nature studies. Occasionally she would give classes that summed up or reviewed the course material. Pupils in the upper grades had an excellent knowledge of the chronologies of Polish history, literature, and spiritual development," Sługocka remembered.[4]

Bruczków Palace

[4] Sługocka, *Bruczków. Tajna…*, p. 51.

Tablet commemorating Wanda Koczorowska and her secret school in Bruczków

Koczorowska stressed patriotic values at her school. She carefully molded and educated the younger generation to "provide our oppressed Fatherland with genuine citizens." She spent all day with her pupils, teaching lessons, personally serving meals, leading every walk, corresponding with parents and guardians to keep them informed of their children's progress, and using every spare moment to impart knowledge—especially the forbidden kind. Her most promising pupils were sent to secondary schools, at Koczorowska's expense. She played the piano and harmonium, embroidered vestments for the local priests, knitted scarves and caps for her charges. Among the latter was Maria Kurcmann, the daughter of a former director of the Raczyński Library in Poznań and a later teacher and director of the state school in Bruczków.

As Ludmiła Sługocka points out, the eight-year program at Koczorowska's boarding school cost pupils and their parents nothing. Everything a pupil needed for daily life—clothing, school supplies, even toys—was provided free of charge.

'Auntie' Rescues Marian

An old topographical map from 1911 shows just how extensive Koczorowska's landholdings were.[5]

This carefully maintained, self-sufficient farmstead—consisting of a central complex of solidly built masonry buildings, including stables, a carriage house, barns, a forge, a carpentry shop and three-story grain silo, a 25-room manor house, assorted outbuildings, a chapel, playing fields for girls and boys, an outdoor summer school and dining area, orchard, flower garden, greenhouse and fishpond—all this, which earlier was at the disposal of Wanda Koczorowska's clandestine Polish school, became during the Second World War a place where children said goodbye to their Polish identity.

Wanda Koczorowska spent 44 years of her life running the place and educating children. She died on January 3, 1927. The only person who spent more time working there was Agnieszka Baszyńska, the cook, who stayed on for years after Koczorowska's death.

In subsequent years, the palace housed a seminary belonging to the Catholic missionary order of Verbists, which according to figures from the Gostyń Museum, trained about 40 boys aged 14 to 18.

Making a brief appearance among them was Marian Pogasz, who later became an actor famous for popularizing the local dialect of Greater Poland. It was quickly decided, however, that young Marian, an orphan, would do better under the care of Maria Kurcmann, who quickly took him under her wing.[6]

---

[5] Sługocka, *Bruczków. Tajna…*, p. 28.

[6] MAZ, "Marian Pogasz – Stary Marych", *Gazeta Poznańska*, May 23, 1997.

In 1940 the palace in Bruczków was converted into a transit camp for local priests. Several dozen clergymen were held at the facility pending transport to Dachau and Buchenwald.

Before they were sent away, the priests managed to prepare a group of children for their first communion. A souvenir photo survives. Marian Pogasz isn't in it. As Jan Figielek explains in reminiscences about his school chum, the Germans were already taking an interest in him.

"Orphans with features like Marian's were being taken away to Germany. 'Auntie' Kurcmann saved him from deportation by bribing the Gestapo with a grand piano," writes Figielek.[7]

Germanization Factory

Fifteen years after Koczorowska's death, in late 1941, this very same site, with its beautifully situated palace once converted into a children's home and school, and later into a theological seminary, saw the arrival of children abducted from Polish orphanages and families and destined for Germanization. Those fit to be absorbed into German society were to be chosen, after careful examination, by Dr. Hildegard Hetzer, a reputable Austrian psychologist who had been brought to Bruczków on the personal recommendation of Heinrich Himmler, SS Reichsführer and Reich Commissioner for the Consolidation of German Nationhood.[8]

Bruczków area residents with snapshots of people who lived and worked at the palace before the war.

[7] Jan Figielek, "Wieczornica poświęcona Marianowi Pogaszowi, związanemu z ziemią bruczkowską", *Ziemia Borecka*, nr 3 (13), March 2000, p. 11.

[8] Herrmann, *Hildegard Hetzer in Polen*, p. 3.

The Bruczków complex's seclusion and ample accommodations made it ideally suited for a Germanization center.

Such operations in Wartegau were directly supervised by Arthur Greiser, the local Gauleiter or Nazi party leader. It was on Greiser's initiative that Bruczków was turned into a Germanization facility. As Edmund Nowak writes, Greiser played the leading role in implementing Germanization policies in Greater Poland.

"In 1942 I received a summons to appear with my granddaughter Teresa for a physical exam at the Social Welfare Department on Piotrkowska Street. (...) My granddaughter was held at the Kopernika Street shelter and deported a few days later. They wouldn't give me any information, except that my Teresa was of German blood and therefore had been taken to a German school. I managed to track down two girls who were in Teresa's group. It turned out they were together at the children's home in Bruczków, and then the whole group was sent to Munich. I've had no news of her since."

Julia Kucharska[9]

"As early as October 1939, [Greiser] himself declared which ethnic groups should be incorporated into the Greater German Reich. A new Central German *Volksliste* Office was established under the Gauleiter, operating in three presidential regencies—Inowrocław, Łódź and Poznań," Nowak said during the unveiling of the memorial plaque at the Bruczków palace.[10]

Adapting Wanda Koczorowska's former property to its new function presented no difficulty due to its earlier use as an orphanage and boarding school. The infrastructure for a children's facility was in place and ready.

Jan Sulisz, a child from Łódź who ended up in Bruczków, recalls his own experiences:

"In 1940, four boys—all with light blond hair, like me—were taken from the Sienkiewiczówka orphanage to the Health Department for testing. We were immediately transferred to the local children's shelter on Przędzalniana Street. They took blood, skin and hair samples and measured body parts from head to toe. Afterwards, I was sent to Bruczków. There were about 70-80 children, all over the

---

[9] Statement by Julia Kucharska, 11 May 1946, in Kacperska, *Germanizacja...*, AAN, karta nr 97.

[10] Lecture by Edmund Nowak, chairman of the Borek Wielkopolski branch of the ZBoWiD veterans' association, on the unveiling of a memorial plaque to the victims of Germanization at the palace in Bruczków, September 1, 1971, excerpt from Władysław Stachowski prepared by B. Latosińska of the Gostyń Museum.

age of three. At Bruczków we were taught German and forbidden to speak Polish. After a few days, some kids were sent to Luxembourg, some to Ludwików, and I went back to Łódź. They tested me again for "race", after which I returned to Bruczków and then six weeks later was sent to Niederaltreich, to Regensdorf… I was put in an SS school… Besides a crash German course, we were taught shooting and riding, ran and carried stones as physical exercise. For going to church or speaking Polish they'd beat you and stop your meals. That's where we were given new surnames and told we would become Germans. After this camp we were allocated to various farmers. We were told to call them "father" and "mother" to help us quickly forget where we came from. My name was supposed to be Johann Suhling."[11]

Under the watchful eye of the matrons—Ludwig, Schramm, Schulz, Bochweld, Burchardt, and Eisler—the children's memories were carefully erased as they absorbed German language and culture. A souvenir photo taken for headmistress Johanna Zander's birthday shows the young teachers erect in studied poses, standing beside a crystal punchbowl.[12]

"The teachers were preoccupied with their duty to the Fatherland. Every child was examined on arrival by Dr. Hetzer. Based on her observations and those of the caregivers, a selection evaluation was made: suitable or unsuitable for Germanization. In the second case, children were sent back to Łódź, to the infamous concentration camp for Polish children—*Jugendverwahrlager der Sicherheitspolizei in Litzmannstadt* (…) While at Bruczków, children who qualified to join the master race were stripped of their documents, photographs and keepsakes and given German first names and surnames. Children who until now had been called Janek, Czesiek, Terenia or Jaga suddenly became Hanses, Adolfs, Gretas and Trudis. Not just their names were changed, but also their character, thinking and habits. Young minds absorbed a new language and new truths. In this way, new citizens were readied for the Third Reich," Nowak noted.[13]

---

[11] Statement by Jan Sulisz, 13 May 1946, in Kacperska, *Germanizacja dzieci…*, AAN, karta nr 93.

[12] Zenon Bosacki, Maciej Siejak, "Tajemnica pałacu w Bruczkowie", *Gazeta Poznańska,* nr 10, January 12, 1967.

[13] Edmund Nowak lecture, September 1, 1971.

Antonina's letters

The last contact parents had with their abducted children came through a Polish cook working at the facility, Antonina Nowicka, then using her maiden name of Borowczyk.

"She worked at the Germanization center as a kitchen helper. She used to describe how she would post letters from children to their parents when she went to town to buy bread. She slipped them into the letterbox—when no one was looking, of course. Apparently, she was never able to send many letters. The whole correspondence was collected by journalist Jerzy Zielonka in 1971," says Nowicka's daughter in law, Lucyna Nowicka.

"Many names faded from memory over the years, but a few stuck. The cook sent letters from Teresa Frąckowiak to Rogóźno, from Tekla Dudzińska and Maria Grzymalska to Poznań, and from sisters Anna and Maria Olszacka to Zduńska Wola. Sad letters from sad, solemn-faced children giving their families a last shred of hope," Zielonka wrote in *Gazeta Zachodnia*.[14]

The palace in Bruczków

Going to town was not easy to arrange, since the palace had its own vegetable garden and was virtually self-sufficient.

---

[14] Jerzy Zielonka, "Tajemnice pałacu w Bruczkowie", *Gazeta Zachodnia*.

Antonina Nowicka collected mementos from the Bruczków children in a scrapbook. Among them was a picture of a group of girls with nuns and children's ID photos with inscriptions beginning "Dear Mrs."

"As time passed, they began to forget their families, but their families never forgot about them. Mothers arrived bearing food and toys, having discovered who knows how where their children were being held. None were allowed through the palace gates. So they tried to smuggle these tokens of love and remembrance through the few Polish members of the menial staff—laundresses, cleaners, cooks. They offered enormous sums for help in kidnapping their own children. Unfortunately, it was impossible to get these kids out of Bruczków, or later, Kalisz. One of the former Polish staff at Bruczków remembers an unsuccessful escape attempt by a group of older boys, about 10 years of age," Zenon Bosacki and Maciej Siejak wrote on the pages of *Gazeta Poznańska* in 1967.[15]

Anna Rudzińska also refers to this children's revolt: on Arthur Greiser's orders, all the boys were taken to a site near Poznań and shot.[16]

Hildegard Hetzer's "Polish beer"

What do Bruczków residents know about Hildegard Hetzer today?

Very little. Neither former Bruczków inmates who came back to tell the story, nor the village chief, nor the local school director have heard anything about her.

Yet the Austrian psychologist's achievements and honors have been written about by German and Austrian authors. From a lengthy text by Theo Hermann, a psychology professor at Mannheim University, we learn more about the career of the researcher so esteemed by Heinrich Himmler.

Shortly after the war began, Hetzer took a job with the National Socialist People's Welfare (*Volkswohlfahrt*, or NSV) in Berlin. Among other duties, she headed an educational counseling unit for the German National Socialist Workers' Party (NSDAP).

---

[15] Bosacki, Siejak, *Tajemnica pałacu…*

[16] Anna Rudzińska, "Losy gostyńskich dzieci w okresie okupacji niemieckiej", *Nowa Ga- zeta Gostyńska*, nr 38 (281), Sept. 21, 2008, and nr 39 (282), Sept. 28, 2008.

17 Herrmann, *Hildegard Hetzer…*, p. 2.

In early March 1942, Hetzer was transferred to Poznań. Himmler wanted her to investigate the racial and psychological suitability of children at Bruczków for Germanization.

Hetzer, as she later testified, was convinced that her task was to examine neglected German children. As a rule, however, she was dealing with small children who were only starting to learn the German language. Would a woman with so much professional experience be likely to mistake a non-native speaker for a German? Moreover, as Hermann remarks, she was encountering children who mostly had Polish names.

A month before arriving in Poznań, Hetzer must have known about her job at Bruczków. In an 8 February letter to Hildegard Knies, a former colleague, she writes cryptically about "having to drink the Polish beer", using an idiom that means "facing the music" or "reaping what you sow". She needed an assistant at Bruczków and was asking Knies to join her.[18]

Hermann writes that Hetzer's activities at Bruczków were preceded by intensive preparations in Berlin. While writing to Knies, Hetzer must have known that Bruczków had been established as an "observation home for new candidates to be turned into German children" (*Beobachtungsheim für die neu zu deutschenden Kinder*). Crucially, she stressed in the letter that the Reichsführer SS had personally ordered psychological studies of the children. Could Hetzer have known Himmler's precise instructions on February 8, 1942? After all, his notorious Regulation 67/I, outlining plans to Germanize Polish children who met the racial criteria, was not issued until 19 February.

Hetzer is specifically named in the document, as shown by this excerpt:

"Children who have been racially examined by the SS Race and Resettlement Main Office and deemed fit for Germanization will be given a careful medical examination by State Health Department offices, including a Wasserman test, X-rays, tuberculosis test, thorough de-lousing, etc. Medical results of children considered suitable for Germanization based on previous selection testing should be forwarded to the *Warthegau* Reich plenipotentiary (District Authorities). The Reich plenipotentiary in Poznań will place these children in the district children's home at Bruczków (Gostyń district). At the Bruczków *Gaukinderheim*, Professor Dr. Hildegard Hetzer (of the NSDAP), Reich leadership, People's Welfare Main

[18] Herrmann, *Hildegard Hetzer*..., p. 4.

Office, will conduct psychological testing of the children. In addition, the children's home director (assisted by the caregiving personnel), will issue an evaluation of each child's character. Children are to stay at Bruczków for about six weeks. Upon completion of testing at Bruczków, the *Warthegau* Reich plenipotentiary will forward the results for children at the district children's home to the plenipotentiary in Poznań..."[19]

After the war, Hetzer maintained that she had not known about Regulation 67/I, learning of its existence only on December 22, 1949.

She began work at Bruczków on March 1, 1942, without help from the coworkers she had so counted on.

Hetzer's first encounter with children who had been selected as racially valuable occurred on March 14, when a transport arrived with 14 girls and 13 boys from Łódż. The children were aged from five to 12 years.

During the children's stay at Bruczków, the most important task was to teach them German. They were all given new German names. Speaking Polish was strictly forbidden, and any violations were severely punished.

One of the children Hetzer examined was Zyta Suś, whose stay at the facility and negative psychological evaluation by Hetzer were described by Ines Hopfer-Pfister in her book, *Geraubte Identität* (Stolen Identity).[20]

Zyta, along with two boys—Jan and Bolesław—was sent back to Łódź on April 3, 1942 as unsuitable for Germanization. She returned to Bruczków on May 27, 1942. Subsequently, all three children were deemed eligible to join German society.

The Bruczków center was supposed to decide whether the children delivered there met racial, medical and psychological criteria for Germanization and adoption in the Third Reich. A final report was prepared for each child. Professor Hetzer signed each psychological evaluation. She judged character traits, and classifying children on their ability to fulfill certain tasks and attributing shortcomings to "lack of inner content" or "flaws in internal content."

A local history of the Gostyń district (*Dziejów ziemi gostyńskie*) states that the Bruczków facility could accommodate 45 children and employed 13 personnel, of whom 10 were Germans. The ages of the children varied. For example, of 24

---

[19] Regulation 67/I, in *Biuletyn Głównej Komisji w P*, v. 5, 1949, IPN Archive.

[20] Ines Hopfer-Pfister, *Geraubte Identität,* Böhlau Verlag, Wien, Köln, Weimar 2010, p. 112.

children registered in October 1942, six were between three and six years old, while 18 were aged from six to 14.[21]

"My mother died in 1940, and my father in 1942. The four of us children were taken in by my mother's sisters.... After a few months, we all got a summons to report to 113 Piotrkowska Street for testing. There we were weighed, X-rayed, photographed, carefully measured, and given blood tests.... One week later, we were taken to Bruczków, where we spent another five weeks. The whole time we were taught to read, write, and sing in German. Speaking Polish was forbidden, they took away your food for that. About 40 children were at the facility."

— Barbara Mikołajczyk[22]

After their stay, which typically lasted from six to 12 weeks, most of the older children were sent to Germany for further education at boarding schools or to Hitler Youth and League of German Girls [*Bund Deutsche Mädel*, or BDM] facilities.

Physicians who visited the children at Bruczków were less interested in their health than in the development of personality traits and general predispositions that would "allow them to be adopted by the "Great German People". One of the most frequent visitors to Bruczków and Kalisz was a physician by the name of Barthel, accompanied by a female physician-psychologist named Reisch.

After two months at Bruczków, Professor Hetzer was suddenly transferred to Poznań. No explanation for the move was given. According to Hetzer, the transfer may be explained by her "vigorous" insistence after the appearance of two mothers at Bruczków that their children be returned. The NSV Head Office then summoned Hetzer to Poznań, where she took up a specialized department leader's post.[23]

From Bruczków to Kalisz

When a children's home with a separate registration office for abducted children was established at Kalisz, the Bruczków center changed to a third-level facility.

---

[21] Stanisława Sierpowskiego, ed., *Dzieje ziemi gostyńskiej*, Wydawnictwo Naukowe Uniwersytetu im. Adama Mickiewicza, Poznań 1979, p. 391.

[22] Statement by Barbara Mikołajczyk, 11 May 1946, in Kacperska, *Germanizacja...*, karta 91.

[23] Herrmann, *Hildegard Hetzer...*, p. 8.

This meant it received only pre-selected children who met the racial criteria, were promising psychologically, and had been successfully Germanized. They were simply awaiting transport to Germany.

> *"I was seven when they took me from the Copernicus Street orphanage, where I'd been placed, for a medical examination at Piotrkowska Street. Afterwards they sent me to Bruczków, where I stayed for more than a year. I remember a camp in Salzburg where they gave me a card with the name Malknecht and my date of birth. That was to be my name from then on. Afterwards, they handed me over to a farmer."*
>
> — Zenon Małkiewicz[24]

A document at the Modern Records Archive [*Archiwum Akt Nowych*, AAN] in Warsaw indicates that two sisters, Barbara and Mirosława Rzetelska, were placed in a Łódź orphanage after their mother died. In November 1947, the Polish Government's Plenipotentiary for the Recovery of Abducted Children, Roman Hrabar, asked Social Welfare in Łódź "to resolve the case of the Rzetelski children."[25]

Hrabar had obtained information indicating the girls had been taken in August 1942 to the Bruckau (Bruczków) facility near Poznań. They had then been transported to Achern to be Germanized. In 1943, they were put under the care of the Mayer family in Sandhausen, Germany.

Barbara and Mirosława became Baerbel and Hilde Rätel.

Their Germanization was so successful that after the war, they didn't want to come home.

Hildegard Hetzer's Postwar Reckoning

Professor Hetzer had difficulty finding employment after the war. After a two-stage de-Nazification procedure, however, she was reinstated in the civil service. Nothing untoward was seen in her activities involving Germanization of Polish children or on occupied Polish territory.

---

[24] Statement by Zenon Małkiewicz, 13 May 1946, in Kacperska, *Germanizacja…*, karta nr 80.

[25] Letter from Roman Hrabar, Plenipotentiary for Abducted Children, to the Łódź Municioal Social Welfare Department, Child Recovery Section, on the Rzetelski sisters case, November 21, 1947, *Dokumenty Ministerstwa Pracy i Opieki Społecznej*, AAN, sygn. 375, karta nr 143.

In 1949, Hetzer was again subjected to an inquiry in Hesse concerning her record at Bruczków. It was found that Hetzer was "more a less a witness in her own case", which substantially distorted the picture of her true activities. In the end, it was ruled that there were no grounds for prosecuting her.

Memorial plaque

"Polish society's greatest tragedy under German occupation was the abduction of Polish children, torn from their home environment and transported into an alien and hostile society," said Edmund Nowak during the unveiling on September 1, 1971 of a plaque commemorating the victims of Germanization in Borek Wielkopolski.[26]

A few isolated clues in the archives lead back to Bruczków. "The municipal office had some old registry records from 1939 and before. I wanted to find out if a German teacher lived there who had employed my mother—then 13 years old—to stoke her furnace. Those pages were torn out. Somebody must have deliberately removed them. Not a trace of those Germans remained, not a single document," says Maria Jańczak.

"The Germans destroyed everything when they left, they were covering their tracks," adds Bruczków resident Teresa Szymczak.

"My mother-in-law, Antonina Nowicka, was taken away along with the children to the Germanization center in Kalisz," recalls Lucyna Nowicka.

Antonina Nowicka's home was then occupied by Mrs. Kurcmann, together with the boy she rescued from Germanization: Marys. Later they moved to Bogdaniec, and Mrs. Kurcmann changed her name to Karlińska.

After the children were removed from Bruczków, the palace was taken over by an official and his family, along with a tailor who made uniforms for the German army and his five children. There was also an older married couple and two ladies with their grandmothers. They were supposedly from Berlin and stayed until the war ended.

Before she died, Antonina Nowicka, who had smuggled children's letters out of the Bruczków facility, remembered how some men had visited from Germany. They said they had lived at Bruczków as children.

---

[26] Edmund Nowak lecture, September 1, 1971.

***

The story of Bruczków was told by:

Teresa Szymczak, Maria Nowakowska, Janina Janicka, Lucyna Nowicka, Maria Jańczak, Stanisława Grzeszczak, Elżbieta Guszczak, Urszula Michalak, Anna Marcinkowska, Hieronim Michalak and Leszek Chałupniczak.

Kalisz: Ghost Stop for Stolen Children

It was likely on the third floor—the school library. Sister Ruth Kawa, of the Sisters of Nazareth, and I perch on a ladder and peer out the window. It's May, and an orange expanse of tiled roofs stretches out below us. The nun gestures with her arm: "The laundry was there, and higher up, on the second floor, is where the children taken by the Germans slept." From a different window we see the broad convent grounds, enclosed by a thick, ivy-covered wall.

In 1942, when the Nazis set up a Germanization facility at the convent with its own secret civil registry office, the nuns were already gone – sent to the forced labor camp at Bojanów. That's when the Germans began bringing in abducted, racially suitable children who had been snatched from their families, shelters and schools. Their stay in Kalisz was brief, just a few weeks. Later they were shunted to other facilities and stages of Germanization. The process lasted until they ended up with a German family or employer.

We stroll along the convent wall. It's a hot day. The smell of roses lingers heavily in the air.

***

"My daughter got a notice to appear at Obornik in early August with her birth certificate. She was seven and a half years old. At Obornik, the children had their profiles measured, first one side and then the other. After four weeks they called me back. They took a blood sample from my girl and did racial tests. They were taking children with blond hair and blue eyes. Then they smeared something on her side and said come back in three days, when the pustules start to appear. She caught a fever… We went to the railway station and the children were sent to Kalisz," said Bronisława Ewertowska in her testimony at the 1946 trial of Wartheland Gauleiter Arthur Greiser.[1]

Asked whether she demanded the return of her child, Ewertowska replied:

---

[1] Testimony of Bronisława Ewertowska during the 1946 trial of Wartheland Gauleiter Arthur Greiser, Kalisz State Archive [hereafter: APK], Tadeusz Martyn collection (1241), sygn. 167, karta nr 1.

"I screamed and cried, but they didn't want to give her back. I gave the child a postcard and she mailed it to me from Ostrów, which made it clear she had gone to Kalisz. After that, I didn't get any word from or about my daughter. She never came back, and until today I don't know whether she's alive or dead. She vanished like a stone in a pond."

Sisters of the Holy Family of Nazareth convent, Kalisz

Garden path along the convent wall in Kalisz, with Józef Kicała's home visible (background left).

***

Confidential letter from the Third Reich Ministry of Interior to Wartheland Gauleiter Arthiur Greiser, 10 December 1942:

"At the direction of the Reichsführer SS, the Lebensborn organization is to carry out Germanization of Polish children. To this end, the aforementioned children will be dispatched to the *Gaukinderheim* in Kalisz (Warthegau) for examination as to their racial, genetic and psychological suitability. In case they prove suitable for Germanization, these children will be placed in the appropriate facilities."[2]

This was the document that officially founded the District Children's Home in Kalisz.

***

We enter the former *Gaukinderheim*. The ground floor is sunny, with the summer heat seeping through the open windows. If we were to transport ourselves back to 1942, one door would lead to the salon where the youngest children spent most of their day. Behind the other is the former refectory, which served as a dining and common room.

The former refectory where the children ate their meals.

[2] Regulation of 10 December 1942 on registering children at the *Gaukinderheim*, APK, Kalisz municipal records, sygn. 61, karta nr 3.

***

"I remember we still had china plates with swastikas on them in the early 1990s," Sister Ruth says.

"They were used in the convent?"

"Yes, for a while, until they landed in the basement—they were quite heavy."

"The sisters didn't object to the swastika?"

"It was on the reverse. We saw things differently then."

The corridor windows look out on the courtyard. There stands a white sculpture of the Holy Family, since the order's official name is the Congregation of the Sisters of the Holy Family of Nazareth. On the first floor, the courtyard is lined by a row of windows. One is smaller, tilted open. Sister Ruth is just about to tell us about it.

View of the convent courtyard. The smaller window on the second floor opens onto a room used to punish disobedient children, according to sisters assigned to work at the Gaukinderheim during the war.

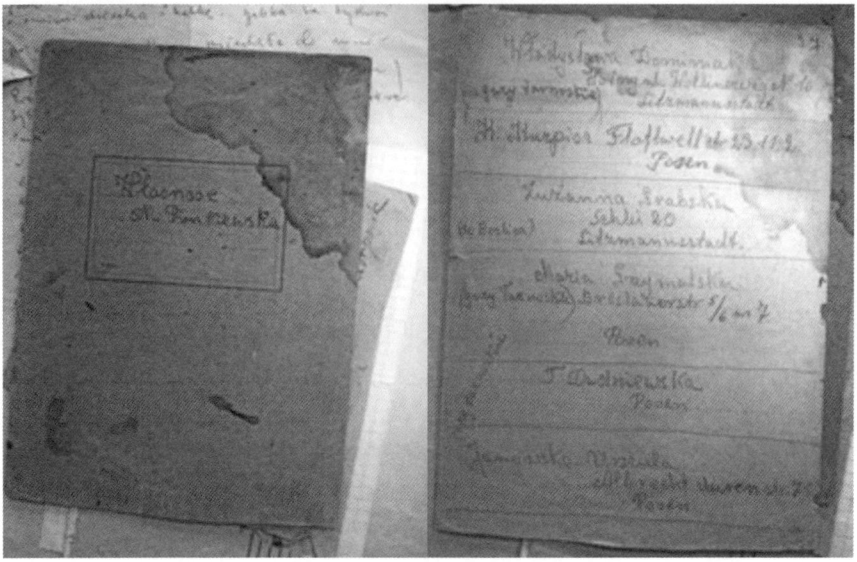

Maria Pinczewska's notebook about the Gaukinderheim in Kalisz

***

The State Archive in Kalisz has a little, yellowed notebook in which children's names and addresses are inscribed. Its pages are brittle, as if they were about to crumble into dust.

***

The police took Czesław Wojciechowski directly from home in 1943. They told his mother he would be fine and that nothing would happen. He remembers being taken with the other kids to Kalisz, to a facility in a church. He remembers his stay as tightly organized, with every slot on the daily calendar filled.

As Kacper Poldek testified in June 1946, "I had a Mommy and a Daddy, sister and a brother. The Germans came for me at school.... They took two other boys from my class and my sister, too. Straight from school to the station."

Władek Ostrowski: "I was taken by some SS men straight from the pasture where I was tending cattle. They took me to Kalisz. I was beaten there for speaking Polish."

Mietek Domański: "I was six when the Germans took me from home. My Mommy didn't want to let me go but they told Mom they would kill her."[3]

> *"In 1940 my wife died, leaving me alone with two boys. Both of my sons fell ill with typhus in 1942. After a hospital stay, they were placed in a children's home on Brzeźna Street [in Łódź], while I was sent as an invalid to an old age home, In the winter of 1942-1943, the boys told me that they had been given a "race" exam and photographed and would be sent to Germany. I never saw my sons again and they didn't write. The lady director at my old age home told me the boys were in Kalisz and doing well. Now I've heard from Social Welfare that they are in Salzburg. The names of my sons are Henryk and Leszek."*
>
> —Jan Olejnik[4]

Prime candidates for Germanization were children who had passed the racial and psychological examinations and were specimens of good health. They had to be obedient and intelligent. The children were tested and careful observations made. From a partial registry of children who passed through the *Gaukinderheim*, it appears that those in Kalisz were from two to 14 years of age. They came for a stay of approximately six weeks before being sent on. Neither they nor their families were ever told the destination.

***

7:00 a.m. – Reveille. The children dress and wash in cold water. They must be toughened up. Warm water is provided on Saturdays only. Morning calisthenics.

8:00 a.m. – Breakfast.

Younger children go outside to play, older ones help tidy up.

1:00 p.m. – Dinner, followed by lessons.

6:00 p.m. – Supper.

---

[3] Testimony of children who underwent Germanization, APK, Tadeusz Martyn collection, syg. 157, p. 8, karta nr 11.

[4] Statement by Jan Olejnik, 25 May 1946, in Kacperska, *Germanizacja dzieci...*, AAN, karta nr 66.

After supper the youngest children are put to bed, while older ones learn German. Songs and reciting poetry help them acquire the new language.[5]

Wiesiek Kuligowski can't get the hang of German and receives multiple beatings from his instructors.[6]

***

The open window is not of standard size. Sister Damiana "did not personally witness children being beaten, but she heard about such beatings from Konstancja Kosmalska and Jożefa Twardowska, especially in a room on the second floor just off the attic stairs. They were beaten for speaking Polish," Sister Ruth says, citing Sister Damiana's testimony.

Briefly, we pause before some frescoes recently discovered during a renovation and peer again at the half-open window across the courtyard, into what was allegedly a child punishment room. Sister Ruth takes a cautious view of claims that children were violently abused at the facility. She has no desire to embellish previous accounts.

Sister Ruth points to the second floor dormitory at the Kalisz Gaukinderheim

---

[5] Jadwiga Ruth Kawa CSFN, *Czas wielkich spraw. Wojenne losy kaliskich nazaretanek,* Congregation of Sisters of the Holy Family of Nazareth, Kalisz 2018, p. 92.

[6] Wiesław Kuligowski, *Ja – Claus Kugler*, Fundacja "Moje Wojenne Dzieciństwo", http://www.mojewojennedziecinstwo.pl/pdf/02_kuligowski_ja.pdf

"Taking a young person from their home and uprooting them is a sufficient act of violence. Along with feeling foreign and alone," Sister Ruth says. "The children have every right to the worst possible memories of a dark, gloomy convent."

Not every child proved suitable for Germanization. As Janina Kossowska, or Sister Vianney, recalls, "the more resilient and spiritually strongest children were sent back. As were those deemed morally unworthy to belong to the German nation – for example, three girls caught sneaking into the pantry."

***

"In the summer of 1943, children of single mothers, orphans and half-orphans from the village of Rogoźno in Greater Poland were sent to nearby Oborniki to appear before a commission composed of SS officers. The commission was to test and select children. After a thorough exam, an SS officer instructed the secretary to put me and my younger sister Urszula on a red card. The names of some other children were entered on a white card. As it turned out, everyone on the red card were designated for transport to a Germanization camp," remembers Regina Kiziak (maiden name Jabłońska).[7]

The first transport of children from Rogoźno to Kalisz was organized in the autumn of 1943. Regina was placed on the second transport, in January or February 1944.

"We were escorted by a young German woman dressed in the black habit of the Sisters of Mercy. On arrival at the convent, we were first led to the dining room, where a portrait of Adolf Hitler hung. On the side walls were photos of Hermann Göring, Heinrich Himmler, Joseph Goebbels and others. We were told that from the instant we set foot in the *Gaukinderheim*, our father was Hitler and he would take care of us," Regina recalls.

She remembers caring for a nine-month-old girl, the daughter of a female clerk. The girl's name was Heidi.

Regina also remembers young children being brought to Kalisz, three- or four-year-old kids. She didn't know their names or where they were from. They were mute with fright. "They cried and called for their Mommies, and we were just helpless," she recalls.

---

[7] Jacek Zduńczyk, "Skazani na wynarodowienie", *Kalisia*, nr 11 (42) November 1997.

***

"One must reckon with the fact that relatives and acquaintances will try by various means to locate and track down the children. Such searches are possible through applications to the police registry office but potentially jeopardize the pre-established goal of Germanizing these children. All possible measures should thus be taken to eliminate pedagogical difficulties attributable to the influence of these relatives and friends. For this purpose, I order the establishment of a special police registry office at the specified *Gaukinderheim*, which should be given the name: Second Police Registry Bureau in Kalisz (Warthegau). This institution's cooperation with existing posts such as the registry office is essential and necessary. The whole matter should be treated as confidential and is not for publication in any form," according to a document from the Third Reich Interior Minister date December 10, 1942.[8]

> *"My adopted daughter Anna Żakowska was summoned to the local Landrat and then sent to Łódź for racial testing. When we didn't send our daughter to a second examination, gendarmes came to our home and made me take the little girl to the railroad station (...) She was sent to Kalisz. I went there but the people in Kalisz hadn't heard about any facility for Polish children. I was able to find the place and saw my daughter. My appearance there caused a considerable stir and great agitation. They kept asking aggressively how I had obtained the address. That was the last time I saw my daughter. Recently a young boy returned to Zgierz who had seen Anna. He told me that after a short stay at Oberweißbach in Thuringia, they had been parceled out among the local Germans. He said the children were treated as German orphans, it was forbidden to say they were Poles. I've received word that my child is in Salzburg."*
>
> — Stanisław Żakowski[9]

Special responsibilities were given to the *Gaukinderheim* director, who was charged with supervising the secret registry bureau. This clandestine office registered children but was not empowered to certify residence, while names were omitted in the official registry. Formally, these children did not exist. Following Ministry instructions, facility personnel were listed in the official registry, so we see entries for

[8] Letter from the Interior Minister of the Third Reich, 10 December 1942, APK.

[9] Statement by Stanisław Żakowski, 29 May 1946, in Kacperska, *Germanizacja dzieci*..., AAN, karta nr 72.

staff—but not for children abducted to be Germanized. It was if they were never in Kalisz or had ever even been alive.

The system of institutions and authorities entrusted with Germanization worked efficiently. Confidential instructions were drafted and issued to individual facility and office directors. Children's personal data were altered, with surnames sometimes changed twice. Those slated for Germanization were registered in a bureau known only to authorized personnel. Old identities are erased—for many, irreversibly.

***

Sister Ruth opens a door on the ground floor. Zosia Arden, Olek Szalata, and Ania Szczotka used to run up and down these steps daily, along with the Witaszek sisters, Krysia Szafranek, Józia Pielucha and Adaś Spławski. These are just a few names from a partial list of children who passed through the *Gaukinderheim*.[10]

The stairs are steep, with a rickety handrail along the right-hand wall. Children descended them every morning from bunk bed dormitory on the second floor. Perhaps to the refectory, with its lovely, vaulted ceiling. Bright sunlight spills from large windows over the arched masonry. The kitchen was the domain of a German matron, Anni Gloser. She was assisted by Antonina Borowczyk, transferred from Bruczków, and Anna Breś, whose testimony as Sister Damiana we have heard.

After dinner the children do the dishes. Perhaps today is 14-year-old Zygmunt Światłowski's turn for kitchen duty. At the facility, he has been renamed Hans. Zygmunt/Hans quickly drew interest from a German family. But there is a problem. The facility staff believe Zygmunt has shown poor behavior by always speaking in Polish, which is forbidden. Johanna Zander enters the room and orders him in German to follow. Hans goes along to the refectory. There one of the girls has been bound with string to a bench as punishment for speaking Polish again. The other children have been gathered to see an "example" made. Terrified, they watch the scene play out. With a gesture, Zander instructs Zygmunt to hit the girl. She's to receive 20 lashes with a riding crop.[11]

---

[10] The children's first and last names come from a registry of children staying at *Gaukinderheim*, APK, Kalisz municipal records, sygn. 61, karta nr 5.

[11] "Ośrodek germanizacji polskich dzieci", *Słowo Powszechne*, nr 203, 1991.

The crop is then handed to Hans Huerlemann, which is Zygmunt's new name. He knows what he's supposed to do and is admonished to get on with it. Hans draws back and lashes the riding crop across her face with all his strength. But he does not strike the girl. The face belongs to Director Zander.

We know what happened next thanks to Maria Pinczewska's testimony and a 1991 newspaper article in *Słowo powszechne*. "Frau Zander dragged the boy down to basement, where the generators and power cables were located, and threw him onto the exposed wires.

The stairwell used daily by children at the Gaukinderheim. Their bedrooms were located upstairs, while the staff and doctor lived on the ground floor.

Gaukinderheim staff in Kalisz.

Zygmunt screamed and his body was instantly charred black. The German police were informed that the boy had stumbled onto the cables by accident.[12]

***

"Do you recognize this picture?"

"No."

On her laptop, the sister has pulled up a group photograph of the *Gaukinderheim* personnel in Kalisz.

Director Zander is smiling at us. There's nothing unusual about her. She stands in the middle, a kerchief on her head.

Her old room is behind the stairs. It's large and named for St. Raphael, the patron saint. A window opens out onto the garden, where today the fragrant meadowsweet is blossoming.

The ground floor with its spacious rooms was assigned as living quarters to the staff and doctor. Zander must have had exactly the same view as Sister Ruth and I, sitting a couple of windows down in the convent visitors' room. She would have seen not just the garden, but a section of the wall and the tenement house built by Józef Kical. Until 1935, the nuns rented space there for classrooms and faculty quarters.

---

[12] "Ośrodek germanizacji…"

During the war Sister Ewangilista lived there, as one of the few nuns the Germans chose not to send to the Bojanów work camp. She was judged unfit for labor due to wax burns on her hands. Despite Sister Ewangelista's infirmity, she made a living as a seamstress. She also kept a watchful eye from her room on what was happening behind the convent wall.

Sister Ruth points to the tenement windows that provided an excellent vantage to observe the convent grounds.

"'Keeping an eye on the convent' from there would have been a pretty sharp lookout," Sister Ruth assures me.

***

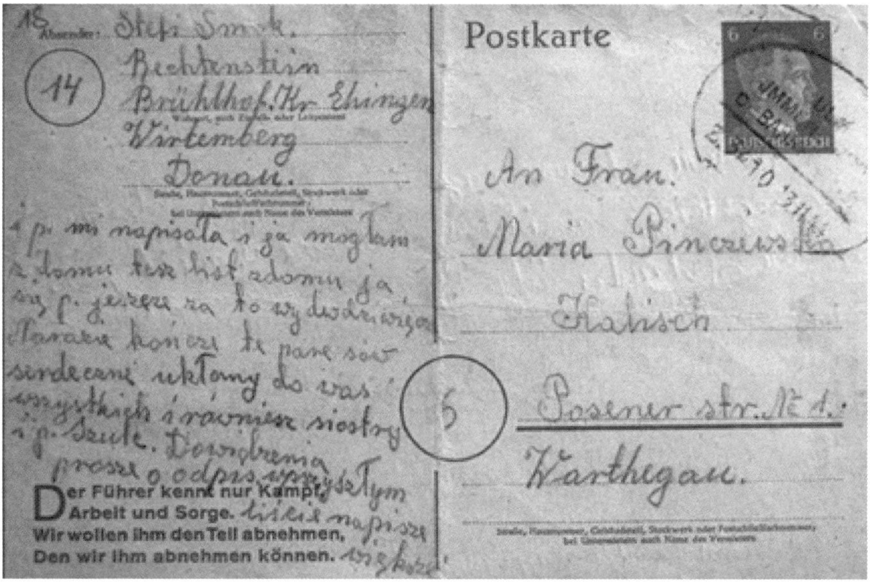

Postcard to Maria Pinczewska

"The children were allowed no correspondence whatsoever. I had three sister nuns living in Kalisz who received letters and packages for them. These I collected and passed on to the children in secret. I would call them into the lavatory, read the letters to them aloud, then tear them up and flush them down the toilet," Sister Damiana said later.[13]

---

[13] Testimony of Anny Breś, Ostrów Wielkopolski, 10 November 1975, APK, Tadeusz Martyn collection, sygn. 155, karty nr 1–2.

As she pointed out, other staff members had similar contacts and also delivered letters to the children. In Bruczków, as mentioned, this role was played by Antonina Borowczyk, who made trips to town to post illegal correspondence.

"Upon arriving in Kalisz, we were taken to a church on Dworcowa Street. At that time, the church had been converted into a dormitory. (…) One time, a nun secretly showed me a letter from my mother. It turned out the nun had written to Obornik and given mother the address where I was living and information about what was happening to me. I don't know the identity of the nun, however. I was kept at the facility until January 1944," testified Kazimiera Habicht, neé Chuda.[14]

***

We stand beside the mortuary chapel, which the *Gaukinderheim* staff likely used to lock up disobedient kids.

During the occupation, Maria Pinczewska lived next door to the convent.

"They kept bringing children, from where, I don't know. At first, they were escorted by Germans only, but after a while a few Polish nuns showed up. Of these nuns, I only knew Anna Breś. This sister passed on to me various bits of information," Pinczewska testified in Kalisz on February 23, 1967.[15]

Before Sister Damiana of the St. Elisabeth Order arrived in at the Germanization facility in February 1943, two Ursuline nuns—Sisters Vianey and Laurencja—were already working there.

---

[14] Testimony of children who underwent Germanization, November 1991, APK, Tadeusz Martyn collection, syg. 167, karty nr 28–29.

[15] Interrogation transcript of Maria Pinczewska, Kalisz, 23 February 1967, APK, Tadeusz Martyn collection, sygn. 155, karty nr 6–7.

The mortuary chapel in Kalisz where children who disobeyed the Germanization facility's rules—by speaking Polish, for example—were locked up.

After a stint at the Bojanów work camp, the two were transferred to the Kalisz *Gaukinderheim* in November 1942.

We have these sisters to thank, along with Maria Pinczewska, for much of our knowledge of what happened behind the walls of the *Gaukinderheim*.

"When I climbed up to the third floor of our building, I could see what was going on. One day Sister Breś told me to observe carefully what was happening at the '*Heim*'. I noticed the dead body of a boy. His corpse was blue, as if he had been electrocuted. Sister Breś told me that the home director had been on the lookout since he was always greeting people in Polish, even though that was forbidden (...). I saw how the director's husband took a photograph of that boy's body. Later, at the cemetery, Mrs. Maciejewska's husband lifted the lid of the coffin and I saw him," Pinczewska testified.

Based on an entry in a little notebook, she was able to identify the murdered boy as Zygmunt Światłowski from Łódź. "After the war, his grandmother visited me to ask about her grandson. I told her where to find the grave (...). The boy's parents had died in a camp. He must have been 13 or 14 years old."

The grave of Zygmunt Światłowski at the Majków military cemetery, Kalisz.

The utility gate for removing garbage from the convent. This was probably the route used by Stanisław Kulczyński to smuggle out children designated for Germanization, hidden in trash cans.

The military cemetery at Majków, where Zygmunt is buried, is a short drive from Kalisz. The boy's grave is close to the front gate, wedged behind much larger Gypsy family tombs with life-sized portraits of the deceased engraved on their marble slabs.

Zygmunt's headstone is inscribed: "Boy scout Zygmunt Światłowski, 1930–1944. Murdered by Germans at the Kalisz *Gaukinderheim* because he did not want to be a German."

***

On the Śródmiejska Street side of the convent is an old wooden gate—a utility entrance for tradesmen. It has a built-in flap that gives a view of the convent out-buildings or what is happening outside the grounds.

The second-floor dormitory for children at the Gaukinderheim.

"The wooden gate was used for removing garbage," says Sister Ruth. Sometimes, those trash bins were used for removing kids as well. The children were packed inside by a carpenter on the staff, Stanisław Kulczyński, who helped some of them avoid Germanization and return to their families.

Standing beside the heavy, rough-hewn gate, as if on guard, is a luxuriant acacia tree.

***

Before Sister Damiana arrived in Kalisz, she had been sent to work in Kobylin, at the *Jugendlager für Polnische Kinder* [Youth Camp for Polish Children], where 265 children were kept.

"Was that a Germanization center, too?"

"Yes, though it appears that Kobylin contained mostly older boys more suitable for work than for adoption. But the first thing they did was to kick the Franciscans out of the monastery," says Sister Ruth.

On March 13, 1940, the Gestapo brought a group of children to Kobylin from the Wolsztyn nursery, followed later by others from Poznań, Lisków, Pleszew and Zduny. The full name of the facility was "*Jugendlager für Polnische Kinder in Koppelstadt, Kreis Krotoschin.*"

"Children who were determined by the Commission to be of Nordic extraction were separated and sent to the Reich for Germanization. The other children remained in the monastery until the facility was liquidated by the Gestapo in August 1943," I read on the monastery's website.[16]

After the Kobylin facility was closed, Sister Damiana was transferred to the *Gaukinderheim* in Kalisz. Forced to work there as a kitchen assistant, she went out of her way to speak with the children. She had the older ones tell her their first and last names and place of residence. She collected from them letters written to their parents and passed these on to Maria Pinczewska, who posted them with her return address. Responses came back. She noted down everything in a little notebook, which she kept hidden in her straw pallet.

That notebook is now at the Kalisz State Archives. Its stained cover bears the inscription "Property of M. Pinczewska" and its pages are covered with entries about children kept at the facility, written in pencil.

Both today and 76 years ago, those pages contained information about the monastery's youngest residents.

***

Sister Ruth shows a photograph of an attractive young nun. Her name is Angelina Podemska. She arrived at the convent on July 18, 1966, as a visitor. She had wanted to see the place where she had been taken by the Germans during World War II as a 12-year-old girl who fulfilled the racial criteria. At the *Gaukinderheim*, she went through the whole procedure of denationalization.

"The sobbing young girl (born 1931) was noticed by Sister Evangelista from the other side of the garden wall. When she was able to make contact the girl, it turned out she was from the Kępno area. Efforts to get in touch with her uncle and smuggle her out of the facility came too late, as she was shipped out to Germany," Sister Ruth writes in her book, which cites the convent records.[17]

After liberation, Angelina found herself in the American occupation zone. With the help of an American soldier, she emigrated to the United States, where she was

---

[16] http://www.franciszkanie-kobylin.pl/index.php/zarys-dziejow

[17] Kawa, *Czas wielkich spraw. Wojenne losy…*, p. 104.

18 Statement of Stefania Smok, 29 May 1946, in Kacperska, *Germanizacja…*, AAN, karta nr 71.

entrusted to the care of the Sisters of Nazareth. Many of the nuns came from Polish immigrant families.

***

At least five transports of children were organized from Kalisz to Germany, each of about 30 to 40 children.

After the war, inquiries came in from all over Poland. Parents and institutions wanted to know what had happened to these deported children.

"We respectfully inquire whether the orphanage still has any of the children who were deported from Poznan by the occupation authorities for denationalization purposes."

In 1945, the Gniezno Social Welfare Department had the names of Mirek Sziwa, Henryk Wojciechowski, Jan Dapsuk, Olek Szalaty and Maciek Dąbrowski on their search list. "Please apprise whether the above-mentioned children taken from Gniezno are still there or, alternatively, where they were sent." This was the Polish Red Cross headquarters inquiring about whether its Kalisz office knew anything about what happened to children kept in local facilities during the German evacuation. They were also looking for a Stanisław Limański.

Meanwhile, the Pabianice municipal authorities were asking for the whereabouts of Krystyna Niewiadmoska, Józef Niewiadomski, Jadwiga Szafrańska and Jan Kusak—all "racially suitable" children from Pabianice who were delivered to the Kalisz orphanage.

What happened to Stefania Sława from Środa and Jan Cehner from Toruń?

And the answers came back: "We don't know", "we have not been able to ascertain", "she was not present", "she was not registered at Kalisz."[19]

[19] Children present during the occupation at the *Kalisz Gaukinderheim* and correspondence on lost children, APK, 11/19/0, Kalisz municipal records, Series: 4.2, Wydział Administracyjny, sygn. 61.

Alodia Witaszek (L), who as a child was sent to the Gaukinderheim in Kalisz.

The Fatherland School: An Ordeal for Polish Girls

No uniforms could be found for Halinka and four other Polish girls—perhaps because nobody was expecting them. Or perhaps this time there were more Eastern arrivals to the Reich than usual?

It's late summer, 1942. Teachers at the German Fatherland School at Achern, a town in Baden, are fussing over the latest transport from Poland, helping the kids get undressed and bathe. It is essential that they have a tidy, modest appearance. After their bath, the girls' hair is plaited into tight braids. If it's long enough, that is. Some girls' hair is too short, sometimes much too short. They're ones from orphanages and camps where children's heads are shaved bald.

Barred windows

After more outfits are ordered, Halinka and the Polish girls finally get their own white blouses, black ties and black skirts. This is the obligatory uniform of the *Bund Deutscher Mädel* [League of German Girls, or BDM] the female arm of the Hitler Youth. However, these fashionable clothes are only worn on holidays and special occasions, such as Nazi ceremonies. Everyday work in the fields and the kitchen is performed in much coarser attire.

Such hard labor is quite beyond the strength of an eight- or even 12-year-old child. Their stay in Baden is not meant to be an idyll but stern training that will turn them into real Germans. Soon they will learn what it means to be placed in an "institution of national-political education." The German Fatherland School in Achern is located at Illenau, a complex of neoclassical buildings gracefully situated among lawns and flowerbeds shaded by stately old trees. The girls take in this view through the barred bedroom windows.

For more than 100 years, since the mid-19th century, the Illenau psychiatric clinic was famous for its pioneering treatment methods. Hundreds of patients sent there in the 1940s, however, never got to experience these therapies. Instead, they were made to disappear because invalids and cripples did not fit into the image of ideal man propagated by the Nazi state.

The former Fatherland School at Achern-Illenau.

Historical marker telling the story of Halina, Ilona-Helena, Zyta and other Polish girls at the Fatherland School in Achern

In 1939-1945, about 200,000 people, many suffering from mental illness or physical handicaps, were murdered in the so-called T4 Program, with most of the euthanasia administered by poison gas.[1] The places occupied by these superfluous individuals were to be occupied by "full-fledged" Aryans. As with many similar facilities, the Illenau clinic disposed of patients deemed "unworthy of life" while simultaneously admitting "racially suitable" girls who would augment the Aryan race. Among them were several dozen girls abducted from occupied Poland.

Many years later, in June 2017, children of about the same age played the roles of these kidnapped girls in Achern school pageants. Dressed in long skirts, with hair neatly brushed, they performed on an improvised stage at the local museum.

The scene they enacted was an arrival in a strange, foreign town. Feigning terror, the young actresses shouted: "Where are you taking us?" "When will I see Mommy?" "Why are the windows barred?" "I'd better behave or they'll lock me in the cellar!"

Stealing German Blood

But in 1942, for Zyta, Halina, and Ilona-Helena, this was not theater but reality. They were forbidden to speak Polish and still found it difficult to communicate with each other in German. At the dining hall, the Polish girls sat apart. The other girls were mainly from the South Tyrol, whose inhabitants were required to choose between Italy or Germany under a bilateral agreement signed by Hitler and Mussolini. The parents of the girls in Illenau picked Germany, and as children of loyal *Volksdeutsche*, they had been accorded the status of prospective German women. As loyal followers of the Führer, they were to be drilled at the Fatherland School in Achern. But at least these girls did not have to be forcibly Germanised like their Polish classmates; they already spoke German, even if with a characteristic southern lilt. They just needed to be inculcated with certain values they had not acquired at home, like an adoration for Adolf Hitler.

These girls were among the 80,000 Tyrolean *Volksdeutache* who opted for Germany and thus heeded Hitler's call to "come home", in keeping with the principle that "people of the same blood should be in the same Reich."[2] As part of this plan,

---

[1] Götz Haydar Aly, *Obciążeni: „eutanazja" w nazistowskich Niemczech* [original, *Die Belasteten. „Euthanasie" 1939–1945. Eine Gesellschaftsgeschichte*], trans. from German by Viktor Grotowicz, Wydawnictwo Czarne, Wołowiec 2015, pp. 9, 21.

[2] *Wysiedlenia, wypędzenia i ucieczki 1939–1959: atlas ziem Polski.* Wydawnictwo Demart, 2008.

more than 800,000 people of German extraction were resettled to Germany from various parts of Europe in 1939-1944 to help make good the Reich's growing losses on multiple battlefronts.

It was all in keeping with the ideology expressed by SS Reichsführer Heinrich Himmler, who openly declared his aim "to rob and steal German blood wherever I can."[3]

Children of the East

German Fatherland Schools, such as the one in Achern, were mentioned in a 1942 decree from the Reich Main Office for the Consolidation of German Nationhood. The document concerns "the Germanization of children from Polish families and former Polish orphanages" and recommends that children "suitable for Germanization" undergo selection based on racial and psychological testing before being placed "from the age of six to 12 years in German Fatherland Schools".[4]

Girls from South Tyrol and Poland (distinguishable by their short hair) together with School Director Klara Keit.

---

[3] Speech by Heinrich Himmler, 8 November 1938, at a conference of SS grüppenführer in Munich, translated by Monika Sieradzka from Heinrich Himmler, *Geheimreden 1933 bis 1945 und andere Ansprachen hrsg. on Bradley Smith*, Agnes F. Peterson, Ffm 1974, p. 37 ff.

[4] Regulation nr 67/I in Józef Wnuk: *Dzieci polskie oskarżają,* Wydawnictwo Lubelskie, Lublin 1975, p. 14 ff.

5 Georg Lilienthal, *Der „Lebensborn e.V." Ein Instrument nationalsozialistischer Ras-senpolitik*, new edition by Fischer-TB, Frankfurt 2003, p. 47.

The children brought from Poland did not come from ethnic German families, but that is how they were presented to prospective adoptive parents. Taking in an orphaned *Volksdeutsche* child is considered an acceptable choice for good Germans or Austrians. No self-respecting citizen would credit stories that Germans were involved in the crime of child kidnapping in Eastern Europe. Many of those who adopted so-called "children from the East" never had any idea they were abducted. Perhaps they preferred not to know.

Zyta, Halina and Ilona-Helena had all gone through hell by the time they arrived at the Achern Fatherland School in autumn 1942. Each girl might have experienced a different version of hell, but they all shared one quality: deep inside, they had long ago stopped being children.

Zyta

Zyta Suś, born in 1934, was an orphan almost from birth. Her mother, a worker at a Łódż textile mill, died of tuberculosis just three months after she was born.

One of her mother's friends took in Zyta, but only for a little while. She was also a millhand and had to work her daily shift at the factory. Since she could scarcely be expected to cope with a child, she gave Zyta up to an orphanage. On Zyta's birth certificate are the names of her godparents: Stanisława Olszak and Władysława Wesołowska. Both godmothers were employees at the orphanages. Until she was a very old woman, Zyta never met a single relative.

Zyta was unlucky to end up in an orphanage, because these were the first places the Germans looked to take children "suitable for Germanization". No heartbreaking scenes of parents refusing to give up their children. Afterwards, it was rare even for anyone to ask after them.

"After breakfast the Germans entered the orphanage. From the hall we could hear loud shouts and orders. All the doors were opened wide and we were stood along both sides of the corridor. One of the Germans walked back and forth down the middle of the hall, peering closely at us and twitching a whip against the shafts of his boots. He had on a black uniform with a swastika armband. He ordered all the children sent the next day to a municipal bathhouse to be washed and have their heads shaved. So the next morning we went with our matrons on a long trip through the city of Łódż until we came to a great enclosure. The matrons turned over our documents at the gate. We had to strip naked and be examined by a medical commission. Then we were given blouses, dungarees and wooden clogs.

That made us look like real orphans! After that, we had to trudge back across the city to another gate," Zyta remembers.

Zyta no longer remembers where she stayed and where they took her next. Over the next few months, she spent time at orphanages in several German cities, a process she was later able to laboriously reconstruct in the 1970s by writing to various archives. The documents indicate that she arrived at Bruczków, near Kalisz, in the spring of 1942. She had already been classified as a child "suitable for Germanization". Here the selection process was supervised by the Lebensborn organization, under the aegis of the SS. Polish children picked from various orphanages underwent further evaluation.

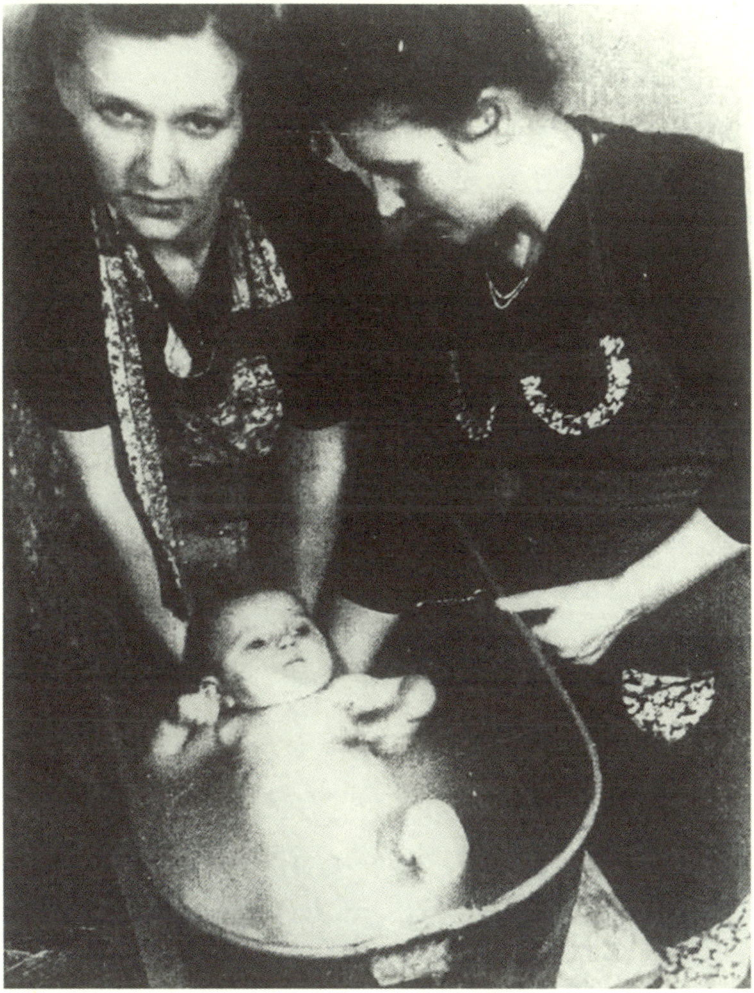

The only surviving photo of Zyta Suś with her mother (woman on the left), summer 1934

Dr. Herzer's Evaluation

At Bruczków, Zyta didn't make a good impression. "Dirty, undisciplined, unhesitatingly does whatever she pleases, disliked by her classmates, whom she shoves and pinches from behind. Unmoved by any attempt at correction. Suffers from delayed development." This harsh evaluation was delivered by the esteemed Austrian psychologist, Dr. Hetzer.

At Lebensborn centers Dr. Hetzer, a specialist in psychology and social pedagogy, played a crucial role because her scientific pedigree lent credibility to the ideology of Aryan racial purity. Before the war, she had devised tests to isolate children with delayed development from the rest of society, thus contributing to the official policy of eugenics.

In Viennese care facilities, for example, Hetzer's tests were used to determine which children were deserving of further therapy and which should be killed or used for medical experiments. After the war, Hetzer focused on her academic career. In 1972, she was awarded the Federal Order of Merit, First Class, and she remained a popular lecturer at Justus Liebig University Giessen in Hesse until her 90th birthday, in 1989.

The evaluations Hildegard Hetzer and other psychologists gave to children at Lebensborn facilities determined their fates. Those considered problematic from the educational point of view or not Aryan enough were sent to the children's camp on Przemysłowa Street in Łódź.

Zyta Suś, despite Dr. Hetzer's negative opinion, stayed in Bruczków because she had already been evaluated favorably by the SS Race and Resettlement Main Office (RuSHA) in Łódź, which judged her suitable for Germanization.

Many decades later, Zyta still can't understand how she could have been considered the Aryan type. "Fair hair? I certainly didn't have it, so why did they classify me that way?"

I didn't know Hitler was God

The unruly Zyta was sent by train from Bruczków via Berlin to Achern, where her real problems begin. At the entrance to the dining hall, she saw a huge poster of Hitler, which began to irritate her. One day she simply ripped it down. Another time, in a fit of rage, she put the paddles used for spanking children into the furnace. She didn't care what would happen to her. Zyta was simply fed up with being treated like a trained animal. She was brought before the commandant, who explained that Hitler was her father and provider, whom she should repay with love.

"I didn't know Hitler was God," she answered.

Upon hearing these words, the commandant slugged the eight-year-old girl, who flew across the room and struck her head against the doorjamb. Zyta was then punished by spending several days without food in the ice-cold cellar.

The director of the Fatherland School in Achern, Klara Keit, had seen enough of this girl. She preferred obedient children who didn't cause problems. These she tried to hold on to as long as possible.

Families kept applying to the school for permission to adopt one of these "Eastern children", but director Keit was not at all eager to give them up. The children must be properly Germanized first. In addition, the girls, once they matured, were expected serve as baby-making machines to incubate new generations of Führer-loving children.

Zyta didn't deserve this honor because the director didn't like her. Indeed, Frau Keit was astonished that a girl with dark hair and dark eyes should have been sent to her in the first place. "Gypsy child" is what Zyta remembers being called.

Frau Keit had been known to send unsatisfactory children back to Poland. Those who "failed to meet Nordic racial requirements" or too obviously "flaunted their Polishness" were packed off to Łódź, or more specifically, to *Jugendverwarhlager Litzmannstadt*, a special camp for children and teenagers. It was inevitable that Zyta, as an incorrigible child, would end up there, too.

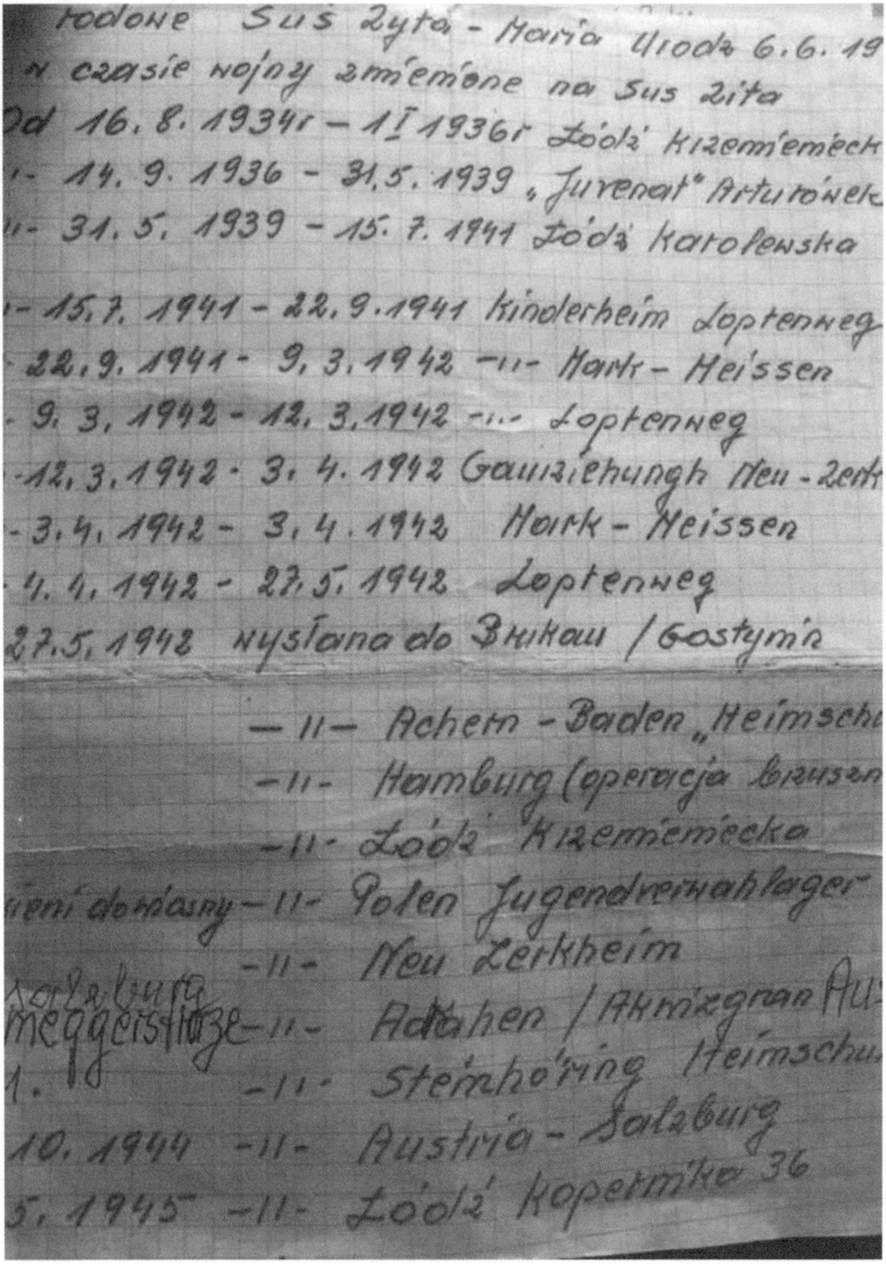
rodone Suś Zyta - Maria Łódź 6.6.19
w czasie wojny zmienione na Sus Zita
Od 16.8.1934r - 1.I.1936r Łódź Krzemieniecka
- 14.9.1936 - 31.5.1939 „Juvenat" Artutówek
- 31.5.1939 - 15.7.1941 Łódź Karolewska
- 15.7.1941 - 22.9.1941 Kinderheim Loptenweg
- 22.9.1941 - 9.3.1942 -11- Mark-Meissen
- 9.3.1942 - 12.3.1942 -11- Loptenweg
- 12.3.1942 - 3.4.1942 Gaueinziehungh Neu-Zerk
- 3.4.1942 - 3.4.1942 Mark-Meissen
- 4.4.1942 - 27.5.1942 Loptenweg
27.5.1942 wysłana do Brikau / Gostynin
-11- Achern-Baden „Heimsch
-11- Hamburg (operacja
-11- Łódź Krzemieniecka
ieni domasny -11- Polen Jugendverwahrlager
-11- Neu Zerkheim
Salzburg meggeisflaze -11- Aachen / Akmizgnan Au
1. -11- Steinhöring Heimschu
10.1944 -11- Austria - Salzburg
5.1945 -11- Łódź kopernika 36

Years later Zyta reconstructed her odyssey.

First Encounter with Death

At the camp, she remembers being beaten for the smallest infractions, such as speaking Polish. Standing for hours at roll call was a daily routine.

Hunger was rampant. For dinner, each child received an ounce of meat, four ounces of potatoes and two ounces of kasha—all in a watery soup.

Zyta remembers a girl called Gienia, who was so frightened by the camp personnel's brutality that she wet her bed three nights in a row. Each time, supervisor Eugenia Pohl punished her by flogging.

"Gienia had to lie down on a special bench used for beatings, basically a plank set on four wheels. Her arms were pulled upwards. She had to count off the blows in German and was not allowed to cry. The second time we carried her back to the barracks, she was barely alive. We watched over her the whole night. In the morning, Gienia declared she was going to die. I kissed her and begged her not to do it. A few minutes later she was gone. That was my first encounter with death."

A few times Zyta also found herself stretched out on the flogging board. Supervisor Pohl was particularly fond of whipping children on the soles of their feet, which quickly turned into raw, open wounds that left the victim unable to walk. She also liked to jam children's fingers into the floorboards until the splinters drew blood.

After the war, Pohl felt secure enough to remain in Łódź, where she worked as a kindergarten teacher under the slightly modified name of Poll. She was finally unmasked and sentenced in 1974 to a 25-year prison term for causing the little girl's death in the children's camp.

Well before serving her full sentence, Pohl was given an early release for good behavior.

Steinhöring: Breeder of Supermen

When Zyta returned to Łódź and the children's camp, her situation appeared hopeless. The *Jugendverwahrlager* was a place where you checked in but never left. Zyta, however, was sent once more to Germany, this time to the "Hochland" Lebensborn facility at Steinhöring, near Munich. Lebensborn's chief medical officer, Dr. Gregor Ebner, was personally in charge. This son of a Bavarian restaurateur had dreamed since childhood of wearing a uniform. He fulfilled this ambition during World War I, when he served as a medical officer. After the war, he could not reconcile himself with Germany's defeat and, like thousands of other demobilized young Germans, signed up for one of the many paramilitary units, or *Freikorps*, springing up at the time.

Afterwards, Ebner made a career in the Nazi party and the SS, becoming the personal physician of Heinrich Himmler, with whom he shared an ambition to "rescue the Nordic race". By 1937 he was the chief physician of Lebensborn, stationed at Steinhöring, the organisation's oldest and largest facility. Here German mothers could bring their offspring into the world in comfort and privacy, even when they were illegitimate. Lebensborn was a weapon in the struggle for a higher birth rate. By providing care to mostly unmarried expectant mothers, the state was also protecting them from social ostracism.

Dr. Ebner did not confine himself to his medical responsibilities, showering his wards with maternal and paternal care. This benevolent attitude is apparent from the correspondence preserved in his file at the International Tracing Service archives in Bad Arolsen. Dr. Ebner was genuinely interested in the welfare of mothers who gave birth under his watchful eye.

On Sept. 3, 1944, the "Dear Oberführer" is addressed in a letter from Gisela Gorges, who four years earlier had given birth to a daughter, Elke, at "beautiful Steinhöring".

Fraulein Gorges is sending the joyous news that she has become engaged to a Luftwaffe lieutenant. "My fiancé is very kind to my little Elke, and she is already allowed to call him Papa. It will be good to have the little one back with her mother and back in the bosom of her family, since right now she is with my mother."[6] Ebner scrupulously replied to the letter.

In October 1944, he sends encouraging words to his "National Socialist sister" Ruth Bader, who had been assigned to work in a Lebensborn facility in Norway. "Dear Sister Ruth, I am very well acquainted with that facility and can imagine your delight at its magnificent surroundings. Lebensborn's tasks abroad differ from our own at home. I allow myself to hope that you will find use there for everything you saw and learned while with us," Dr. Ebner writes to the nurse.[7]

[6] Ebner correspondence, ITS Archive, Bad Arolsen.

[7] Ebner correspondence.

Greeting cards to "dear Dr. Ebner", the chief medical officer of Lebensborn

Like all "National Socialist sisters" at Lebensborn, nurse Ruth is equipped with special powers. In her work, she is required to place the welfare of the "national community" over that of the individual. This means exercising the right to decide which lives are worth sustaining and which aren't. Ruth learned these lessons under the watchful eye of Dr. Ebner. Several years later, this esteemed boss and skilled physician, the would-be breeder of supermen, stood before the Military Tribunal at Nuremberg. The judges did not find that he had participated in a criminal war machine. After the war, Dr. Ebner conducted a private medical practice in Munich for many years.

A Happy Childhood

In 1943, Zyta spent very little time in Dr. Ebner's domain. After a scant two months, she was adopted by a young, well-to-do, childless couple. The nine-year-old was now called Zita Sus instead of Zyta Suś. After years of rough schooling, she spoke almost fluent German. Her few linguistic lapses could be forgiven, especially since her new foster parents believe this "child from the East" came from a *Volksdeutsche* family.

At the start, Zyta aka Zita was beside herself with happiness at her new home.

"There were roses in the garden, so beautiful that to this day I try to grow similar ones on my balcony. Behind the house was an orchard. On the porch was a wicker table, and on the table, a basket of oranges. I didn't even know then what oranges were."

But she was not destined to stay here long.

"A room was prepared for me. There were shoes, a neat row of dresses in the wardrobe, and toys. And that's when I saw the doll that made me want to leave. It looked exactly like the doll that was taken from a little girl standing beside me in Łódź, when we were presented naked to the medical board. Maybe it was the same doll? Perhaps it had been confiscated from there?"

In tears, Zita returned to the Lebensborn facility. "Since you won't like rich people, maybe a poor couple will have you," was what she heard as a welcome back. She ended up with the Bliem family in Salzburg and began her only happy period, which lasted from autumn 1943 until the summer of 1945. Not quite two years of normal childhood.

Zita began attending school and helped Frau Bliem knit wool sweaters for the Wehrmacht. She loved to play in the garden under the tall walnut and pear trees. She became an enthusiastic participant at meetings of the Nazi League of German Girls. Meanwhile, her command of Polish and memories of Poland slowly faded.

One day Zita ran into Janek, a boy a couple of years older whom she knew from the camp in Łódź. Janek had also been adopted by a Salzburg family. He tells her: "Remember you are a Polish girl." Zita never forgets those words.

Another abduction

In August 1945, an elegant limousine pulls up in front of the Bliem home in Salzburg. A man and a woman get out and ask if a child from Poland lives in this house. Zita bursts out with a reply in German: "Yes, I'm a Polish girl." After all, that's what Janek told her to say. When she's invited into the car, she jumps right in, happy at the prospect of a ride. As the car pulls away, she doesn't understand why her adoptive parents are crying on the porch. Only hours later does she grasp the situation, when she finds herself sitting in a cattle car with dozens of other *Ostkinder* whom the Polish government has decided to recover after the war from German and Austrian homes and institutions.

The children are of various ages, all crowded together in freight cars that travel with virtually no rest stops. Finally, they halt at some kind of checkpoint. The doors fly open and a Soviet soldier peers in. "Are there any German children?" Once again Zyta boldly pipes up: "*Ich bin Deutsche*!", because now she'd give anything to be out of that terrible boxcar and back with her Austrian *Mutti*. The soldier tells her to get out, but the Red Cross matron starts begging him to leave the little girl alone. Afterwards, Zyta hides under a bench, where she spends most of the rest of the trip. She cries and says nothing. She has no family in Poland and is travelling into the unknown. Before the Germans took her away, she had been in an orphanage. Did that mean she was going back?

Fritzi with an accent

Zyta's worst fears came true. She ended up in an orphanage, pining for her Austrian home – the only one she had ever really had. In Poland, where the war was raging just a short time ago, she is still mocked as a "Fritzi" for her broken, heavily accented Polish. So when a couple the orphanage director said were her parents offer to adopt her, Zyta's joy is boundless. It was the same woman who took care of her after her mother's death, then gave her up to an orphanage. At the time, Zyta believed she was her biological mother. Once again, her happiness was short-lived. The woman's husband was a zealous member of the Polish Workers' Party, and later, the Polish United Workers' Party (PZPR), the backbone of the Soviet-installed communist regime in Poland. He almost immediately took the entire family to Warmia, in former German East Prussia, where he would help entrench communist rule.

In a house confiscated from a German family in the village of Łogdowo, near Olsztyn, Zyta began a new kind of hell. She lived isolated from the rest of the village. Nobody was to hear her harsh German accent. A Polish teacher came regularly to tutor her, while her mother gave her a spanking every time she used a German word.

Zyta is 26 years old when she finally leaves home. In Warsaw, she completes hairdressing school and finds a husband. The marriage only lasts a year before her husband dies. He never found out about his wife's past, nor did her friends or customers at the beauty parlors where she worked for more than 30 years. That's all part of a traumatic past that Zyta wants to forget. She doesn't even want to be Zyta, asking everyone to call her Źenia instead. Not until after the death of her parents does she learn from relatives that they were not her parents at all, and that she was adopted.

"My dream is to find out who was my real mother. Before I die, I'd like to find her grave," Zyta says.

Alone among the living

In 2012, Zyta tells her story on German television. Rainer, a newly retired 65-year-old from Hamburg, is in shock. Like many or even most present-day Germans, he had never heard of the criminal Nazi procedure of kidnapping children. On impulse, he catches a train and visits Zyta's tiny apartment in Warsaw's Praga district. He is greeted by a menagerie, because Zyta loves animals. A dog and a cat are underfoot, several parrots roost in a cage, and Zyta is stirring a large pot of scraps to feed the neighborhood's stray cats. Unlike people, cats have never done anything bad to her.

Conversation is difficult, because Zyta has almost completely purged German from her memory. Rainer from Hamburg promises to stay in touch and send a specific sum each month. He sends her a first letter and Zyta sends him back an introductory Polish textbook. After a while, the correspondence breaks off. Zyta is again alone with her past.

After again spending hours in her Warsaw apartment telling her life story to a visitor, 80-year-old Zyta carefully stows the documents and photographs into locked cabinets and drawers. Nothing must be left out for the neighbors or the occasional ex-customer to see. Seventy years after the war, she is still afraid of being ridiculed.

"That's how we are, alone among the living," Zyta says pensively.

Halina

Like Zyta, Halina lost her mother to tuberculosis as a child. But unlike Zyta, she had grandparents to look after her. Halinka's grandmother received a welfare payment for the child, which meant she was on a list at the local *Jugendamt*, or Child Welfare Agency. That's how Halina fell into the clutches of the German bureaucracy. Their calculation was that families at the bottom of the social ladder were less likely to put up a fight when their children were taken away.

Halina Bukowiecka was called for a medical examination. They took measurements of her facial features and cranium from various angles. It turned out that her dimensions met Aryan criteria and that decided the child's fate. Halina didn't come back after her second examination. Fortunately, however, her grandparents had friendly German neighbors who were able to find out where the little girl had been sent. Her grandmother began to pay her clandestine visits. When she tried to follow Halina to Bruczków, she discovered that the girl had already been sent to Achern, in Baden, and that she was no longer called Halina Bukowiecka but Helene Buchenauer.

Unpronounceable Polish Names

Special instructions on Germanizing surnames had been issued to all Lebensborn facilities from the SS Race and Resettlement Main Office (RuSHA). For Klara Keit, the headmistress of the Achern school, it was a relief not to have to deal with Polish phonetics. After the war, she claimed it was a voluntary procedure: "Usually they chose German names for themselves when they were with me, or else they got them from their German schoolmates. Polish names were difficult for us to pronounce."

The whole thing was done in proper style. When the little girls had acquired an adequate command of German, Keit would testify in later years, Lebensborn passed them on and their new adoptive parents collected them from directly from the centre.[8] The reality was less idyllic. The children were assigned German first and last names, and they were expected to forget how they had been called in Polish, Czech or Slovenian.

The RuSHA instructions called for the new Germanized names to be as close as possible to the originals. Typical German Christian names should be used, rather than old Norse ones. This technique was intended to make it easier in the mind of a young child to blur the distinction between old and new identities. In her testimony at postwar trials, Klara Keit acknowledged that any resistance on the part of the children was punished. "Four girls were sent back to Łódź as unsuitable for Germanization, in part because they deliberately flaunted their Polish identity. I never heard anything more about those girls."[9]

---

[8] Volker Koop, *Organizacja Lebensborn. Rozrodcze stajnie Himmlera [original: Dem Führer ein Kind schenken]*, translated from German by Barbara and Daniel Luliński, Bellona, Warszawa 2014, p. 221 ff.

[9] Koop, *Organizacja Lebensborn.*

Photos of Polish girls from Museum in Achern-Illenau

Who Am I?

On arrival in Achern, Halina—now called Helene—is falsely informed that her whole family is dead. She cries constantly, but in contrast to the incorrigibly rebellious Zyta, is docile and obedient at all times. She heeds the words of her beloved grandmother, who told her such behavior would get her through any situation. One day, the girl hears terrifying shrieks, which go on for hours. It turns out they had come from some of the older girls, who had made contact with forced laborers on nearby farms to try and get word back to their parents in Poland. The girls were tortured as punishment.

Halina took this as a warning. Don't think too much and do what you're told, just as grandmother said. Beatings and torture were part of the daily routine at Achern. A girl fainted at roll call, so after that she is regularly doused with cold water and forced to stand in wet clothes until roll call is over. Children with scuffed shoes or improperly folded underclothes are slapped in the face and called dirty pieces of trash. Every week they are issued seven handkerchiefs, and whoever doesn't bring back seven dirty ones at the end of the week is punished. Wherever you looked, fear was in the air. Polish was heard only rarely. By these methods, the teaching staff accomplished its objective—the children's real identities were gradually erased from their consciousness. Halina no longer knows whether her real name is Halina or Helene, or whether she Is Polish or German.

A Nazi Child

Halina's life suddenly changes in the autumn of 1943, when she is sent to work on a nearby farm. The Huber family treats her like their own daughter. She attends school and has her First Communion. But after two years, she must board a repatriation train to Poland.

Halina's frightened, because over the past two years she has become convinced that her whole family is dead. She has also almost entirely forgotten how to speak Polish.

Before going back to Poland, Halina spends a short time with Stanislaw Jargus, a Pole living about 100km from Achern. Jargus realizes the problems these children will face on their return and tries to prepare them for re-acclimatizing themselves to Polish life. They take Polish lessons but still talk among themselves in

German. It already feels like their native language, showing that Germanization has worked.

Once she's home, Halina moves in with her grandfather. He can't believe what has been done to his beloved granddaughter. Now she's a real "Nazi kid" who doesn't speak Polish. He makes poor Halina read the Polish newspapers every day, even though she doesn't understand a word. School is just as bad, because the other kids mercilessly mock Halina's thick German accent. The Russian teacher, who still has visions of the German who killed her family, calls Halinka a "Fritzi" and singles her out from the rest of the class. Decades later, Halina is still traumatized by the experience.

Ilona-Helena

While Zyta and Halina were attending the Fatherland School in Achern, one of their classmates was Ilona-Helena Wielganowicz. She had been taken from an orphanage in Pabianice during one of the German bureaucracy's periodic roundups of Aryan genetic material.

"They took a lot of blood samples, then they photographed me and measured my head." She remembers being taken to a train station, which was swarming with children and SS-men with dogs. The children boarded a train and their parents were told they were going on vacation for a few weeks. They ended up at Achern. The beginning was the worst, especially the humiliating medical examination.

Ilona-Helena was kidnapped from a Pabianice orphanage and sent to Achern

"For the initial exam, I had to strip naked and parade around that way from one room to another. It was horrible, which was why I remember it so well."

After an awful year of indoctrination at the Volksdeutsche school, she managed to land a job at a local farm, where she was treated like family. After the German surrender, when French soldiers try to take her back to the Achern school, where Polish children are being kept before being repatriated, she resists.

Ilona-Helena is 14 years old and knows perfectly well what she wants, or at least what she doesn't want. She certainly won't allow herself to be sent God knows where. This is her home now. Ilona-Helena already feels German. She stays in Achern, where she tries to lead a normal life.

In the 1980s, she is one of the first people to try to make a political issue out of the story of abducted children—perhaps the only group victimized by the Third Reich that never received any compensation or reparations. She never received a reply to any of her letters. Instead, Ilona-Helena has to endure comments from her neighbors that she should be grateful to live in prosperous Germany rather than in communist Poland.

Living Death

Today the Polish girls' dormitory at the Achern-Illenau complex has been converted into private apartments. Before that, it was part of a psychiatric clinic for "disturbed men". Among the last of those disturbed male mental patients were the murdered victims of the T4 euthanasia program.

A historical marker stands in front of the building with the following information: "Reichsführer SS Heinrich Himmler wanted to ensure for the 'German nation' what he termed 'worthwhile natural increase'. To this end, based on their 'Aryan appearance', thousands of children are abducted from their families to be 'Germanized' and then handed over to German families. On June 13, 1942, the first such girls arrive in Illenau, with the final transport arriving on Oct. 30, 1942. Of 57 girls, the youngest is seven years old, the oldest is 13. They live in a former psychiatric ward for men, which still has barred windows."

The marker is illustrated with photographs of Zyta, Halina and Ilona-Helena, who endured their own ordeals behind those bars. Their childhoods were stolen, and something inside of them dies. Years later, Zyta observes: "You can die without being killed."

"I Regretted I Wasn't A Fly"

Once again, I've messed up. This time my punishment is being locked in a cabinet. It's dark inside as I sit quietly and wait. I'm terrified, because I know what's about to happen. In just a moment, I hear him. My heart is about the leap out of my chest. I peer through a crack in the door: "the Monster" is coming my way.

I scream.

***

Today I know that it was just someone in costume. But then I was only five years old. Or maybe seven? The only thing I remember is being frightened to death. I cried, while he lectured me about good behavior.

***

It's evening and we're trying to sleep. There are about 20 children in the room—little kids like me, four- or five-year-olds. Our eyes are closed tight but we can't sleep. The silence is oppressive—nobody dares to make a peep. I just remember the sound of his steps—the "Monster". He's walking between the beds, checking whether we're being good. Whether we're asleep.

***

Another time, in Austria I think, they shut me in a cellar for three days. Alone, in the dark. I was really scared then. I remember regretting I wasn't a fly, because then I could just buzz off instead of enduring this torture.

I don't remember what they were punishing me for. I guess I was just a little rascal.

***

Maksymilian Jadoch knows he was born in 1936, somewhere in Poland. Where exactly, he doesn't know. About his hometown, he hasn't a clue. He has no idea who his parents were. He doesn't even know if he came from an orphanage. For a long time, he believed he was German.

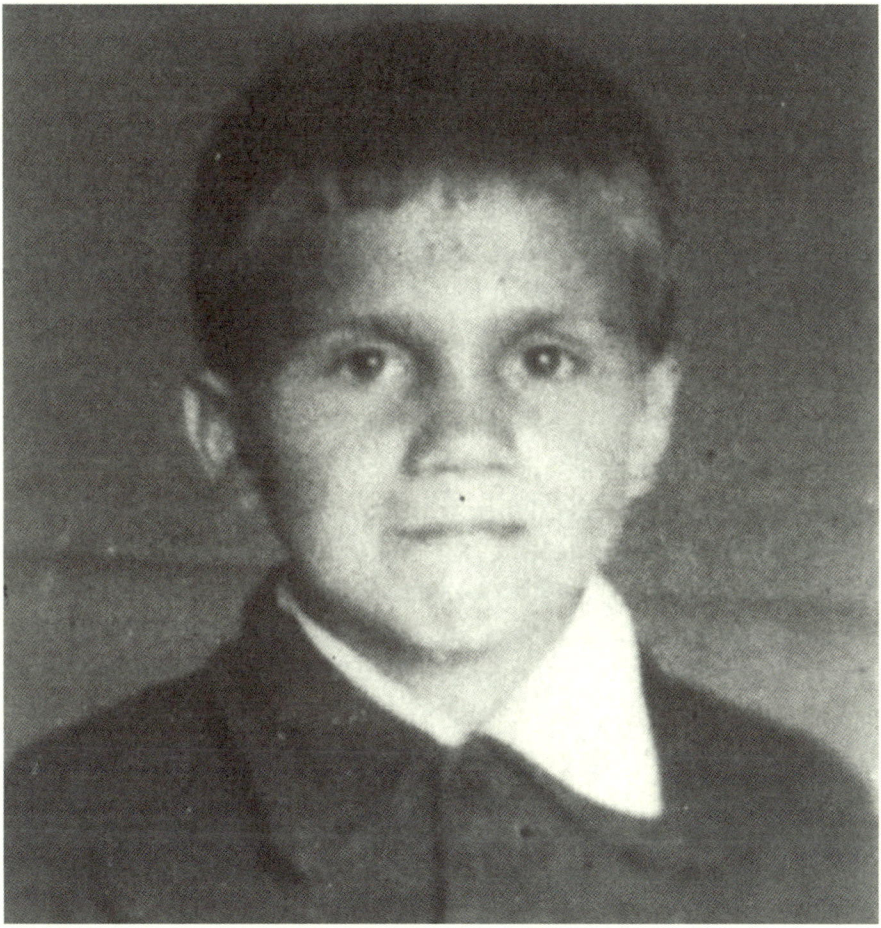

Nine-year-old Maximilian Jadoch, Barcelona, 1946

***

What I mainly remember from the Bielsko orphanage is "the Monster". He made my flesh crawl. To this day, if someone touches me unexpectedly, I scream.

Even so, life in Bielsko was pretty good. We went on outings to the mountains and they taught us to swim.

It wasn't my first orphanage. Before that I lived at another one, I don't know where. The only thing I remember is that nuns took care of us.

***

During World War II, the Upper Silesian city of Bielsko was incorporated into the Third Reich as Bielitz. The Nazi bureaucracy installed German administrators in orphanages and children's homes. These institutions were mainly supervised by the National Socialist People's Welfare, or NSV. In keeping with Nazi racial theories, children in these institutions were reclassified as Germans and immediately subjected to Germanization procedures.

Max doesn't remember the orphanage he was in before Bielsko. Perhaps it was the shelter on Nowokościelna Street in Tychy run by the St. Elizabeth Sisters. In 1941, the institution was taken over by the NSV, which removed its Polish personnel and transferred some of the children to Bielsko. Max could have been one of them.

***

The Bielsko orphanage was run by Germans. They brought us there by train. There were about 60 or 70 of us, all from Poland. But none of us spoke Polish, it was strictly forbidden. The only language I ever heard was German. So I believed I was German. I spoke German, went to a German school, sang the German national anthem.

It seems to me now that I was never a Polish speaker. It was not until a few years later, after I arrived in Barcelona, that it began to dawn on me that I wasn't a German at all.

***

I met her in Bielsko. I remember standing on the patio in front of the orphanage when suddenly I saw a woman, standing in the metal gate. I had a feeling she was my mother. It seemed to me that I recognized her. I started shouting: "Mutti! Mutti!" I couldn't believe that she had finally come to visit. I was convinced that she would rescue me.

Her name was Elisabeth, but she called herself Elsa. I called her "Mutti". She didn't object, so I believe she was my Mom.

She'd come to visit every so often. She would bring toys and take me for short outings. I met her friends. She spoke perfect German.

After they told us we'd be taken to Prague, Elsa promised to find me there. She was pregnant at the time. She said the child would be my brother, Hans.

***

From Prague they took us to Austria—to Linz, I think. I remember the constant bombing. We would spend the night in air raid shelters. As soon as the sirens went off, we'd start running. It was almost a mile to the shelter. I can still hear our attendants shouting at us: "Run, faster!"

***

After that was a resettlement camp in Salzburg, with a bunch of other Poles. This was right after the war.

I have no idea why I wasn't sent back to Poland. The rumor was because of the communists. Supposedly there was even a chance we'd be sent to Australia, but no orphanage there wanted us.

At first about 45 of us kids—all from Bielsko—were sent to Arco, Italy. We lived in a big barracks there together with Polish troops. They would come to see us and try to speak to speak Polish. At first I was scared of them, especially because I only spoke German.

Then they put us aboard a ship in Genoa and we sailed to Barcelona. The trip took a day and a night. A lot of kids were throwing up from seasickness. That's how we got to Spain.

***

Max arrived in Barcelona with the first transport of Polish children. The trip took months to organize.

Polish children in Barcelona, 1946

The idea of taking in Polish children came from people involved with the Polish Legation in Barcelona. The project was submitted to the Foreign Ministry of the Polish government in exile in London. In July 1945, the Spanish Foreign Ministry agreed to accept 40 children and preparations began.

Politics intervened, however. In November 1945, Spain came forward with an initiative to take in 50,000 children for several months from the most war-torn countries. The Spanish government turned to Great Britain, France and the US for help in organizing the program.

The Allies weren't nearly so enthusiastic about the proposal, however. In part, this was because both the Americans and the European powers suspected the Franco regime had an ulterior motive and wanted to rehabilitate itself after its wartime cooperation with Nazi Germany.

Even so, in late 1945 the Spanish offer was accepted, but only under the condition that the particulars be agreed with the Allied powers and international relief organizations.

In the case of the Polish children, this posed a serious problem. Under the official British interpretation, the new government in Warsaw was considered an "Allied power". This was not the position of the Franco regime, which refused to recognize the legitimacy of the postwar communist authorities.

An attempt was made to arrange the transfer through relief groups. The British wanted to use the United Nations Relief and Rehabilitation Administration (UNRRA), but this proved impossible because Spain was not a member, while the Polish government in exile regarded UNRRA as too susceptible to communist pressure from Warsaw. It was therefore decided to turn to the Geneva office of the American Polish War Relief, established in September 1939 by the Polish American Council.

This allowed preparations to pick up speed. By March 1946, the Polish Red Cross in Salzburg had completed a list of children, prioritizing victims of the Germanization program. Several days later, the children were issued visas and on April 16, the Barcelona municipal government assigned the Poles a spacious villa on the Calle de Angli in Barcelona.

On April 24, 1946, the Spanish merchant ship *J.J. Sisters* docked in Barcelona harbor. On board were 35 Polish children, aged six to 16.

***

At the start we were all living together—boys and girls—in an enormous, beautiful home. Older children from the next transport went to live somewhere else. Later we were split up, girls in one building, boys in another. Many of the children spoke Polish and only some spoke German. We were teased for that.

I don't blame those kids; nobody was around to explain things to them. The teachers didn't know or care. They had their hands full dealing with more children than they could handle. I had to take care of myself.

But it was thanks to the teachers that I slowly began to realize I was a Pole. It was terribly hard to accept. Especially because I had absolutely no memories—no Polish words, no songs, no traditions. Only in Spain did I start to learn all that.

It was a very active life. We had a lot going on—Polish lessons, Spanish lessons, school, sports, excursions to various places. We celebrated Christmas and Easter in Polish style.

We also went to church every day. There was a priest, Father Worek, whom I really liked. After a while he had to leave, which made me very sad.

I had friends who also left. They returned to Poland after their families managed to locate them. Each departure had a devastating effect on me. I walked around depressed for weeks.

Nobody was looking for me. Nobody tried to get in touch, not even my "Mutti".

Children and teachers, Barcelona, 1953

***

Two more transports of Polish children arrived in Barcelona in June and October 1946. The children lived in two villas—at the Calle de Angli address and at a residence in Vallcarca. By November 1, 101 children were living at the two locations. There would have been even more, but in the meantime, some had been reunited with their families in Poland, while about 20 of the older children were sent to Italy.

Personnel records indicate that one of the biggest problems faced by the teaching staff was language. Because some of the children could only speak German, Polish language instruction became a priority.

Another huge challenge was the trauma inflicted on the children by their wartime experiences. Nightmares, depression, delight in malicious destruction, claustrophobia and the experience of real starvation all left their mark. So much so, indeed, that the facility's regulations contained explicit instructions for the staff each night to inspect children's' bedding for "leftover food hidden under their pillows". As time passed, more letters started arriving from families seeking their children. Sometimes the letters came from parents or other relatives, sometimes from foster parents or children's home workers. As these children began to depart for home, the numbers in Barcelona dwindled. By the time the last repatriation transport left on Aug. 19, 1952, only 52 children remained in Spain.

"For them, every empty bed is like a fresh blow, an ever-widening breach or dark cloud overshadowing their future", noted Wanda Tozer, one of the most committed volunteers at the orphanage who for many years served as the chief liaison between the Polish consulate and the Spanish authorities.

***

It wasn't until 1964 that I arrived in Poland. Earlier, I received a telegram from "Mutti" that broke my heart. She wrote to say that she wasn't my mother. I came anyway. I'd been waiting 20 years for her.

Hans collected me at the airport and took me home. When his father-in-law saw me for the first time, he mistook me for Hans. We looked so much alike.

She didn't appear for three days. I don't know why she took so long. For the next five weeks, it was just the three of us—Hans, myself and "Mutti". It felt good to be together.

She told me she had been a nurse in Auschwitz. I was a Jewish newborn she had rescued. An orphan.

I believed her then.

***

I hate the word "orphan". When we got to the States, they took us to a park where the local Polish-American community had gathered. They asked us to sing something for them in Polish. Afterwards, the woman who brought us explained that we were "orphans" and asked whether anybody would like to adopt us. I felt ashamed and humiliated, like a nobody. I just walked away.

Afterwards the sound of the word "orphan" became very familiar to me. For example, from my in-laws. It was always the refrain: "You poor orphan, you poor orphan!" My God, can't they just give it a rest?

My wife, on the other hand, was a wonderful woman. We met by a very strange coincidence. It was love at first sight. I was walking in a park in Buffalo and caught sight of this wonderful girl. I looked at her and she at me. I was smitten. But we didn't say a word to each other.

Two weeks later, she walks into the jewelry store where I worked. We recognized each other right away, and this time the words came....

***

The Barcelona kids grew up and started to lead their own lives. Each year fewer remained at the orphanage. The volunteers wondered how to give them a secure future. Again, the Polish-American community came to the rescue.

The first transport to the US left Gilbraltar on December 5, 1951. Seven days later, the young Poles arrived in New York. Thanks to help from the Polish-American Council's Buffalo District, they found places to live and jobs.

Maximilian Jadoch with his wife, Buffalo, 1962

Max was in the final group of 18 children who left for the US on July 7, 1956. They travelled through Madrid to Lisbon, and then by plane to New York, arriving on July 23.

***

In America, I again landed in an orphanage. After four weeks, they moved us into a boarding house, where we rented rooms.

I felt completely lost. I didn't know the language or the customs. I had no idea what to do.

It wasn't at all like Barcelona, where it was easy to get to work. I wanted to stay in school, but the lady who supervised our orphanage didn't want to give me the money for train fare. I had no way to get to classes. So I found work at a printing house. It was a good job. The boss liked me because I was a hard worker.

POWITANIE SIEROT POLSKICH NA POLU LOTNICZYM — Grupa Sierot Polskich przybyła wczoraj krótko po godzinie 6-ej wieczorem do Bufalo, z Hiszpanii. Opiekę nad nią sprawować będą Katolickie Dobroczynności, a tymczasowo zamieszkują w Sierocińcu Polskim w Cheektowaga, N. Y., pod opieką Wiel. Sióstr Felicjanek. Później starsza młodzież umieszczona zostanie w domach prywatnych. Zdjęcie przedstawia sierotki polskie w otoczeniu osób które wyszły na ich powitanie. Na lewo widzimy Przew. ks. Bolesława M. Woźniaka, dyrektora Katolickich Dobroczynności; w Przew. ks. prałata M. T. Bogackiego; na prawo, Wiel. Siostry F. S. M. Generosa, przełożona zakładu w Cheektowaga; S. M. Caris M. Fidelma; Stanisław P. Turkiewicz, prezes Okręgu 8-go R. P. Jan Juhasz, dyrektor Wydziału Wysiedleńców Kat. Dobroczyn

Osiemnaście Sierót Polskich

się będą do czasu aż do starszego wieku.

Umieszczeniem kich w domach się

Newspaper clipping documenting the arrival of Polish children in the US

But I always wanted to study. My ambition was to get an education and be somebody. The dream didn't happen for me, but my son fulfilled it.

***

I got the job at the jewelry store after moving out of the orphanage. They taught me how to repair, set and polish rings. English I learned on my own. After work, I'd go back to my room and hit the books.

I spent five years in the boarding house. After getting married, we moved into an attic at my sister-in-law's. It was seven years before we decided to buy a house. It scared me to death because I'd never owned anything. I lived with a lot of anxiety. The whole time I was worried about whether I'd be a good provider for my family.

My first car was inherited from my friend Witek Drożdż. We knew each other from Spain. He was another Germanized kid, and after coming to the States, we stayed in touch. He often came to visit, since he didn't have any family of his own.

One day I got a call from his lawyer. He said Witek had committed suicide. I was stunned. Later I found out that he had cancer.

The lawyer said that I should come since I was in the will. And that's how I got my first car.

***

The whole time I couldn't get over the Auschwitz story. I even watched a documentary once about conditions in the camp. There was absolutely no way any nurse was going to smuggle a child out of there. I tried to get the truth out of Elsa, but she kept changing her story every time. Finally, in one of her letters, she wrote that I will never find out who my parents were.

But in that case, why did she come visit me in Bielsko?

Today we don't talk to each other. She's told me too many lies. I keep hoping to find something out when she dies. I'm waiting for my own "miracle on the Vistula".

***

Sometimes I get angry that all this had to happen to me. Other times, I just feel terribly empty. But I try not to give in.

My wife died 20 years ago. For the first year, I was depressed. Then I read an article where somebody wrote that "life is for living" and I thought—that's enough. Why keep brooding and dwelling on the past? It's over and gone. Time to start living again.

Because life is for living.

Parsch, Austria: The Last Stage Of Germanization

After the Anschluss of 1938, Germany treated newly acquired Austria as an integral part of the Third Reich. The territory of the Federal Austrian Republic seized by Adolf Hitler was designated for propaganda purposes as the "Eastern Marches" [*Ostmark*], a reference to the medieval Holy Roman Empire, or First Reich. Among the organizations active in Austria under Nazi rule was Lebensborn, responsible for Germanizing children abducted from occupied Europe. A crucial role in this procedure was played by the resettlement camp at Parsch.

Lebensborn was founded as an association to aid German mothers, but by 1942, Reichsführer SS and national police chief Heinrich Himmler had decided to make it the main conduit for children harvested from territories conquered by the Third Reich. Making use of orphanages and other educational facilities put at its disposal, Lebensborn indoctrinated and prepared these stolen children for life in German society, following the precepts of Nazi "blood theory" allowing them membership in the Aryan race. This process, however, was not restricted solely to Lebensborn facilities.

The Parsch resettlement camp was located in what is today a suburb of Salzburg. Formally, it was merely a temporary holding facility for so-called "ethnic Germans" [Volksdeutsche] awaiting resettlement to the Reich. In reality, however, Parsch was the final stage of Germanization for abducted children assigned to the northeastern regions of Austria.

Officially, the Parsch camp was completely independent of Lebensborn. In practice, however, it cooperated closely with "Alpenland", an Austrian children's home operated by Lebensborn, along with a Luxembourg-based branch office of the organization.

"What enchanting little creatures"

The treatment of abducted children at Parsch is described by Ines Hopfer-Pfister in her book *Geraubte Identität* [Stolen Identity], which among other things tells the story of 60 Polish children brought to the camp in 1943.

Austrian and German customs officials tear down a border barrier near Salzburg after the 1938 anschluss

For these children, Parsch put the finishing touches on Germanization. Earlier, they had spent at least a year in Lebensborn educational and custodial facilities. As described *in Geraubte Identität*, despite a regime of indoctrination, constant surveillance and tight personal supervision, inmates at Parsch still managed inside the camp to carve out for themselves a measure of relative autonomy.

"What enchanting little creatures" is how these children were remembered by Waldemar Luser, the adoptive father of one of the little girls cited by Hopfer-Pfister in her book.[1] According to Luser, the children's behavior gave no hint that they were being held at the camp against their will.

[1] Ines Hopfer, *Geraubte Identität*, Wien, Köln, Weimar 2010, p. 137.

The real reasons for the children's assignment to Parsch and other Germanization facilities was not disclosed by the Nazi authorities. Luser himself was told that the children had been brought to Austria to ensure their safety.

Germanizing through Education and Practice

Appearances aside, it was clear from the start that the children had been sent to Parsch with one aim in mind—ruthless Germanization. The whole process was based on swift language acquisition. All children at the camp were given an intensive crash course in German. The language lessons lasted several hours each day, with strict punishments handed out for every utterance of a Polish word.

"All conversations at the camp were German only. We were also taught to read and write," remembers Mirosław Cieślak, one of the Polish inmates.[2] "Whenever we were caught speaking Polish, they beat us or made us do painful calisthenics".

The children were also kept occupied by frequent inspections and racial testing, along with regular brainwashing in Nazi ideology, administered by employees of the SS Race and Resettlement Main Office. Every attempt was made to induce these children to forget Poland by describing their homeland in disgusting terms, while praising the triumphs of the Third Reich. This indoctrination aimed to impress on these children that their future was inextricably linked with the *Ostmark*.

Children assigned to Parsch had already passed successfully through the Lebensborn program at other Germanization centers, which included a heavy dose of Nazi ideology. In most cases, their command of German was already more than adequate. Often Polish surnames were the only remaining trace of their true heritage. At the Salzburg camp, these names were replaced with German ones.

Creativity with Surnames

The choice of surname rested with the SS Race and Resettlement Main Office. The procedure for changing personal data was accompanied by an elaborate ceremonial that was supposed to lend the occasion a solemn majesty.

"The children were made to stand at attention," says inmate Barbara Mikołajczyk in recollections cited by Hopfer-Pfister.[3] "After each child received a

---

[2] Ines Hopfer, *Geraubte…*, p. 137.

[3] Ines Hopfer, *Geraubte…*, p. 138.

little tag with their new name, they were supposed to shout 'Heil Hitler!' I got a tag inscribed with my date of birth and the name Barbara Micker."

The children's new surnames were devised in one of two ways.

In certain cases, the first few letters of their original last names were preserved while adding a suitably German suffix, creating a similar-sounding German name. In this way, Barbara Mikołaczyk became "Barbara Micker", while Renata Sosnowska turned into "Renata Sosemann". In some cases, Polish surnames were simply recast into German phonetic spelling, such as "Piontek" instead of Piątek. Another technique was to use literal translations of suitable surnames. For example, the Polish surname Ogrodowczyk [Gardener] became "Gärtner", while Młynarczyk [Miller] turned into "Müller".

With the adoption of a new surname, the final element of a new German identity was in place, successfully completing the Germanization procedure. All that remained was to find an appropriate foster family and place the child.

A New German family

The duration of a child's stay at Parsch depended on several individual factors: psychological makeup, physical health, behavior and—above all—the availability of suitable foster families.

Some children spent a month at the camp, while others were placed with German families within a week. These stays might seem extremely short, especially when compared with 12 or more months typically spent by children in some Lebensborn orphanages.

The Parsch district in Salzburg, circa 1890-1905

Most Polish children were split into smaller groups at Parsch and then taken by bus or train to their new foster families. Most were placed with farm families, as one of the unofficial purposes of the camp's orientation program was to help fill a severe shortage of agricultural labor.

Arrival in a new family evoked mixed feelings. On the one hand, there was an exhilarating feeling of freedom at escaping the close confines of re-education centers and camps. Yet coming under the permanent care of total strangers was also a major cause of stress.

The handover itself went off without much ado. As Irene Majeski describes it to Hopfer-Pfister: "The first time I saw my foster parents in Salzburg, they lined us all up in a row and told the adults to pick out whomever they liked. Three weeks later, they came back and fetched me to Bischofshofen".

It's not clear whether the new foster parents knew the origins of the children placed under their care. Waldemar Luser, mentioned earlier, was convinced that his little girl was a war zone evacuee. Irene Majeski, on the other hand, suspected that her foster parents knew her case history, even though they never revealed any details to their adopted daughter.

“Even Today I Could Find My Foster Home”

The house was on the corner. We lived on the second floor, but the building itself was taller. The front door opened onto a corridor, the kitchen was to the left and the living room straight ahead. You walked right through it into another room. To this day I can still recall the layout. But not what “Mutti” and “Papi” looked like. I mean Elise and Franz Glück, the Austrians who were supposed to make a German out of me. They picked me up from a Germanization center. They’d lost a son in the war.

That’s how at the age of nine I came to live in Salzburg. My name was Hans Gluck. I went to a German school. I spoke German. I sang German songs.

At home there was one more boy, younger than me. He played the violin. He was supposed to be my brother, but I don’t even know if he was the Glucks’ natural son. What was his first name? Did we play? Did we even like each other? It’s all a blank to me now.

I barely even remember the Glucks. Did they treat me well or badly? The only thing I can recall is going back to their house once, after the war. This was after I had been taken away and placed in a repatriation camp. At the camp they gave us candy, lots of hard candy. I saved mine and wrapped them in a little package. I bundled it all up in a handkerchief and took it to the Glucks. But they weren’t at home, so I left the candy hanging on the doorknob and went back to the camp.

Would I have stayed if they’d opened the door? I don’t know.

From today’s perspective, I guess not, since the camp personnel would have showed up right away and taken me back. But as for what I felt then…. Probably yes. They were my first real family. My first Mom, my first Dad… Before that, I’d been a stranger to those kinds of emotions.

***

There’s a click as the electric kettle shuts off—the water to make coffee is on the boil. “Almost forgot—I’ve got something to go with it,” says Jan and wanders out of the room. I pour water over the coffee grounds and wait. He comes back with sliced cake on a tray.

We sit down again opposite each other. We're in a downstairs room at a vicarage in Poznań. Jan is 84 years old, with grey hair and blue eyes. Correction: not just blue, but a clear-sky azure.

Jan Dopierała

Jan works at the church next door. He does the Christmas and Easter decorations. On the table is a small stack of documents he's collected about his past: a letter from the Polish Red Cross confirming that he was a Germanized child, a snapshot from Barcelona showing him grinning broadly and hugging his two best friends—also victims of German racial policies; a Spanish-language child health booklet.

According to the Polish Red Cross, Jan was born on Jan. 16, 1934 in Zduny, near Poznań. During World War II he was "deported to Germany in order to be Germanized."

***

Years later, I traveled to Krotoszyn to look at the parish records. I know that my real name is Jan Dopierała. My mother's name was Zofia. My father's name wasn't entered in the book, and to this day I don't know who he was. At some point, I was advised to give my father's name as "Jan" in the questionnaires, which I did. Later for some reason the name "Czesław" cropped up. It must have been a mix-up, since Czesław is my middle name.

I was raised by nuns at the Zduny orphanage. I don't know when I got there or how old I was. I only remember my teacher, Stefania Wiśniewska.

***

After the war broke out, I was evacuated with the rest of the kids from our orphanage to Kobylin. That's where the Germans found me. I don't remember any racial testing, but I must have gone through it, because they took me to the Germanization center in Kalisz. Probably in 1941 they transferred me to a similar facility at Oberweis, in Germany. Then to Salzburg, in Austria. Later I met the Glucks, but you already know about that. I remember even less about the period before Austria than I do about Salzburg. There was horrible treatment, abuse, German lessons, punishments for speaking Polish, roll calls, bunk beds, some kind of big room… But I can't keep it straight whether this was Kalisz or Oberweis. I only know that at that time I was called Johann Dobermann.

***

Jan tries to recall more details, but time and pain have effectively erased his memories. Besides, as he says, how much can a little kid remember?

Sometimes Jan is helped by his adoptive son, who has joined us in the meantime. He's heard the story often enough to prompt his father or supply a date, filling in the broader context.

From a Polish Red Cross document: "He was placed at the German Gaukinderheim Children's Facility in Kalisz, from which he was sent in 1941 to Oberweis near Gmunden, and then to Salzburg Parsch, Zigmunthoffstr. 2… The aforementioned individual is registered among the children repatriated to Poland after the liberation."

Children of former slave laborers wave from the window of a repatriation train from Germany, Braunschweig, May 1945

***

I became Jan Dopierała on returning after the war. They came to get me at the Glucks. I don't even know who they were. I don't remember if I resisted. They took me to an American-run camp near Salzburg.

A year later, by a complete accident, I was sent to Spain, to sunny Barcelona. The authorities in Madrid had allowed the Polish Red Cross to set up a center for Polish children there. It was supposed to be a short-term stay, just so we wouldn't have to be shuffled around resettlement camps. But the ones who went unclaimed stayed there for 10 years.

I don't have too many clear memories of Barcelona, but I feel those were the happiest years of my life. After the nightmare of war, there was finally peace and quiet. We had enough to eat and other children around who shared our experiences. We all understood each other.

I had to re-learn Polish, which I had completely forgotten. But I never lost the awareness that I was Polish. It's hard for me now to say how this was possible. Perhaps because they punished us so severely in Kalisz and Oberweis for speaking Polish.

A group of boys from the Polish children's home, Barcelona, 1947

***

The first time I went to the movies was in Barcelona. I even remember the film: Tarzan. We were amazed to see something like that.

I joined the Scouts and we often went camping or to jamborees. I remember bringing back two feathers from one camping trip. Maybe they were parrot feathers, I honestly can't remember. But I still have them. Basically they're all I have, because I brought very little back with me from Spain. We were ordered to come home from Barcelona. They said "go", so we went.

***

It turns out my old teacher from the orphanage tracked me down. She said she would take care of me, so I arrived back in Poland on Oct. 25, 1948. To be precise, to Olsztyn, because that's where the sisters and Ms. Wiśniewska moved after the war.

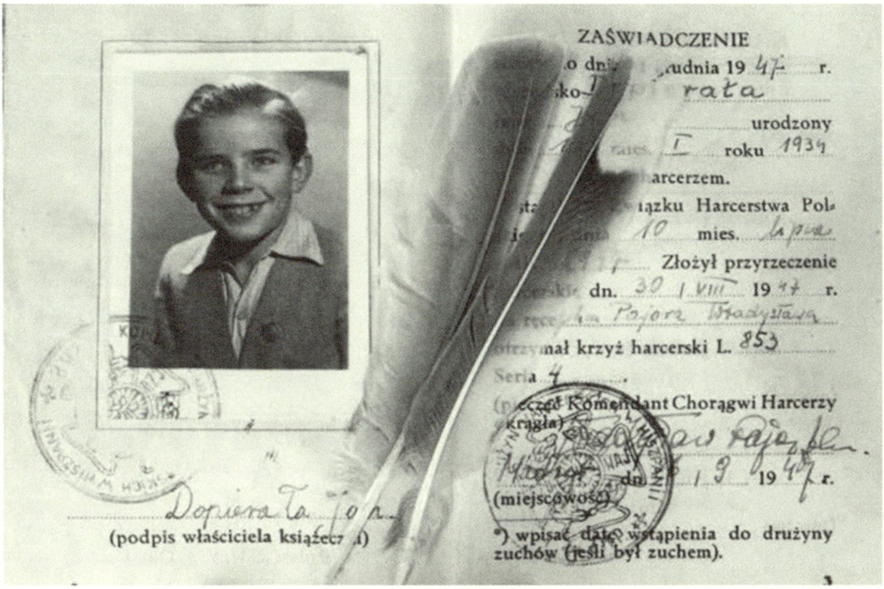

Jan Dopierala's Scout Book and two feathers – probably from parrots

It's difficult for me to say today whether I held it against her at the time. I didn't know what was happening to my friends who stayed behind in Barcelona. Besides, I don't believe even then I thought very much about why I was being repatriated.

I was 14 years old. At that age, I should have already finished primary school, but instead due to the constant interruptions and school transfers I was put back into the early grades. When I finished, the sisters got me enrolled at a trade school in Piła, where I learned metalworking.

Times were tough. At Piła I was on my own. The girls and boys I was going to class with were always talking about their homes, parents and relatives, while I didn't have anybody. They went home for Sundays and holidays. The only place I had to go was back to the orphanage.

It still hurts today. That's why I'm crying.

***

A long silence falls, which I don't interrupt. Jan's son places a hand on his shoulder and squeezes. He also knows what it's like to be alone.

***

Later I had my military service and work. I moved away from the sisters at the orphanage.

But in 1970 I came back. That's when one of the nuns introduced me to a girl from a family she knew. Not long afterwards, we got married and moved to Września.

My wife was basically the only person who knew about my past. Except for the nuns. I preferred not to talk about it because it was too upsetting. Besides, people who haven't gone through it themselves wouldn't understand. Now I live in Poznań and help decorate the church. I have an adopted son—he doesn't know his father, either. That shared experience has brought us together. I know what it's like when you can't get to know your own parents.

***

My whole life has been dictated by other people. Either I was following orders or accepting whatever fate dished out. I got used to it. Maybe that's why I don't feel any anger or regret about what happened to me.

I still have two dreams—to see Barcelona again, and Salzburg. Even today, I think I could find my way to the Gluck house. I'd like to see who's living there now.

If I could travel back in time, that's where I'd go. Barcelona was sunny, but it was just a bunch of kids. In Salzburg, I had a family.

***

The son walks me to the door. He'd like to fulfil his father's wish and take him to Salzburg. "Maybe it'll still work out," he says with a smile.

Resettlement camp run by British occupation authorities, Hamburg, May 1945

Three Brothers from "Sunny Meadow"

"This isn't a story our town wants to boast about," admits Corinne Schulze, director of the Kohren-Sahlis Museum in Saxony. She's referring to the "Sunny Meadow" [*Sonnenwiese*] Lebensborn facility, once situated in a sprawling building on a hill overlooking the town. Today it's a German Red Cross residential home for people with disabilities.

What happened at this place has been hushed up over many decades since the war. Even so, the subject hung in the air, until the silence was broken in 2016 by a student at the local gymnasium, who wrote a term paper about Sunny Meadow's history. A year later, a historical marker was installed in front of this former Lebensborn center, telling about the events there.

In 1939, the building was occupied by an old age home, whose tenants were soon required to leave. A few died in the infamous T4 Program, intended to liquidate people with chronic illnesses or disabilities via euthanasia or gassing. The Reich had no need for such people. The former residents of Sunny Meadow were forced to make way for younger occupants whom the Nazi's considered "worthwhile" human material. The building was taken over the by SS-run Lebensborn organization, which took in pregnant women so that they could bear children in safety and comfort.

That was far from the sole aim of Lebensborn, however.

Children from Nazi-occupied countries who had been kidnapped due to their Aryan appearance were also brought here.

For most of this period, up to 130 children under the age of three were kept here, though there were older kids as well. The SS didn't skimp on personnel costs—three teachers and more than 40 nurses and caregivers helped with the children. Pay was well above normal rates. At a time when the average German monthly wage was 140 Reichsmarks (then equivalent to $55), the Sunny Meadow director earned 380 RM, while caregivers and secretaries were paid 200 RM a month. For this "breeding ground" of future *Herrenvolk*, it was full speed ahead.

Corinne Schulze is unsurprised that the story of Sunny Meadow was kept quiet for more than 70 years. Even now, some former Lebensborn employees still live in the area, along with many children who passed through the facility. For years, Schulze says, there had been concern that digging up the past would be an unnecessary and painful intervention in their private lives, threatening to unearth something they had no wish to reveal.

Interior view of a Model Lebensborn Facility

Romek

Hermann Lüdeking is one of the few victims of forced Germanization unafraid to reveal the past. By recounting his own experiences, he wants to encourage others to emerge from the shadows and openly speak about their suffering. The retired engineer's apartment at Bad Dürrheim, in Baden-Württemberg, is piled high with papers. On his desk are stacks of ballpoint pens, each stamped with the "Seeking Identity" logo and his telephone number. For many years now, this search has given meaning to Hermann's life. After raising a large family and completing a successful professional career, he has time in old age to consider other nagging issues—including the one he finds most vexing: Who am I? Hermann has been able to reconstruct parts of his life, but many question marks remain

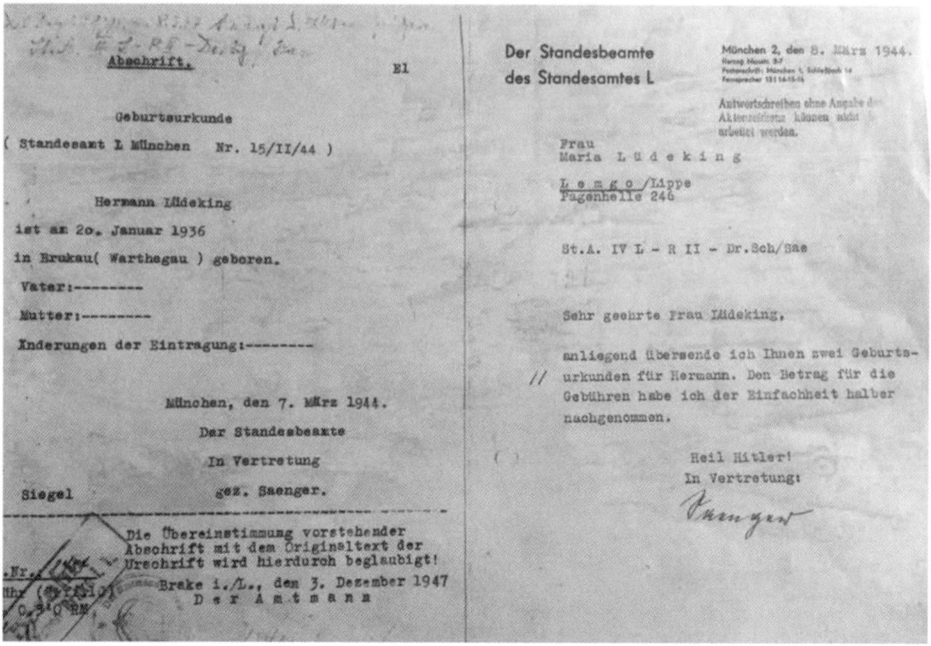

Abschrift. El

Geburtsurkunde

(Standesamt L München Nr. 15/II/44)

Hermann Lüdeking

ist am 20. Januar 1936

in Brukau(Warthegau) geboren.

Vater:--------

Mutter:--------

Änderungen der Eintragung:--------

München, den 7. März 1944.

Der Standesbeamte

In Vertretung

Siegel gez. Saenger.

Die Übereinstimmung vorstehender Abschrift mit dem Originaltext der Urschrift wird hierdurch beglaubigt!

Brake i./L., den 3. Dezember 1947

Der Amtmann

Der Standesbeamte des Standesamtes L

München 2, den 8. März 1944.

Frau Maria Lüdeking

Lemgo/Lippe Pagenhelle 246

St.A. IV L - R II - Dr.Sch/Sae

Sehr geehrte Frau Lüdeking,

anliegend übersende ich Ihnen zwei Geburtsurkunden für Hermann. Den Betrag für die Gebühren habe ich der Einfachheit halber nachgenommen.

Heil Hitler!

In Vertretung:

Hermann's birth certificate with the date of birth altered by lebensborn

Replacement child

After many years of correspondence with the Polish administration and the Polish Red Cross, Hermann knows at least that he was taken from an orphanage in Łódź and placed at the Sunny Meadow facility in 1942, as a boy of six. His memories from these years are unattached to specific dates. In Poland, he was called Roman Roszatowski. Evidently, he was regarded as "worthwhile material from the racial standpoint", which according to Himmler's theory should be found in ample supply among nations living on territory conquered by the Third Reich. Upon his arrival at Kohren-Sahlis, the Lebensborn employees swiftly renamed into Hermann. At first he wasn't assigned a surname, as that would be given when he was adopted by a German family.

Upon the death of her 21-year-old son, Maria Lüdeking decided to apply to Lebensborn for an adoption. "My son has fallen for the Führer on the slopes of Olympus," she wrote in her cover letter, asking to be given a "replacement child". Of course, this replacement should be a suitable and fulfill strict SS racial requirements. The child had to be of "German blood" and "German lineage", with a "predisposition to be of good character". Her application was forwarded to Sunny Meadow, where she was given her choice of two boys.

"I was playing with a classmate when we were summoned," Hermann remembers. "The head nurse said: 'Mrs. Lüdeking, here are two children, would you like to choose one?' And the lady looked at me and said: 'I'll take him, he looks a little sickly and I'll fatten him up.'"

Hermann with his adoptive mother

Maria obtained permission to take the child. Not all were so fortunate, since Himmler believed choosing the right foster parents was crucial to raising German patriots. The Lüdeking family were considered suitable guardians. Frau Lüdeking was the head of the local BDM branch at Ostwestfalen-Lippe in North Rhein-Westphalia, while Herr Lüdeking was an SS member. Both were great admirers of Hitler. In his new home, Hermann started using the last name of Lüdeking.

The procedure for changing first and last names required involvement by the local public registry office, designated in the documents by the abbreviation "L" for Lebensborn. Eight-year-old Hermann was given a falsified birth certificate issued on March 7, 1944, characterizing his biological parents in a terse note: "mother unknown, father unknown". The boy was taken from an orphanage in

Łódź, but it is not at all clear whether his birth parents were really unidentified during this period or whether they were reclassified as such by decision of the Lebensborn office. In any case, the point was to ensure that the abducted children forgot or never found out their true identities, as well as to persuade their adoptive parents that they were German orphans, not Slavic children spirited away from occupied countries.

Eastern children with issues

Maria Lüdeking became concerned about the condition of the boy, who she was convinced suffered from developmental delays. She began to wonder about the accuracy of his birth certificate. Corresponding with the worried woman, Dr. Ebner, the Lebensborn medical director, tried to explain the specific issues that often applied to children transferred from the East. Hermann's small collection of documents found after the death of his mother includes a copy of the letter, in which Dr. Ebner writes: "Your concern about the boy's age is wholly justified. I must admit that these Eastern children often suffer from developmental delays, but with time overcome them".

He didn't mention that these *Ostkinder*, for example from occupied Poland, often struggle with the aftereffects of starvation and torture. He said nothing about little Romek, now called Hermann or "Hermchen" [Hermie] by his doting adoptive mother, having been put through an orphanage and probably the Łódż children's concentration camp. Or even that during Hermann's stay at Sunny Meadow, as he will remember vividly in later life, he was frequently put on short rations. And that perhaps such malnutrition might have been responsible for his visibly lagging development.

The boy was sent for wrist X-rays, which allows Mrs. Lüdeking to obtain a certificate confirming that he is eight years old. But she still knew nothing about his past. And very soon she didn't wish to recall that she had obtained him through Lebensborn. After the war, she would deny any such thing.

Afterwards, life for the boy began to settle down into a normal rhythm, although there was a certain lingering distance in his relations with Mrs. Lüdeking. Hermann felt that he was being treated differently than Maria's other, biological children.

Who Am I?

Maria Lüdeking didn't have an easy time with Hermann. The boy was by now a fluent German speaker, but he still remembered perfectly well that he'd been brought from Poland. He was tormented by the question of his true identity.

"When I was 10 or 11, I asked my adoptive mother who my real parents were. She just cut me off by saying: 'Your mother and father are dead, that's what it says in your birth certificate.' I was too scared to ask any more questions."

When representatives of the Allied occupation authorities come to the Lüdeking's home in Lemgo, North Rhein-Westphalia, to take away their Germanized Polish child, Maria didn't want to give him up. For his part, Hermann wouldn't admit that he came from Poland. He was already in complete denial about speaking Polish and that whole chapter of his life.

"I really don't know who I am anymore, German or Polish."

Forgotten Victims

Unlike many who underwent forced Germanization and later tried to cover up their past, Hermann decided to speak out and seek the truth. It bothers him that the German government refuses to commemorate the victims or offer any compensation. He compares this treatment with examples of other countries where victims of forced Germanization live, and it makes him bitter.

"Why is it that Norway can recognize the harm done and pay damages, while Germany stays silent?"

On the other hand, this silent treatment doesn't really surprise him. Even the postwar Nuremberg trials treated Lebensborn as a charitable organization. As for trying to track down his identity, it's like seeking a needle in a haystack—especially since a large chunk of Lebensborn records were destroyed after the war, while others were scattered around various local Youth Offices all over Germany, none of whom were interested in revealing the identities of abducted children.

Perhaps Hermann would not have taken up the fight for victims' rights had it not been for his meeting with a teacher from Freiburg, Christoph Schwarz, an avid amateur historian and founder of the "Stolen Children – Forgotten Victims" Association. For years this group has been making its way through the labyrinthine German bureaucracy. They want recognition for the victims and some kind of moral compensation, with a strong emphasis on the latter.

Hermann Lüdeking with a childhood snapshot

In 2013, the German Federal Finance Ministry, in response to a letter from the Association, acknowledged that what happened to these abducted children "affected many families during the war and resulted from military strategy," adding as an extenuating circumstance, however, that the policy of forced Germanization "did not have as its primary intention the destruction or incarceration of individuals".

Rejections from the German Bundestag's Petitions Committee follow.

"The point was a symbolic recognition of the harms done to us. We were forgotten, simply ignored. It's a sad thing, pure ignorance. Those 'gentlemen' don't give a damn about abducted children. For me, they don't have any conscience at all."

Hermann is fond of the term "gentlemen", which on his lips acquires a special connotation. After all, he was a victim of Nazi ideology, the push to augment an "Aryan master race". To this day, Hermann, aka Romek, feels like a stranger in his own land.

"Germany doesn't want to know, because it will cost them. They will delay as long as they can, until we're all dead. In a few years, simple biology will solve the problem. I've been looking for my parents my entire life. I keep asking myself: who am I, where did I come from? And I know I'll never find the answer."

Relentless

Christoph Schwarz, Hermann Lüdeking, Alexander Orlow, and other protesters before an Administrative Court hearing in Cologne, June 21, 2018.

In June 2018, the Cologne Administrative Court ruled that, under German law, there was no reason to classify the victims of abduction and forced Germanization as entitled to financial compensation. The German Federal guidelines of 2011, referenced in the ruling, concern repressions against ethnic groups consider to be "less worthwhile" or inferior, which cannot be said of Germanized children. Besides, the right to demand compensation applies only to those who were citizens of Germany or ethnic Germans at the time the alleged harm occurred. And who, precisely, was Hermann while he was being shunted between various Germanization facilities? Was he still a Pole or a newly minted German? But Hermann isn't giving up. He's already planning an appeal.

"I'll just keep doing my thing".

Folker

Like Hermann, Folker Heinicke has been in relentless pursuit of his own identity for years. His birth certificate was also falsified by Department "L", so he can't give an exact answer on his age.

"I feel like I'm 85. Lately it's a little better, if only because I have cancer, and that means I start to fight. My family never believed in being sick, you can't give in. I'm not going to let a little cancer get me down."

When we met at his Hamburg home in the late 2017, Hermann was getting ready for a chemotherapy session the next day at the hospital. He didn't let it spoil his sense of humor.

Himmler—a family friend

The villa in Hamburg's Harburg district is almost a century old. It's surrounded by a spacious garden and lawn, with chickens scampering about. Three, to be precise. There used to be hundreds, because Folker's adoptive father, Adalbert Heinecke, was a passionate poultry breeder. Beneath the mirror in the entryway, there's a jar filled with thinly sliced frankfurters. Folker takes a handful and scatters them on the terrace.

"They're for the chickens. Those chickens of mine are leading the good life."

Folker with adoptive mother

Almost 70 years ago another poultry breeder stood on the same terrace—Heinrich Himmler. Folker was only a few years old, but he remembers the man in a black coat, maybe a uniform. He remembers the Reichsführer SS chatting amiably with Adalbert Heinecke.

"This must have been shortly before the end of the war. Himmler was standing here and telling my Dad he should build more henhouses, but absolutely not on a north-south axis, they needed to be oriented east-west. And that's what Dad did."

Aryan race

A much bigger interest of Heinrich Himmler's was breeding people. Supermen, anyway. When his Hamburg friend Adalbert Heinecke turned out to be sterile due to a bad childhood case of scarlet fever, Himmler decided to help him out. In 1943 he referred Heinecke to the Sunny Meadow Lebensborn center in Kohren-Sahlis. For the past few months, they'd had a towheaded, blue-eyed boy from Ukraine by the name of Aleksander Litau. He would become Folker.

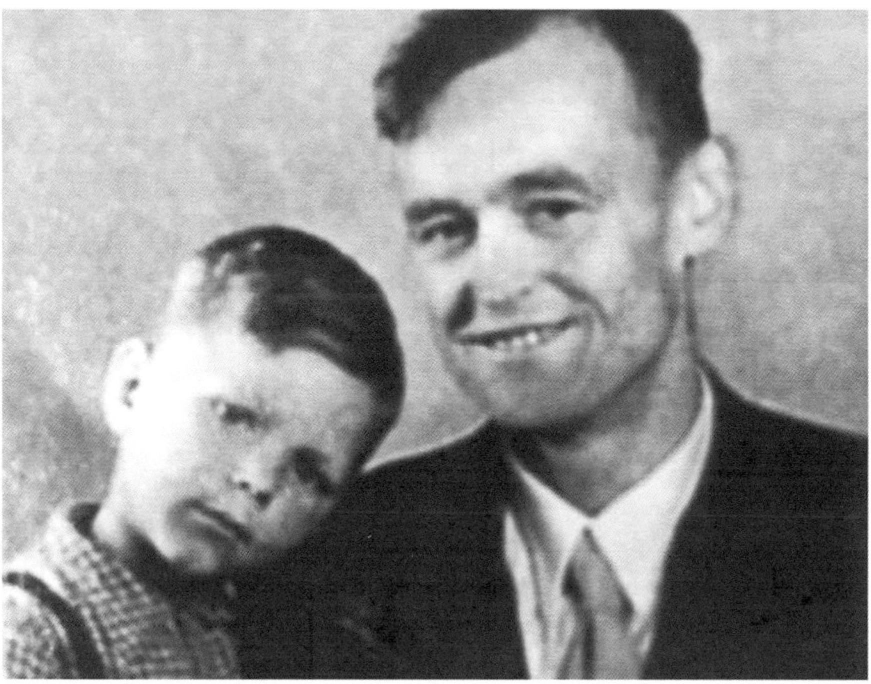

Folker Heinecke with his adoptive father

"There must have been about 30-40 of us boys, so they could take their pick. I ran up to my future father and rested my head on his knees. So they picked me.

'We'll take this one, he's our type,' they said. Almost like picking out a dog from a kennel.'"

When the Heineckes took the boy back to Hamburg, their new son was already a veteran of the Łódź children's camp and the Lebensborn centers at Kalisz, Bruczków and Polczyn-Zdrój. What came next, according to Folker, was heaven.

"My relations with my folks were good, maybe they even treated me better than if I had been their natural child. Everything ran like clockwork: breakfast at 7:30, dinner at one, supper at 7:30. Mom took care of everything, we had a big house and two gardeners. If I came back late from school, dinner was waiting for me under a special cozy Mom had to keep it warm. As a family we were very close, my parents liked taking everyone on trips together."

Only one thing spoiled this childhood idyll.

"Neighbors always know the family dirt. Kids from the whole neighborhood used to hang out at our house because we had a pond. Once, when I was seven, my buddy Wolfgang says to me: "You aren't your parents' son." For me it was like the sky was falling, because I didn't think anyone knew. I never told my parents, because they would have felt bad about it."

Uprooted

It was only around the age of 50, long after his parents had died, that Heinecke began to unearth his own history. When I ask about his regrets in life, he answers that he has just one: that he didn't start looking earlier.

Did Folker's early history, despite his happy childhood, have an impact on his later life? Folker is convinced that it did, if only because it's difficult to build anything permanent if you've been uprooted. When his wife left him after 13 years of marriage, taking their two-year-old daughter, he found it hard to enter a new relationship.

At a certain point, the fact that he never knew his real parents became Folker's main problem. An inquiry at the Moscow archives yielded information that 200 people by the name of Litau were living in Crimea in 1940, when he was born. Folker wanted to travel to Crimea and meet people who could be his relatives.

Folker Heinecke in 2017

He was informed about a possible gravesite for his father, or rather of a man who could have been his father. He was killed at Stalingrad. Folker would like to see the place.

"I would feel calmer if I could get a sense of closure by standing at the grave of one of my parents."

He'd be happier if he could take the trip with his brother Hermann. Maybe he'd take Janusz, his other brother from Sunny Meadow, as well.

Janusz

At Janusz Bukorzycki's apartment in Łódź, his wife Zosia is still the lady of the house. She may no longer be alive, but without Zosia, Janusz would not be who he is. That is 84-year-old's answer for why he seems to be so happy to be alive. He met Zosia after the war at an adult education class, and she made him the home he had so longed for during his childhood and youth.

A Street Kid from Łódź

In 1933, on Zawadzka Street (now Próchnik Street) in Łódź, somebody left an infant in a bundle. It was a usual drop-off spot, just a stone's throw from the local community shelter. The babies were usually abandoned by young single mothers, ashamed of their bastard children and without the means to support them. The little boy was placed with a foster family, Anna and Józef Konieczny. But he kept the surname Bukorzycki. To this day, Janusz has difficulty explaining why. Perhaps the name was written on a card pinned to the bundle he was wrapped in. When he was a young boy, it was not something Janusz bothered his head about. HIs first 10 years of life with his foster family were idyllic.

Then, in 1943, the Gestapo came knocking on the Koniecznys' door.

"In June a woman from the Gestapo came and ordered us to report for a physical examination. They called it 'anthropological' or something like that. I had to go from doctor to doctor, walking around naked as the day God made me. They checked my measurements and took a full vial of blood."

After a few days, a man and a woman in Gestapo uniforms appeared and took the boy to a special assembly point that had been operating for more than a year to process abducted children from all over occupied Poland. Anna Konieczna makes the whole trip there on a streetcar, gripping her adoptive son's hand. Janusz is holding on for dear life. But at the assembly point gate, Janusz has to proceed alone. They won't let his foster mother inside. That moment is the beginning of his ordeal.

Unruly Johann

"From that moment, Janusz Bukorzycki ceased to exist. My new name was Johann Buchner. We slept on iron beds in a factory hall with boarded-up windows. They made us stand outside in the rain. One boy tried to run away through the gate and they shot at him. He fell and didn't get up."

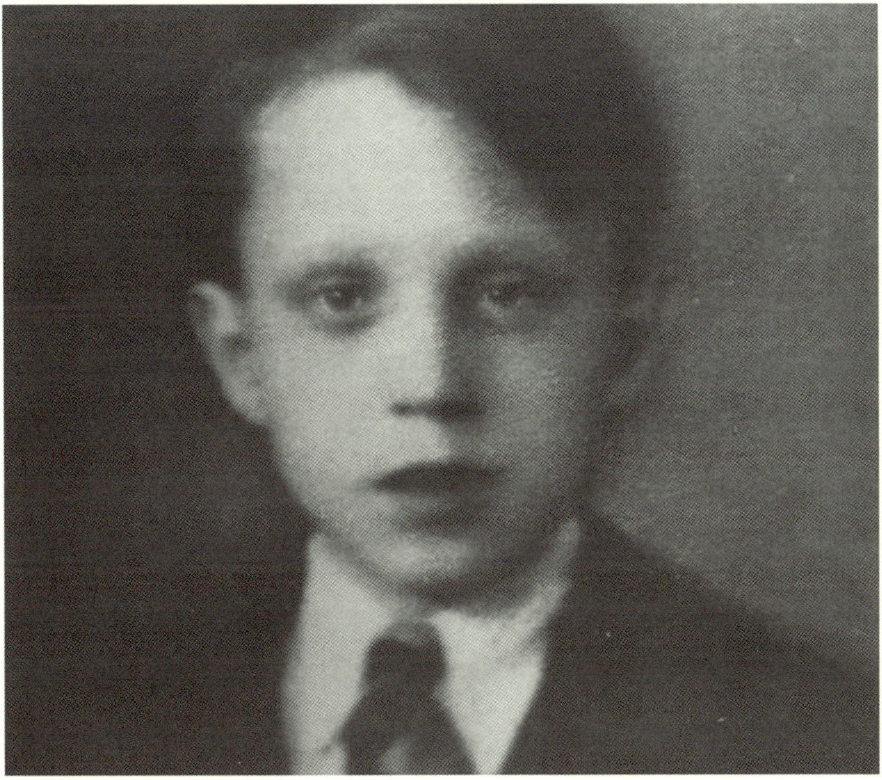

Johann Buchner, aka Janusz Bukorzycki

Afterwards came the Kalisz children's home, where Janusz spent two weeks.

"They always treated little Hansi as a bad boy. One day for lunch, they served us potatoes swimming in some kind of disgusting dark slop. I fished out a potato and tossed it at the portrait of Hitler hanging in the dining room. I hit the Führer right in the eye with my first throw. My second caught him in the other one. For that, I got three days' detention with no food."

These three-day isolation stints with no food, and sometimes no sleep as well, turned out to be standard operating procedure at the Lebensborn "Alpenland" facility in Oberweis, Austria, which was the next stop in the Łódź orphan's odyssey. Speaking Polish was forbidden at "Alpenland". But the older kids, some of them 15 years old, made sure the young ones didn't obey.

"We were caught in middle, between a rock and a hard place. If we spoke German, we got a beating from the older kids. What were you supposed to do? I can't bear to even speak about it, please believe me."

Janusz's childhood experiences are exhausting, but they are so deeply imprinted on his mind that he can't stop talking about them.

Janusz Bukorzycki at home in Łódź holding a family history written by his wife

"Once the boys got in trouble for stealing some money, and I was also caught with 20 Reichsmarks. They have us three days detention with no food or water, and then we were so hungry we ate pig slops and potato peels."

Children to the front

At Oberweis, Johann Buchner was forced to drill in a Hitler Youth uniform.

"They took us on winter marches that left our shoes soaked through. When they dried, the shoes were so misshapen that we couldn't wear them. They taught us to shoot and we were being prepared to go the front."

But the war ended before Janusz could go into action. Together with a group of children, he was sent to Red Cross convalescent center in Barcelona.

Meanwhile, his foster parents in Poland were looking for Janusz. They quickly found him. Janusz didn't worry about the identity of his real parents – he was happy to be back with Anna and Józef Konieczny. But he would have preferred to have a birth certificate with his mother's first and last names instead of the annotation "N.N." – name unknown. When the time came for Janusz to get married, he asked his stepmother to enter her name as his biological mother, and she instantly agreed. After his stepmother's death, Janusz's stepsister told him that Anna was actually his biological mother. Today, Janusz thinks that as a poor country girl, Anna could have left him at the community shelter and then "adopted" him after she was safely married.

"My guess is that she was my real mother. Anyway, it will be easier to die knowing whose child I am."

In late 2017, Janusz wrote another Christmas card to each of his German "brothers" – Folker and Hermann. And just as happens every Christmas, Janusz received cards back from them with holiday greetings. For better or worse, "Sunny Meadow" had forever linked their lives together.

Recovery

Hrabar's Cupboard

On July 22, 1948, Roman Hrabar – the Polish government plenipotentiary for recovering stolen children – and his deputy Wiktor Pietruszka were just leaving the Red Cross delegate's office in Esslingen, Germany. They left behind a cupboard and desk crammed with scrupulously collected files about Polish children deported to Germany and Austria for purposes of Germanization. The drawers and shelves contained folders and binders of documents concerning the youngest victims of Heinrich Himmler's criminal plans. They provided valuable evidence about a large-scale operation which gained a new definition after the war – as genocide and a crime against humanity.

It was no coincidence that the German delegation of the International Committee of the Red Cross (ICRC) responsible for dealing with abducted children was located in Esslingen. The southern German town is home of the International Tracing Service (ITS), now known as the Arolsen Archives, which contain the world's most comprehensive records on the victims and survivors of Nazi persecution.

Hrabar and Pietruszka were taking a short trip to Poland for a conference. They probably had no way of knowing they would not be returning soon, if at all.

Race against the Age Limit

Two months later, Esslingen received instructions from the ICRC Main Delegation in Spenge along with a personal directive from Franz Emerich, the head of the Main Director's Child Repatriation Department, to seal up all documents in the office of Legal Counsellor Hrabar.[1]

During his absence, the Esslingen office had already received 500 new cases to handle. All involved Polish children, and none were being dealt with at an extremely crucial moment in the search effort.[2] Each wasted day meant that more

[1] Letter from Franciszek Emerich, director of the ICRC Main Directorate's Child Revindication Department, to the Main PCK Delegate for Germany Konstanty Rudziński, 9 January 1949, AAN, PCK Delegation in Germany, sygn. 77, karty nr 143–145.

[2] Statement by Stefan Tyszka, 3 December 1948, AAN, PCK Delegation in Germany, sygn. 77, karta nr 99.

Polish kids fell into the "overage" category of children ineligible for repatriation because they had passed the maximum age limit, as regulated by the statute of the International Refugee Organisation (IRO).[3]

Meanwhile, Hrabar's and Pietruszka's stay in Poland dragged on. "In July and August, circumstances occurred that have momentarily prevented the return of Mr. Hrabar and Mr. Pietruszka to Germany," the Red Cross chief delegate to Germany Konstanty Rudziński wrote in a report on his department's organization and repatriation efforts dated Dec. 31, 1948.[4]

But in a letter dated Dec. 7, 1948 from the Polish Red Cross to the Ministry of Labor and Social Welfare, we learn that the IRO had already asked the Red Cross to return Hrabar's documents, which would allow the organization to resume its repatriation work.[5]

So this was far from a "momentary" problem.

The Cupboard's Contents

On Nov. 28, 1948, three people arrive at Hrabar's office to inspect the sealed cupboard and desk – Franz Emerich, Regina Tatarka and Stefan Tyszka (as the American Red Cross representative for Munich's Pasing district). On Rudziński's instructions, the seals are removed. More than four months had already passed since Hrabar and Pietruszka left Esslingen for Poland.[6]

The cupboard turned out to contain files on Polish children who passed through Lebensborn – segregated between those who had been located and those not yet tracked down. There were also files on repatriated Lebensborn children and a handwritten Lebensborn registry. Also, six folders with the personal files of missing children, three folders with census and search cards from Łódż, three more with found children, and seven with repatriated cases. In addition, there were files with lists of children born in Germany, two files on children registered at displaced persons camps, and a separate folder with "closed cases" – those who died, were

---

[3] Letter on "overage" children from Wiktor Pietruszka, AAN, PCK Delegation in Germany, sygn. 77, karta nr 61.

[4] Report by Konstanty Rudziński, 31 December 1948, on department organization and recovery operations, AAN, PCK Delegation in Germany, sygn. 77, karty nr 42–49.

[5] PCK letter, 7 December 1948, addressed to the Ministry of Labor and Social Welfare, AAN.

[6] Protocol on opening the cupboard and desk of Roman Hrabar i Wiktor Pietruszka, 22 November 1948, AAN, PCK Main Delegation in Germany, sygnatura 77, karty nr 97–98.

found but would not be returning to Poland, or resident in third countries. And much more besides. For example, a valuable file with data on Germanization centers active in occupied Poland and 31 folders of correspondence and press publications.

The desk contained three folders with lists of children deported to Germany who were sought, found and repatriated from the United Kingdom. In the right drawer, a folder with correspondence and other material concerning Lebensborn children was found There were also files with lists of [birth] certificates, instructions and transport manifests. Finally, several hard-to-find books on looting and Germanization.[7]

The three visitors later prepared an official protocol on opening the cupboard and its contents. This document is now in the Polish National Archives [*Archiwum Akt Nowych*] in Warsaw, in a file entitled "Polish Red Cross, Main Delegation in Germany, Reference No. 77". Thanks to this protocol, we still have access to Hrabar's valuable cupboard.

What Happened to the Files on 500 Children?

Hrabar never returned to Esslingen. Pietruszka made it back in late November 1948, just after the cupboard and desk were opened. He began to put the documents in order and update the files on Lebensborn children. Pietruszka's official title was the deputy director of the Polish Red Cross Delegation in Germany's Child Recovery Department. In the official Red Cross hierarchy, he was subordinate to the Polish Red Cross Delegate to Germany, but he was also obligated to report to the Ministry of Labor and Social Welfare in Warsaw. His posting could not be changed without Ministry approval. In the Polish Red Cross budget, he was listed as a senior clerk at the Child Recovery Department.[8]

---

[7] File review protocol, 22 November 1948, AAN, PCK Main Delegation in Germany, sygnatura 77, karty 97–98.

[8] Letter from PCK Main Board, 27 November 1948, AAN, PCK Main Delegation in Germany, sygnatura 77, karta nr 158.

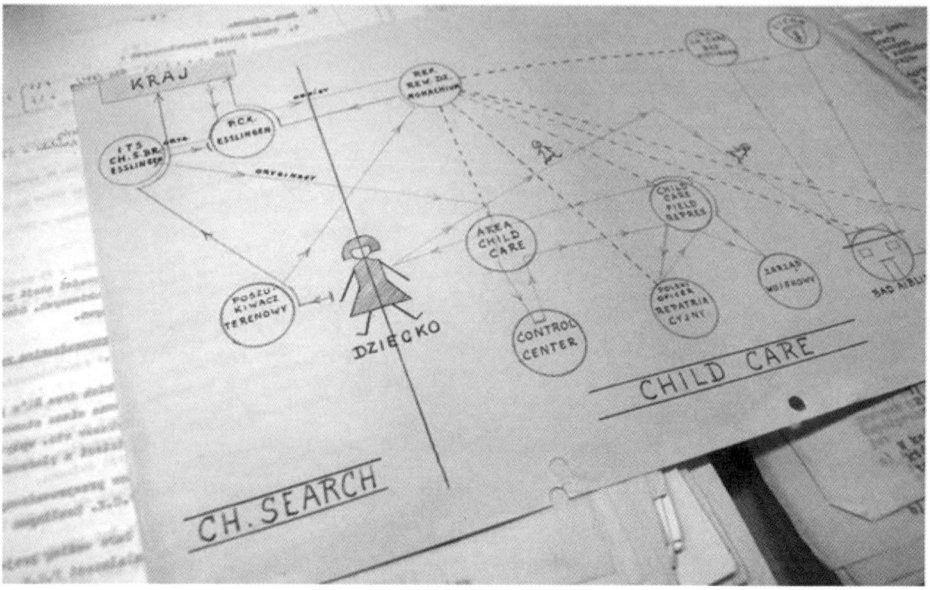

Diagram showing how Polish Red Cross delegations searched and cared for lost children

On arrival in Esslingen, Pietruszka discovered that some of the files had gone missing, and those that remained had been removed from envelopes marked with surnames and case numbers, because these had been deemed mistaken. He complained that during his absence some original documents had been given away to outsiders.[9]

"According to PRC employees at the Esslingen bureau, the cupboard and drawers in the recovery plenipotentiary's office remained unlocked throughout his time there and after his return to Poland…everything was left open and as a result, the documents were available to everybody," Emerich pointed out in January 1949. He described heaps of papers and general disorder."[10]

[9] Report by Wiktor Pietruszka on the period from November 28 to December 15, 1948, AAN, PCK Delegation in Germany, sygn. 77, karta nr 13.

[10] Statement by Franciszek Emerich, 9 January 1949, AAN, PCK Main Delegation in Germany, sygnatura 77, karty nr 149–151.

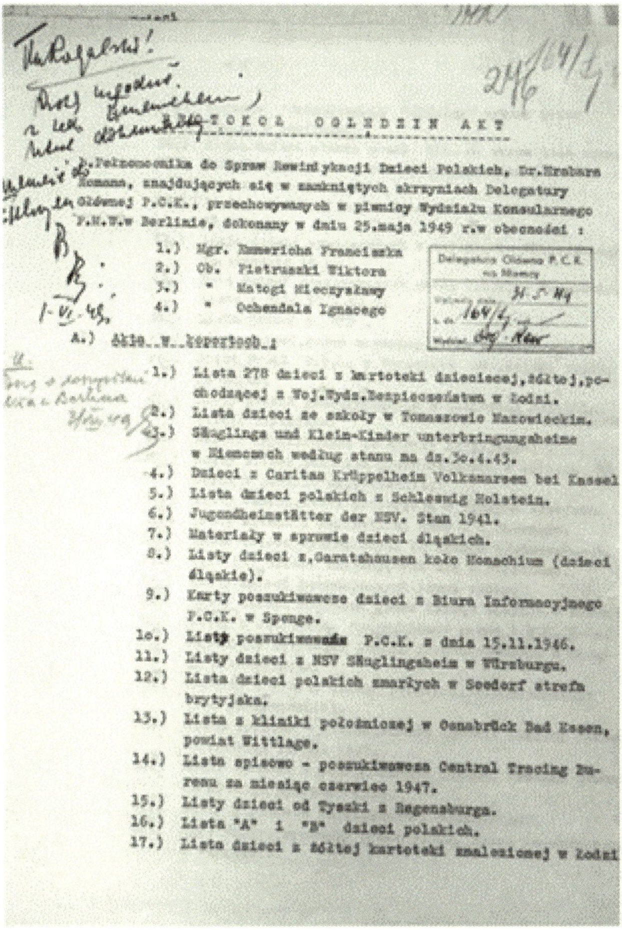

PROTOKOŁ OGLĘDZIN AKT

P. Pełnomocnika do Spraw Rewindykacji Dzieci Polskich, Dr. Hrabara Romana, znajdujących się w zamkniętych skrzyniach Delegatury Głównej P.C.K., przechowywanych w piwnicy Wydziału Konsularnego P.M.W.w Berlinie, dokonany w dniu 25.maja 1949 r.w obecności :

1.) Mgr. Emmericha Franciszka
2.) Ob. Pietruszki Wiktora
3.) " Matogi Mieczysławy
4.) " Ochendala Ignacego

A.) Akta w teczkach :

1.) Lista 278 dzieci z kartoteki dziecięcej, żółtej, pochodzącej z Woj.Wydz.Bezpieczeństwa w Łodzi.
2.) Lista dzieci ze szkoły w Tomaszowie Mazowieckim.
3.) Säuglings und Klein-Kinder unterbringungsheime w Niemczech według stanu na dz.30.4.43.
4.) Dzieci z Caritas Krüppelheim Volkmarsen bei Kassel
5.) Lista dzieci polskich z Schleswig Holstein.
6.) Jugendheimstätter der NSV. Stan 1941.
7.) Materiały w sprawie dzieci śląskich.
8.) Listy dzieci z Garatshausen koło Monachium (dzieci śląskie).
9.) Karty poszukiwawcze dzieci z Biura Informacyjnego P.C.K. w Spenge.
10.) Listy poszukiwawcze P.C.K. z dnia 15.11.1946.
11.) Listy dzieci z NSV Säuglingsheim w Würzburgu.
12.) Lista dzieci polskich zmarłych w Seedorf strefa brytyjska.
13.) Lista z kliniki położniczej w Osnabrück Bad Essen, powiat Wittlage.
14.) Lista spisowo - poszukiwawcza Central Tracing Bureau za miesiąc czerwiec 1947.
15.) Listy dzieci od Tyszki z Regensburga.
16.) Lista "A" i "B" dzieci polskich.
17.) Lista dzieci z żółtej kartoteki znalezionej w Łodzi

Inspection report on files collected by Roman Hrabar.

Emerich and Tyszka claim that Hrabar and Pietruszka neglected to assign anyone to care for the files or ensure their security, which meant that anyone could gain access.

Pietruszka declared, however, that he had shifted responsibility for a portion of his duties and some documents – including about 4,700 recovery files on individual children – to Mieczysław Herdegen, an employee at the PCK Delegation in Esslingen. Herdegen confirms this, but shortly after Hrabar and Pietruszka left, he was relieved of his duties and transferred to another location.[11]

[11] Herdegen letter from February 1949, AAN, PCK Main Delegation in Germany, sygnatura 77, karta 131–132.

In his written description, Pietruszka refers to crates of documents left in the corridor by the entrance to the Esslingen office entrance at the time of he and Pietruszka departed for Poland.

Nobody in Esslingen could say when those crates arrived, where they were from, or who sent them. They contained unsorted PCK files from 1946.

From the documentation collected in Hrabar's office, Pietruszka estimated that upon his return about 500 individual files were missing, most of them concerning recovered children, including 32 from Lebensborn. These included personal files on children named Bartczak and Arden. Also vanished were NSV files from Frankfurt and a report on children born in Germany.[12]

'There was no key'

The office was in an uproar. Serious allegations were made of negligence, sloppy organization, failure to supervise employees, and a generally careless attitude towards the child recovery program.

Upon his return to Germany, Pietruszka discovered a completely new institutional setup.

"Under the methods being used now, more children are lost than found, while children who should be repatriated in the normal fashion are instead subjected to a complicated and tortuous recovery procedure," he notes in a letter dated April 11, 1949.[13]

In Pietruszka's opinion, the new approach took no interest in how a child ended up in Germany, whether by deportation, evacuation or assignment to a Germanization group, on which transport the child had travelled, at which centers he or she had been processed, and what methods had been used to obtain a positive identification. Each side blamed the other as letters flew back and forth.

Tyszka and Emerich accused Hrabar and Pietruszka of lying about the existence of a central card catalogue of Polish children at Esslingen (which they had claimed at a briefing in Berlin on March 19-20, 1948.

---

[12] Report no. 1 on the period from November 28 do December 15, 1948, AAN, PCK Main Delegation in Germany, sygn. 77, karty 139–140; report from Wiktor Pietruszka, January 1949 r., karta nr 94.

[13] Letter on working methods from Wiktor Pietruszka, 11 April 1949, AAN, PCK Main Delegation in Germany, sygn. 77, karty nr 68–70.

The two men's detractors also claimed that they had ignored lists of children prepared by the PCK in Warsaw.

On every trip to Poland, Hrabar and Pietruszka allegedly took "a certain number of documents" with them, without bothering to notify their colleagues about it. Hrabar's accusers say that also happened in July 1948, when he returned to Poland for good.

Tyszka also complained about the "idiosyncratic phonetic system" the Polish-speaking Pietruszka used to arrange files alphabetically, noting that he filed "Zimmerman" under "C" (a letter which in Polish sounds like the German "Z") and Sonnemann under "Z" (which in Polish sounds like the German "S").

Pietruszka shot back that under Tyszka's management, some recovery cases were assigned to an intern.[14]

In short, total confusion.

Pietruszka, asked why he didn't think to lock the cupboard even when he left for Poland, simply replied: "There was no key."

The rest of the delegation was gradually drawn into the quarrel. In December 1948 and May 1949, employees made statements outlining further examples of negligence. Barbara Węgrzecka and Roman Tatarka noted that female operatives of the Intelligence Service used the Lebensborn files for several days, fetching whole binders to their office. In general, outsiders were allowed to work on files at the PCK bureau without supervision of any kind.[15]

Five People to 193 Square Feet

On Dec. 1, 1948, Emerich directed the department to take over management of the central card catalogue and correspondence between the Warsaw head office, the local PCK delegations in German and the recovery section in Esslingen.

This last department was housed in an old storeroom measuring 18 square meters (193 square feet), containing five people working at shared desks. Even though 20 typists worked next door in a large hall, the recovery section didn't have a

---

[14] Report no. 1 on the period from November 28 do December 15, 1948, AAN, PCK Main Delegation in Germany, sygn. 77, karty 139–140.

[15] Employee statements, AAN, PCK Delegation in Germany, sygn. 77, karty nr 101–103.

secretary to do its own typing. According to Pietruszka, "the technical working conditions in the section were scandalous."

By this time, the whole Esslingen office was feuding. Employees passed the time by pointing out colleagues' mistakes and informing on each other. Clashing views on how to conduct recovery operations led to constant arguments that paralyzed efforts. In a letter to Rudziński dated May 6, 1949, Tyszka harshly criticized Pietruszka's work and enumerated his errors. He claimed that Pietruszka's team was working on "imaginary" problems. It was no wonder that he wanted to discredit Pietruszka, since Tyszka's preferred method of recovery involved close cooperation with the German "*Suchdienste*" [literally, "Search services"], which he believed were the only ones in possession of a systematically compiled database. Exasperated, Tyszka complained that his efforts to achieve such cooperation are being "held back."[16]

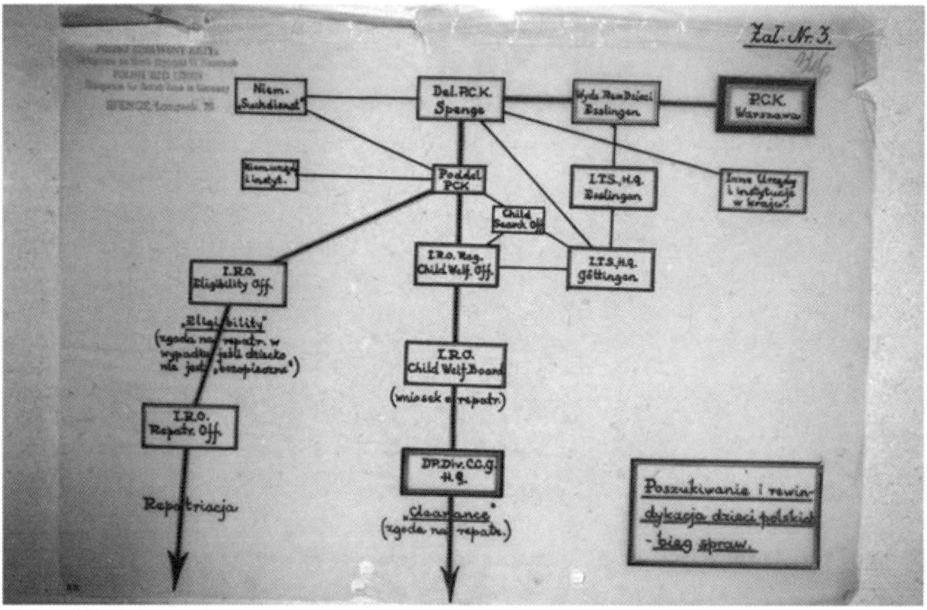

Offices and institutions involved in child search and recovery operations

[16] Letter from Stefan Tyszka to the Main PCK Delegate for Germany, 5 May1949, AAN, PCK Main Delegation in Germany, sygn. 77, karty 10–14.

***

After returning from the conference in Poland, Pietruszka reported that "the department is not planning operations or looking into the Germanization, deportation, evacuation and extermination of Polish children; it is not keeping up-to-date reports of its activities; it is not conducting, correcting, instructing or supervising operations; it is not collecting books, periodicals and documents pertinent to operations; it is not investigating centers for Germanizing, deporting, evacuating and exterminating Polish children; it is not studying deportation routes; and it is not drawing conclusions from its experience."[17]

Operation interrupted

Our current knowledge about abducted children is largely based on Roman Hrabar's work. To this day, researchers rely mainly on the numbers compiled by the plenipotentiary for child recovery. We know from Hrabar that the Germans may have taken some 50,000 to 200,000 Polish children to be Germanized. For more than 70 years after the end of World War II, no time or money could be found to verify these figures and to complete the work of tracking down these children and organizing the documentation.

The recovery operation was stopped at a moment when it could still have succeeded. When I asked why, Jacek E. Wilczur, a colleague of Roman Hrabar's, told me simply: "It was for lousy reasons".

[17] Report by Wiktor Pietruszka on application submissions, 5 January 1949, AAN, PCK Main Delegation in Germany, sygn. 77, karta nr 105.

Lousy Reasons

"You absolutely must get in touch with Professor Wilczur," I keep hearing while looking for traces of the stolen children. It's a subject he knows a lot about. Wilczur worked with Hrabar and was an investigator with the Main Commission for the Investigation of Nazi German Crimes in Poland. He's definitely a man to see.

They say Professor Wilczur has an amazing setup in his apartment, which he's turned into an archive. The documents are stacked everywhere, so many that you have to squeeze between tall piles to move around.

"Why don't you try calling? It might work," I'm told. They give me an address and telephone number.

Weeks go by. Perhaps something's happened to him? Maybe he doesn't live there anymore. Finally, the professor answers his phone. We have a long conversation – first one, then two and three of them. Finally, we make an appointment.

***

Professor Wilczur's cramped flat does in fact look like an archive. From the dark stairwell, one passes through a reinforced, burglar-proof door into a modest interior of a Warsaw high-rise apartment building.

Only the coat hanger and shoe rack indicate a human lives here. We creep along a narrow path to the coach and some chairs, sharing the space with stacks of documents, back issues of newspapers, research materials, valuable artefacts rescued from rubbish heaps in the Bieszczady mountains that villagers had intended to burn, and dozens of snapshots of the Professor's relatives clustered around a few paintings the walls. They stare at us from the past, and we stare back from the present.

The other room is lined with bookshelves, and on these shelves Professor Wilczur has arranged his private archive. Thousands of documents, organized by subject and grouped in sets of 10 or 15, each labelled with a cardboard tab.

The middle shelves containing information on concentration camps and German processing centers, On the left are materials about resistance fighter Jan

Piwnik (pseudonym Ponury, or "Gloomy") and Home Army resistance operations in the Świętokrzyskie [Holy Cross] mountains, the Nazi movement and the SS. To the right, more shelves on the Allied powers, intelligence, counterintelligence, the East German Stasi, the Israeli Mossad, Chinese special forces, Upper Silesia, the Owl Mountains, secret installations, the Nazis' secret Riese tunnel complex, and the legendary Amber Room looted by the Germans from the Catherine Palace in Tsarskoye Selo.

Professor Wilczur in his apartment

Jack Wilczur as a teenage soldier in the Home Army (AK)

"My daughter asks me who is going to inherit all of this stuff? And I tell her not to worry about it."

Hanging on the wall is a family heirloom – an antique mirror in a heavy, hand-carved wooden frame. I'm told something of its history and how it got here. History is something palpable in this place.

These token souvenirs from the past come mainly from city of Professor Wilczur's birth, Lwów – now a part of Ukraine. In his small apartment, he has re-created a small replica of his former world, a tiny fragment of his hometown.

In Lwów, his entire family was killed by Nazi occupiers, leaving him orphaned and alone. He tries not to break down while telling the story. It simply wouldn't do to lose his composure. After the death of his loved ones, Wilczur – still a 15-year-old boy – enlisted in the Home Army. He became what they called an *egzekutor* – a hit man or assassin sent to kill Nazi officials and collaborators. He killed, Wilczur stresses, for his mother and his brothers.

***

"Bean soup is my favorite, because that's what I was fed as a child. And bright red *barszcz* (Polish borscht) with potatoes. By the end of the war, I was in England, but I came back. Later I had many opportunities to emigrate. The thing is, I don't like leaving Poland. For all our faults, we are a wonderful people. Where else on earth am I going to find a decent bowl of *barszcz*? For that alone, I'd never leave," he laughs.

"Besides, we have a special way with children. Something I've seen only with the Belarusians, Russians and Ukrainians. What they taught me back at elementary school in Lwów is that a child is a sacred thing."

"When the Nazis murdered my little brothers, I was on my own. Alone in Lwów, my hometown. Well, maybe not entirely. The whole nation was with me. And my loved ones aren't dead, they're up in heaven. The people we keep in our memories and our hearts don't die."

***

The professor sits on the couch. Behind his head, a few small paintings show wolves crouching like sentinels, as if they're guarding him.

"I was one of thousands of people who lost their families to the Nazis. I hate fascism and Nazism. But I'm no enemy of the German nation, because the current generation isn't made up of Nazis but of normal people. Due to my professional responsibilities and research, I have a lot of contact with young Germans. They are anti-fascists, hate Nazism and are ashamed of their parents' history. This is a generation that grew up in a Europe liberated from Nazism."

"Nazis, not Germans" is a phrase I hear frequently from Professor Wilczur. "The first victims of Hitler and the SS were Germans. When Hitler came to power in 1933, the first thing he did was to murder his own. I bow my head to the Germans who died on the chopping block, just as I do to other victims."

"We don't remind ourselves often enough that there were also good Germans."

***

"Let's start with the numbers, because even after all these years, they raise some doubts."

"But I was the worst in my class at math."

"How did you do in history?"

"Oh, I was the best in history and languages. I guess my gift with languages was supposed to make up for being a fool at math [laugh]."

"The published figure for Polish children stolen to be Germanized ranges from 50,000 to 200,000. Is that accurate?"

"It is, except we're talking about a Germanization figure closer to 220,000. I know, because I've worked with the sources and the documentation is clear. Still, at heart I'm an internationalist – I classify people by their character, not by personality. Nationality is incidental."

"How many of these children returned to Poland? 30,000?"

"More. Even so, it's still a very small proportion of those who were deported."

"Why were the recovery operations suspended in 1950?"

"For very lousy reasons."

"Political ones?"

"Yes. After the war, the Polish government wanted to live on the best possible terms with Germany. You can see the sense in that. Today Germany is our largest trade partner, they were instrumental in getting us into the European Union. Germany is our biggest ally."

"Then why was Roman Hrabar removed as child recovery plenipotentiary in 1948? He was operating in Germany at the time and was having considerable success. Suddenly, he leaves for a business trip to Poland and never comes back. He left an office in Esslingen stuffed with valuable documents on stolen children destined for Germanization. And during Hrabar's absence, hundreds of new reports on missing Polish children were piling up. Is this the work of the secret police?"

"Yes."

"Professor, didn't you have the opportunity to work with Hrabar on a book about the extermination of children? How do you remember him?"

"He was an honest man to the core. Like me, he came from the eastern borderlands, so he was big-hearted."

"Who did you find to be your best research collaborators on what happened to children during the war?"

"Hrabar and Zofia Tokarz were the best. We co-authored a book, *Czas niewoli, czas śmierci* [*Time of Captivity, Time of Death*], published in 1979. We were allowed to pick our own topics from the files of the Main Commission for the Investigation of Nazi German Crimes in Poland. Besides my core subject, which was the German intelligence services and their crimes, I chose crimes committed during World War II against children."

***

Czas niewoli, czas śmierci deals, among other things, with how plunder and Germanization operations "were premeditated and centrally controlled, with full knowledge of their criminal character", with how Lebensborn was responsible for issuing false birth certificates, and with how the creation of phantom registry offices allowed all traces of these children to be removed. Just as it was done in Kalisz. If children's data happened to be entered at the local registry office, Lebensborn officials would visit every month to collect the forms and cover their tracks.

"Taking Polish children to Germany for adoption by German foster parents – children who had been forcibly separated from their Polish families — was a standard procedure," the book states.

Children were placed with foster families regarded as ideologically reliable, typically with SS affiliation. This marked the final stage of eradicating their former national identity. "Lebensborn kept up a written correspondence with these families, in which it was careful to maintain an unusually warm and friendly tone," the authors note.

Professor Wilczur is especially complimentary about the historian Zofia Tokarz. "She made an enormous contribution to popularizing this topic," he says. Largely due to her efforts, *Czas niewoli, czas śmierci* was translated into several languages and became well-known.

"The Nazi system of kidnapping children to eradicate their national identity, in its methodology and scope, is unprecedented and without analogy in human history. Its planned and institutionalized nature constitutes a stain on 20th century civilization," the book concludes.

***

"Is today a good time to return to business that we – as a nation – left unfinished after the war?"

"Reviving the issue? Absolutely."

"Could good relations with Germany help us initiate a serious discussion about the fate of these stolen and Germanized children?"

"Sure. Germany is being governed by a new generation that abhors the way their fathers behaved and the crimes they committed on the Slavic nations, Jews and Gypsies. It's a whole new world – a different psychology, different emotions. They don't have our blood on their hands – they're disgusted and embarrassed. We can't hold them responsible for the fact that their fathers and grandfathers were mass murderers."

"Our schools take the easy way out, talking about Hitler and Nazism, about the Gestapo and the SS. They leave out the part about honest Germans. It's wrong to sit in judgment of an entire nation. Every country has its criminals and heroes. We in Poland have had plenty of scoundrels and saints. This is what I try to drum into my students' heads – it's my obligation."

Jacek Wilczur (1925-2018)

Memory Guardian

"Those children were damaged, severely damaged. They were like prisoners, uprooted from their homes and held hostage," says Christoph Schwarz, a teacher and amateur historian from Germany.

In June 2018, the Federal Administrative Court in Bonn began hearing a case brought by the organization Schwarz founded – Geraubte Kinder – Vergessene Opfer [Stolen Children – Forgotten Victims, or GKVO]. Schwarz was trying to demonstrate to the judges and spectators gathered in the courtroom that children kidnapped by the Nazis were the victims of a criminal machine. But German law saw the case in a different light.

Their Day in Court

It had been two and a half years to the day since one of those kidnapped children, GKVO's honorary chairman Hermann Lüdeking, had asked the court to rule on payment of damages to the kidnapped children. During the hearing, judges explained the complexities of German law, which defines groups recognized as victims of the Nazi regime and eligible for financial compensation. According to government guidelines issued in 2011, these are people who had been "subjected to repression as individuals or collectively or suffered harm due to their social or personal behavior" – including, among others, homosexuals and victims of euthanasia. In general, the definition encompassed groups or individuals considered by the Nazis to be "less valuable."

It was to these guidelines that Lüdeking referred in his opening speech, even though they make no mention of abducted children, Nevertheless, his hope was that the court would find sufficient grounds to expand the definition to include this group as well.

Schwarz was also not ready to give up. At the hearing, he patiently tried to explain the scale of the repressions. True, they did not stem – as the regulations stated – from the young victims' "characteristics" or "behavior." Neither were they considered "less valuable". Indeed, it was exactly the opposite, since the Nazis believed these children were worthy of Germanization. It is true that they were not persecuted for their supposed defects, sexual orientation, or national origin. Even so, they were victims.

Christoph Schwarz presents documentation on the stolen children. To his right, Hermann Lüdeking and Alexander Orlov.

"Persecution took place – that's a fact. Their Polish identity was to be eradicated and destroyed. This in turn led to spiritual trauma and bodily harm", he argued.

At the hearing, two binders containing documents Schwarz had collected over many years rested on the podium behind which the judges sat. They contain 600 pages of testimony from several dozen people whose lives were wrecked after losing their homes and families. These documents also show the determination and cynicism with which the Nazi regime tried to remake these stolen children into completely different people. As a plaintiff, Lüdeking's own fate is described in detail. If the court were to award him damages according to the government guidelines, he would have received a one-time payment of about €2,500. But money is not what Hermann was after. He wanted to be officially recognized as a victim.

Nobody was surprised by the judges' verdict issued on July 2, 2018. The court found that abducted children were not eligible for compensation, while Lüdeking, as the plaintiff, "was not persecuted for his behavior or individual characteristics", as we read in the court's opinion justifying the verdict. True, the court had no doubt that the plaintiff suffered "significant harm" from forced Germanization, but it noted that adding a new category to the list of those entitled to payment of damages went beyond the competence of the administrative courts. However, this was a lower court ruling. Lüdeking, with Schwarz's support, plans to appeal.

A Personal Matter

"What happened was a crime. For me, it's something personal. These children should be recognized as victims," Schwarz says.

For the past couple of decades, German historians haven't given up on the case, either. From the moment Schwarz first hear about the tragic fate of children abducted from German-occupied countries, this Freiburg teacher has made it his mission to spread the word in his homeland, where he acknowledges the topic is almost completely unknown. Schwarz himself first heard about it from a Pole who had served in the Wehrmacht and witnessed children being abducted. He began to make inquiries and encountered a woman living in Achern, who as a Polish child had been sent to the local Fatherland School to be Germanized. Her name was Ilona-Helena Lang, who had been doing her best since the 1980s to publicize this topic. Schwarz is disturbed that the German authorities met her efforts with denials or silence. That is what prompted him to found Stolen Children – Forgotten Victims, seek out new witnesses and comment on their cases. Schwarz organized a travelling exhibit that attracts thousands of visitors. He refused to accept the German government's refusal to recognize the stolen children as victims. Thus began a tortuous and sometimes humiliating journey through the German bureaucracy.

Normal Wartime Experience

In 2013, the German Finance Ministry rules that what happened to the abducted children can be described as "a general consequence of the war" that "affected many families during military operations and was the result of wartime strategy." In its statement, the Ministry argued that forced Germanization "was not primarily intended to kill people or enslave people, but rather to acquire them to the Reich's own benefit."

The German Foreign Ministry, for its part, stated that it "possesses no information on this matter" and that "from generally available sources…, it can be concluded that approximately 250 children from Eastern Europe fell victim to abduction and forced adoption." The Ministry added that this information came from "academically unverified" sources. It's true that the figure of 250 children was cited in the postwar Nazi war crimes trials. However, Schwarz was shocked since for decades the academic literature had estimated the number of kidnapped children at somewhere between 50,000 and 200,000.

No Damages for Germanization

Schwarz began to write letters to lawmakers.

"On four occasions since 2012, we've written letters to every single Bundestag member. Two petitions were rejected. Basically, we've been rebuffed on every try, with the explanation that there are insufficient funds."

The 600 pages of courtroom documents prepared by Christoph Schwarz

Not a single MP presented a draft bill to amend the current laws. In 2016, the Bundestag's Petitions Committee declared the matter closed after rejecting a request for a one-time €20,000 payment to victims. The justification is simple: Schwarz's travelling exhibition was paid for in part by Federal funds. In addition, government money had been used to finance a previous exhibit about stolen children and a documentary film production about abductions from occupied Slovenia. At the same time, lawmakers refused to allow Schwarz to show his exhibit at the Bundestag. The official reason is that the Bundestag lends its space only for artistic premieres, and Schwarz's exhibit has already been shown elsewhere. The sole dissenting vote comes from Leftist (*Die Linke*) MP Kersten Steinke, who accuses her follow politicians of cynicism.

A Subject that Won't Let Go

In Schwarz's eyes, these rejections simply heaped more humiliation on the victims.

"Turning down these requests more than 70 years after the war just adds trauma to wartime wounds that have scarcely healed. For the victims, the most important thing isn't money but recognition that they had suffered," Schwarz says.

He admits to being preoccupied for years with the histories of these stolen children. It's a subject that simply "won't let go", a return to the long shadow the war cast over his own early years. His grandmother had been an inmate at a concentration camp.

"The war kept coming up all through my childhood," he says.

That's why he's always had an interest in history. But he never imagined this hobby would start to change the course of his life.

In 2016, the Association of Those Persecuted by the Nazi Regime (*Vereinigung der Verfolgten des Naziregimes*) bestowed on Schwarz its prestigious Alfred Hausser Award. Media coverage of this honor prompted the North Rhine-Westphalia government to give one of the victims living in that federal state a one-time indemnity of €3,600. The authorities in Berlin, however, remain silent.

Identity

Engineer Zoglauer Takes Liselotta

"Hello. In 1942 my grandparents had their daughter, Liselotta Łukaszczyk, DOB 5 April 1941 in Gliwice, stolen from them. She was adopted by a German couple – Franz Josef Zoglauer, DOB 11 February 1893, and Sidonia Zoglauer, DOB 9 December 1903. The child's first and last names were changed to Maria Zoglauer. For the rest of their lives, my grandparents looked for their daughter through the Red Cross, but they were only able to learn that she was married, supposedly ill and likely to suffer harm from a meeting with her real parents. We are in possession of several documents, including her act of adoption, correspondence with the Red Cross, photographs etc. We request help in our search," reads a letter written by Mirosława Sosna to the Interia.pl in response to the website's "Stolen Children" campaign.

***

Liselotta's birth on April 5, 1941 came in a Gliwice clinic. A forceps delivery left indentations on her skull. The baby spent six months in the hospital. Her father had been shot to death at the main railway station in Katowice, while her mother had been sent away on forced labor. The little girl was assigned to the Sauglingsheim infant care facility in Bytom [Beuthen].

In the registry of missing children, an entry for Lukasczyk, Liselotta Gertruda [original spelling] was made on June 9, 1949.

Diminutive or pet names used by the family (before deportation/disappearance): "Kika"

Child's address before deportation/disappearance: Kędzierzyn, at the home of chemical engineer Franz Josef Zoglauer

Address after deportation: Unknown

General appearance, physical features: Plump, blonde hair

Memories the child might respond or react to (alternative means of identification): Unable to remember as she was only three years old

Parents' fate after child's deportation/disappearance: Father killed in the war, mother resided in Legnica, where she was employed as a housemaid

Date and circumstances of child's disappearance/deportation by Germans: In 1944 taken to Germany by her guardian, chemical engineer F.J. Zoglauer, last known address in Kędzierzyn.

Known facts about child's fate after disappearance: [blank]

German institutions with known interest in the child: Chropaczów district council, Sauglingsheim infant care facility in Bytom

Date and place missing child report was filed: 1947, at the Polish Red Cross (PCK) offices in Katowice.

***

Michał Mucha, the second husband of Liselotta's mother, Gertruda, travelled to Kędzierzyn-Koźle after the war to look through the Zoglauers' abandoned flat.

Little Liselotta with her adoptive mother, Sidonia Zoglauer

They'd left in too much of a hurry to pack all their things, leaving documents and photographs for Mucha to find.

***

We don't know exactly when and under what circumstances the engineer Zoglauer first appears in little Liselotta's story. What we do know is that in the Polish Red Cross's "Third list of children taken and assigned for transfer to German institutions, orphanages, adoption agencies and workplaces, as well as to German adoptive families, for purposes of Germanization," prepared by the PCK from official German documents, there is an annotation that the Youth Office [*Jugendamt*] had directed the child to the Bytom infant care facility.

It was there that engineer chemist Frank Josef Zoglauer, resident in Chropaczów, took an initial interest in caring for the girl and later adopting her. Liselotta is soon placed in his custody and Zoglauer, along with his wife and young ward, moves to Kędzierzyn.

Dr. Zoglauer's intention is to adopt the child once she reaches "a suitable stage of development" and in the meantime asks the German local authorities for another girl to be placed with his family. However, Zoglauer's reputation is not the best, and he is refused and asked to return Liselotta to her mother. "After a week, however, the girl felt so poorly that she had to return to Dr. Zoglauer," we read in the file.

The adoption papers identify Franz Josef Zoglauer as a member of the management board of the Schlesiengrube coal mine in Chropaczów. He has a three-room flat with a separate kitchen and bed for the little girl. He earns a relatively high monthly salary of 650 Reichsmarks (then equivalent to $260), allowing his wife – Sidonia née Zinger – not to work. Sidonia, 10 years younger than her husband, has relatives in Łódź and speaks a little Polish. The Zoglauers' live on Admiral-Hipper-Strasse in Kędzierzyn, an address which we will discover is not mere coincidence.

***

In his efforts to adopt little Liselotta, engineer Zoglauer finds an unexpected ally in the person of Chropaczów's mayor. He wrote a letter dated 15 July 1942 to the Bytom care facility, where Liselotta was apparently being kept, requesting that the child be placed in Zoglauer's custody because he had undertaken to care for the child at no charge.

Five months later, Zoglauer wrote from Heydebreck (as the Germans called Kędzierzyn at that time) to the mayor, explaining that he had become attached to little Liselotta and that it would be personally difficult for him to part with the girl, as he was not indifferent to her subsequent fate. He said it would be a shame to remove a child who had become accustomed to her new family and stated that she certainly would not enjoy such good care and living conditions elsewhere. Zoglauer asks the mayor for an honest explanation of the case. His tone is impatient. He suggests that Liselotta's mother write a statement formally relinquishing her parental rights. If she refuses, Zoglauer declares his readiness to give up the child. He asks, however, that the decision be made as quickly as possible, since every day makes it harder for him to bear the loss of the little girl. He mentions a savings book he has set up for her. The funds would be placed at Liselotta's disposal when she turns 20. Zoglauer ends by saying he awaits a quick reply.

***

"Until 1944, when the Zoglauers left Kędzierzyn, Liselotta's grandparents could at least keep an eye on her. They knew the child's whereabouts but were otherwise powerless, since the girl had been taken away and legally adopted. Once the Zoglauers fled, the grandparents completely lost track of her, whereas before they had always managed somehow," says Mirosława Sosna, the daughter of Liselotte's sister, Barbara Pastuszka.

"Did they manage to see Liselotta earlier?"

"They used to follow her when she was taken on walks. My mother had to watch while a German woman fussed over her child – and all the time worry about getting shot by a Schupo," Barbara says.

"*Schupo*?"

"You know, a German."

Schupo is the abbreviation for *Schutzpolizei* – Security Police.

"She was in tears, watching, but she didn't dare approach her own child. It was so sad. They were living right there in Kędzierzyn-Koźle, right by the factory," Mirosława says.

Gertruda and her second husband Michał watched from a hiding place as Frau Zoglauer played with their little "Kika".

Then "Kika" disappeared.

***

Some of the search files relating to Liselotta Łukaszczyk give the alternative version of her name: Maria Zoglauer.

There is a growing correspondence on the subject. The International Refugee Organization (IRO) reaches out to a clergyman in Kędzierzyn-Koźle, Victor Bühl, about Liselotta. Bühl replies that unfortunately he cannot help, because he only served as a chaplain in Kędzierzyn until April 1938, referring the inquiry to his colleague, Wilhelm Malik, who came from Heydebreck, and also gives the name of Adelheid Nitsche, who might know something about the case. From the letter, it is not apparent who Ms. Nitsche was.

The apartment houses on Admiral-Hipper-Strasse in Kędzierzyn were built during World War II. The street has a special status. According to a letter written by Adelheid Nitsche on July 10, 1950, in reply to an earlier inquiry from the IRO, Admiral-Hipper-Strasse was reserved solely for employees at the nearby IG Farben synthetic fuels plant, then known as *IG Farbenindustrie AG Werk Heydebreck*. Later, we will discover that workers from another company also lived there.

Engineer Zoglauer is a highly regarded chemist. According to Mirosława, he was a Czech who signed up for the *Volksliste* as an ethnic German.

***

On July 7, 1949, the Polish Red Cross Main Office sends to the PCK Delegation's Child Recovery Department in Esslingen letter no. 18, containing the names of 15 missing children being sought in Germany. Number 11 on that list is Liselotta Łukaszczyk.

On September 20, 1949, the local Tracing Service in Munich writes that LIselotta had been transferred from a Children's Home (or *Kinderheim*, whereas earlier documents had referred to an infant care facility) to a German family, the Zoglauers, who lived in Chom/Chab/Cheb (Eger). They appear to be uncertain of the locality's exact spelling.

The same day, Herbert H. Meyer from the International Tracing Service (ITS) writes to the Child Recovery Department in Esslingen that "the aforementioned Silesian child is on the Warsaw PCK list of missing Polish children. She is also being sought by her parents, Michał and Gertruda Mucha, currently residing in Pszczyna. In connection with information that the child was taken from an infant care facility in Bytom and put under the care of the Franz Joseph Zoglauer family in Chom, we ask that all known particulars concerning the child's removal to Germany be sent to us, along with her last known address. Since further tracing operations depend on receipt of this additional information, we request a reply as soon as possible."

The Polish Red Cross Main Office sends on all information obtained from Liselotte's parents to the Delegation in Esslingen on December 11, 1949. This is where the report of a forceps delivery appears. The mother, then a resident of Chropaczów, was deported as a forced laborer and her child – without the mother's consent to our knowledge – was given to a German family. "Franz Zoglauer, DOB 11 February 1893 in Blattnitz, Eger County, chemical engineer, last place of work Blachownia, Koźle district, in a synthetic gasoline plant. Sidonia Zoglauer, DOB 9 December 1903, née Zinger, from Gaja, Maehren county. Departed Poland in 1945, taking the child with them. Probable destination Germany or Czechoslovakia, where they had relatives."

In the 1950 correspondence, a variant spelling for Zoglauer's last name appears – Zogalla.

***

Information furnished by Adelheid Nitsche, mentioned above, led to another interesting clue.

On July 26, 1950, Herbert Meyer of the ITS wrote to IG Farben in Frankfurt requesting that their HR department give the Zoglauers' current or last known address.

A reply came back from Hoechst Farbwerke, which stated with regret that its records contained no mention of an engineer by the name of Zoglauer or Zogalla. It suggested the ITS get in contact with the high commissioner of the IG Farben Control Office in Frankfurt or with the Badische Anilin- und Soda-Fabrik (BASF) in Ludwigshafen.

Meyer wrote to these two addresses on Sept. 5, 1950 and got a quick response.

BASF replied on September 12 that it had referred the inquiry to IG Farbenindustrie AG, from which a response should be expected.

Six days later, the IG Farben Control Office high commissioner wrote that he had referred the matter to BASF.

On October 23, 1950, IG Farbenindustrie AG stated that it regretted not being able to help with the inquiry, adding that the stated address provided housing not only to IG Farben employees, but also to those working at the Oberschlesische Hydrierwerke AG Blechhammer [Upper Silesian Hydrogenation Plant, Blachownia]. It suggested that the person being sought may have worked for that company.

This information is key.

***

By the end of 1950, an extensive correspondence is underway between IG Farben (then in liquidation) and Oberschlesische Hydrierwerke AG Blechhammer.

The road to Blachownia Śląska

Nazi Germany made heavy investments in infrastructure needed to provide a steady supply of synthetic fuels. According to Edward Haduch of the Blechhammer 1944 Association, in September 1939 a business consortium from Upper Silesia had agreed to finance such a project, creating a joint stock company called Oberschlesische Hydrierwerke AG Blechhammer, as Blachownia Śląska was called in German.

Ground was broken on the new coal hydrogenation plant at the end of 1939.

"The production technology was based on the method discovered by German chemist Friedrich Bergius, which involved gasification of coal in specially designed reactors that yield synthetic gases which, after further processing, can be turned into liquid fuels, including isooctanes used in aviation fuel," I read.

I get in touch with Edward Haduch, explaining the significance of the Franz Zoglauer and the girl he abducted.

"That's a highly interesting story that bears looking into," Haduch replies. "Let me check our archive for the next few days."

A few days later, I get an answer. "I've been able to find engineer Zoglauer in the old phone directory of Oberschlesische Hydrierwerke AG Blechhammer," Haduch writes. "He was in charge of coking coal production at the plant."

***

On January 5, 1951, Hydrierwerke wrote back with the last known address of Franz Zoglauer – Radvanice 379, Ostrava. They note that this information dates from February 8, 1945. "From that time we have had no news from Herr Zoglauer."

***

In February 1951, IRO gave Zoglauer's address to the tracing bureau of Caritas and the Czechoslovak Red Cross. It also notified them of Zoglauer's employment by the hydrogenation plant in Blachownia, asking for help and confirmation of the Ostrava address.

The Czechoslovak Red Cross in late February supplied further addresses for Franz Zoglauer (who is referred to in the latter as a "former commissioner"). The Zoglauers reportedly fled to the northwestern towns of Rejviz and Bila Vida in Bohemia. The trail breaks off in 1946, and where they went after that is not clear.

***

Where did Liselotta and engineer Zoglauer go? In 1951, documents are sent to the Hamburg *Suchdienst* (trading office) and to Johann Cmiel in Traunstein, who may have been an acquaintance of the Zoglauers and in a position to help. The family does what it can to track down Liselotta. Their only help is a local interpreter.

In April, the PCK Main Office is informed that despite extensive inquiries conducted in Germany and Czechoslovakia, no information has been found on the girl or her adoptive parents.

***

"My parents always stressed that Zoglauer took her from the hospital in Gliwice," says Liselotte's sister.

"Not from the infant care facility in Bytom?"

"No. Perhaps she was at the hospital the whole time and they only sent her papers to the nursery," say Liselotte's sister and niece, who are still looking for her.

"For six months she could have been a Polish child, and then they Germanized her and gave her new papers," her sister says.

***

There is further correspondence in 1978 with the German Red Cross (DRK) *Suchdienst* in Munich, which informs Gertruda Mucha that it has taken over tracing efforts from the Hamburg office and is responding to her inquiry of July 10, 1978.

The Munich office says that it has found in Liselotte's file a message from the Czechoslovak Red Cross, dated July 21, 1959, which states that engineer Zoglauer has been found but does not wish his address or that of his daughter – whom he has raised from early childhood and is recently married – to be disclosed. He stresses that this kind of intervention could cause anxiety to his daughter, who is in poor health.

The file indicates that the Hamburg *Suchdienst* had tried to pass on this information to Liselotte's parents, but the letter was returned to them with the annotation "addressee unknown". The German Red Cross, suspecting the Liselotta may have been living in Czechoslovakia, suggested that her parents contact the Czech Red Cross through the intermediation of the PCK. They noted that the last known address of the Zoglauer family was Radvanice 379 (Moravian Ostrava).

***

Liselotte's parents didn't give up. Together with their younger daughter, they looked for "Kiki" at the addresses given in the correspondence. They went to Poprad, where they found Franz Zoglauer's brother. They also travelled to Ostrava, where they met Maria Hudec.

The engineer's brother said he had no idea what had happened to Franz and Sidonia. Either he didn't know or wouldn't say.

They met Maria Hudec for a long talk – partly in Polish, partly in Czech – at the Zoglauer family home in Radvanice. Somehow, they were able to understand each other. It turned out Maria was a Pole, born in 1942 and adopted by a Mrs. Matusińska.

***

Gertruda and Michał Mucha asked the Czechoslovak Red Cross in Ostrava to help find their stolen daughter.

"We visited the given address in Moravian Ostrava at Radvanice 379, where Franz Zoglauer resided with his wife Sidonia. At this address we encountered the family of František and Maria Hudec. The Zoglauer residence had been assigned to Mrs. Matusińska as the wife of a concentration camp victim. The widow Matusińska adopted Maria in 1951. Maria knows she was Polish, which is of concern to us. She claims to have been born on July 22, 1942. She remembers calling herself Maria Rakoszowa and that she has a brother.... While in Radvanice, we chanced upon some older gentlemen who said engineer Zoglauer had worked at a brickyard near Ostrava. I would also like to inquire officially whether Maria, who has taken her husband's surname of Hudec, is our daughter, and whether she was given on her 20th birthday a certain sum in a savings book as declared by engineer Zoglauer on 9 December 1942."

In 1990, Elżbieta Rejf from the Polish Red Cross Main Office, citing a letter from the Czechoslovak Red Cross, officially informs the family that Liselotta/Maria was not found on the territory of Czechoslovakia and that Maria Hudec's personal information does not correspond with that of Liselotta Łukaszczyk/Maria Zoglauer.

***

Sometime later, however, the Hudec family from Ostrava visited Gertruda and Michał Mucha in Poland.

***

"How long did they go on looking?"

"My parents searched for Liselotta as long as they lived," says Barbara, who along with her daughter Mirosława has continued her parents' quest.

By now, Liselotta would be 77 years old...

Jasia Had a Son

"The documents indicate that your grandmother gave birth on March 16, 1944 in Aurich to a baby boy named Jurek," the International Trading Service in Bad Arolsen writes in 2017 in response to a letter from Piotr Janiak, the grandson of Janina Drygas.

The family had only learned about this child in 1992. Then, Jurek would have been 48 years old. Now, he would be 74 – if he's still alive.

"Just before she died, Grandmother Janina told one of her daughters that while she was on forced labor, she gave birth to a son named Eryk. She also declared that the boy had been taken from her. According to her account, she tried to find him upon her return, unsuccessfully," Janiak wrote to the editorial offices of Interia.pl in September 2017.

Ever since 1992, the family has been looking.

Janina Drygas remembered that she named the child Eryk. So why do the documents refer to Jurek? Photographs still exist of Janina while she was a forced laborer in Germany. There are documents, too – quite a lot of them. The pieces just need to be put together. There are traces, but the person has vanished. The trail breaks off at the hospital in Aurich. It's a small town in northwestern Germany, almost 850 km from Pacanowice in Wielkopolska Province, where Janina used to live until she was transported to Germany as a slave worker.

***

When the Drygas family was forcibly resettled in 1940, Janina (whom the family called Jasia) was 25 years old. They ended up at a collection point, at a school in Lenartowice, near Pleszew. Later they were sent to a textile mill in Łódź, where the family was split up. The Germans first sent Janina and her brother Stanisław to Hamburg, about 800 km from Łódż. There they were separated and sent to different towns.

"During our search, we obtained information from the community of Grossefehn that your grandmother, under the surname Drygasoana [*probably a corruption of "Drygasówna", the Polish form of her maiden name–author's note*], in March 1940 moved into quarters with the Hinrichs family in the town of Ulbargen," reads a letter dated Feb. 24, 2017 from the ITS in Bad Arolsen.

Ulbargen is about 200 km west of Hamburg, only about 40 km from the Dutch border. That's another 200 km farther away from home. The Netherlands remained neutral until May 10, 1940, when Nazi Germany invaded and occupied the country until 1945.

The residents of Pacanowice were evicted – as eyewitnesses record – on August 12, 1940. If the information obtained by the ITS is correct, Janina would have arrived in Ulbargen five months before the resettlement operation. Janina's grandson considers this version to be impossible.

***

There is a snapshot of the Hinrichs household showing a family group sitting close together. On the back of the photo, Jasia wrote:

"Together in our kitchen – me, our pantryman, Miss Hani – a German, our co-worker Ala in front, Zoysia and Kazia."

Miss Hans is sitting with the employees. She looks like a nice person. Grandmother Janina is smiling.

"She was treated properly there," stresses Janina's grandson.

Janina (first L) at the Hinrichs home.

***

In March 1944, Jasia is 29 years old. She travels to the hospital in Aurich, a distance of 13 km from Ulbargen. How does she get there? Does someone accompany her? Who?

In Aurich, she gives birth to the boy, Eryk. She clearly remembers that was supposed to be his name. In the documents, however, he's Jurek. Was that a mistake or a deliberate alteration?

Why did Jasia give birth at the hospital? Was it because a German couple was waiting for the child? Perhaps the prospective parents paid for the pregnant woman to be transported to the hospital? Perhaps that particular clinic was among those cooperating with Lebensborn, which had its own Civil Registry offices that could erase all traces of an abducted child?

***

The newborn boy arrived well after a special decree issued in 1943 by Reichsführer SS and Police Chief Heinrich Himmler had taken effect. This document (entitled "*Behandlung von Ausländischen Arbeiterinnen und der im Reich von Ausländischen Arbeiterinnen geborenen Kinder*") described how the Reichs Commissioner for the Consolidation of German Nationhood intended to deal with "pregnant foreign workers and their children born inside the Reich".

Only under exceptional circumstances was a forced laborer allowed to give birth in a hospital. In other cases, the deliveries were to take place in special wards established in camp infirmaries or on farmsteads, if the German proprietor did not report that one of their female workers was pregnant.

Jasia gave birth "officially" and apparently in what could be called decent conditions.

***

The Germans made a careful distinction between "valuable blood" and that which they considered worthless. Employers were required to report all pregnant women to the local *Jugendamt*. These Youth Offices then investigated the father's origins and conveyed their findings to the local SS and police commanders.

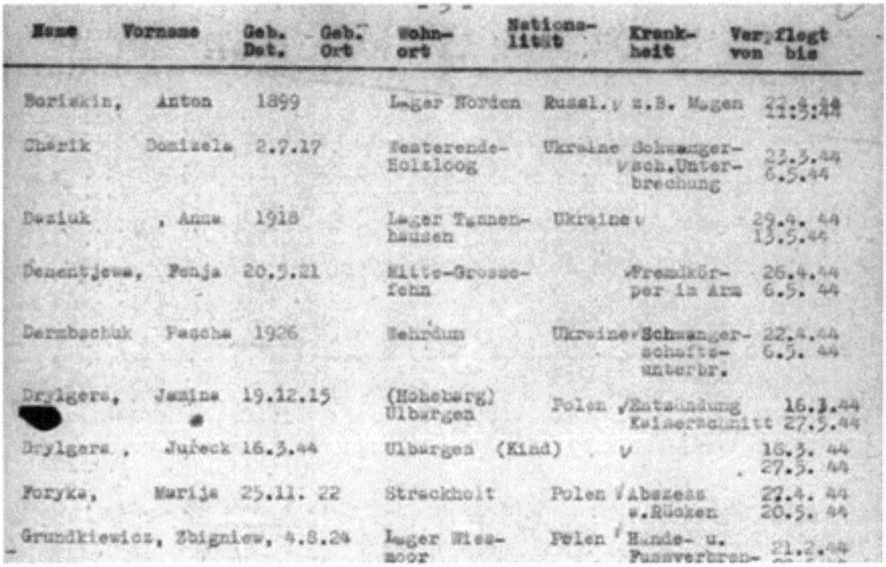

Name	Vorname	Geb. Dat.	Geb. Ort	Wohnort	Nationalität	Krankheit	Verpflegt von bis
Boriskin,	Anton	1899		Lager Norden	Russl.	z.B. Magen	22.4.44 11.5.44
Cherik	Domizela	2.7.17		Westerende-Holzloog	Ukraine	Schwangersch. Unterbrechung	23.3.44 6.5.44
Dziuk	, Anna	1918		Lager Tannenhausen	Ukraine		29.4.44 13.5.44
Dementjewa,	Fenja	20.5.21		Mitte-Grossefehn		Fremdkörper im Arm	26.4.44 6.5.44
Dermbechuk	Pascha	1926		Wehrdum	Ukraine	Schwangerschafts-unterbr.	22.4.44 6.5.44
Drylgers,	Janina	19.12.15		(Hoheberg) Ulbargen	Polen	Entzündung Kaiserschnitt	16.3.44 27.5.44
Drylgers ,	Jureck	16.3.44		Ulbargen (Kind)			16.3.44 27.5.44
Foryka,	Marija	25.11.22		Streckholt	Polen	Abszess a. Rücken	27.4.44 20.5.44
Grundkiewicz,	Zbigniew,	4.8.24		Lager Wiesmoor	Polen	Hände- u. Fussverbren-	21.2.44

Patient records from the Aurich hospital. Janina's surname and that of her son Jurek have been distorted.

The SS Race and Settlement Main Office and local health departments were in charge of racial testing. If the parents were determined to be "racially valuable", the child was placed under the institutional care of the National Socialist People's Welfare (Nationalsozialistische-Volkswohlfahrt e.V., or NSV).

This was a party welfare organization that supervised a network of mothers' and children's homes. It was responsible for Germanizing children of slave workers deemed to be racially valuable, children of parents suitable for Germanization, children of parents qualified to be treated as *Volksdeutsche* or "of German origin", and so-called special cases. As early as two years before the outbreak of World War II, NSV personnel were already learning Polish.

Children earmarked for Germanization were directed to special facilities established for that purpose or were placed directly with German families by the NSV. In keeping with Himmler's decree, mothers incapable of work or their racially worthless children were to be "deleted".

Janina (second from L) during her stint as a forced laborer

***

Janina wasn't "deleted", even though she must have been a troublesome patient. She spent three months in the hospital due to complications from a cesarean section and then was admitted again in August for thrombosis.

Who went to the trouble to fetch Janina, suffering from a high fever, back to the hospital in Aurich for a month-long stay? Why? What small farmer could afford such a prolonged absence during a severe labor shortage? And where was Jurek/Eryk during this time? Had he already been taken away?

In all likelihood, the little boy vanished between Janina's first and second stay at the Aurich hospital. That is what the family claims at any rate.

They've been looking ever since they heard of the child's existence. The Civil Registry office in Aurich even has a record of the birth.

Jurek was the 52nd child whose birth was entered into the Aurich Civil Registry for 1944. The document's original date of issue is unclear, because it was subsequently corrected.

"Unfortunately, the birth certification contains no annotation about a possible adoption or what later happened to Jurek. The Hinrichs family, who employed Janina, told the ITS in Bad Arolsen that they knew nothing about the fate of the missing boy. We assume that the family who took Jurek may have changed his personal information, including his name," Janina's grandson wrote in his letter to Interia.pl.

Janina Drygas (first R), photograph likely taken just before her return to Poland

***

In November 2017, Janina's grandson Piotr receives an answer to the letter he sent the Hinrichs family.

The reply is written by Margareta, who's done her best to help. She's talked with two older people from Ulbargen and Umgebung, asking about Jurek. She's also checked the parish records. Nothing. At the Civil Registry office in Aurich, she does find entries for Jurek and his mother. But we know Janina returned to Poland before the end of the war.

One thing is certain – there were forced laborers from Poland living in Ulbargen.

Margareta's mother could be helpful here, but she's recently deceased. Her father died in 1992. Her aunt and uncle – Tette and Frerich Hinrichs – have also passed away recently. They could have had more to say. "Maybe Jurek left with a family for North Rhine-Westphalia, where it was easier to find work," Margareta writes to Piotr Janiak. But that begs the question – which family?

In cases of adoption by German families, the child's personal information could have been changed several times. In the first instance, Lebensborn falsified documents, altering first and last names, along with places and dates of birth.

After the war, Janina Drygas searched for her son, with no success.

What happened to little Jurek? If he's alive, he would be 74 years old. In all probability, he has no idea that he is one of about 200,000 Polish children whose identities were stolen by the Germans.

***

In February 2017, the ITS passes on to the family some bits of already familiar information. In the letter, we read that "because we see no further possibility of successful tracing, we must close the case file. We remain yours with sincere greetings."

What Happened to the Boy in the Photo?

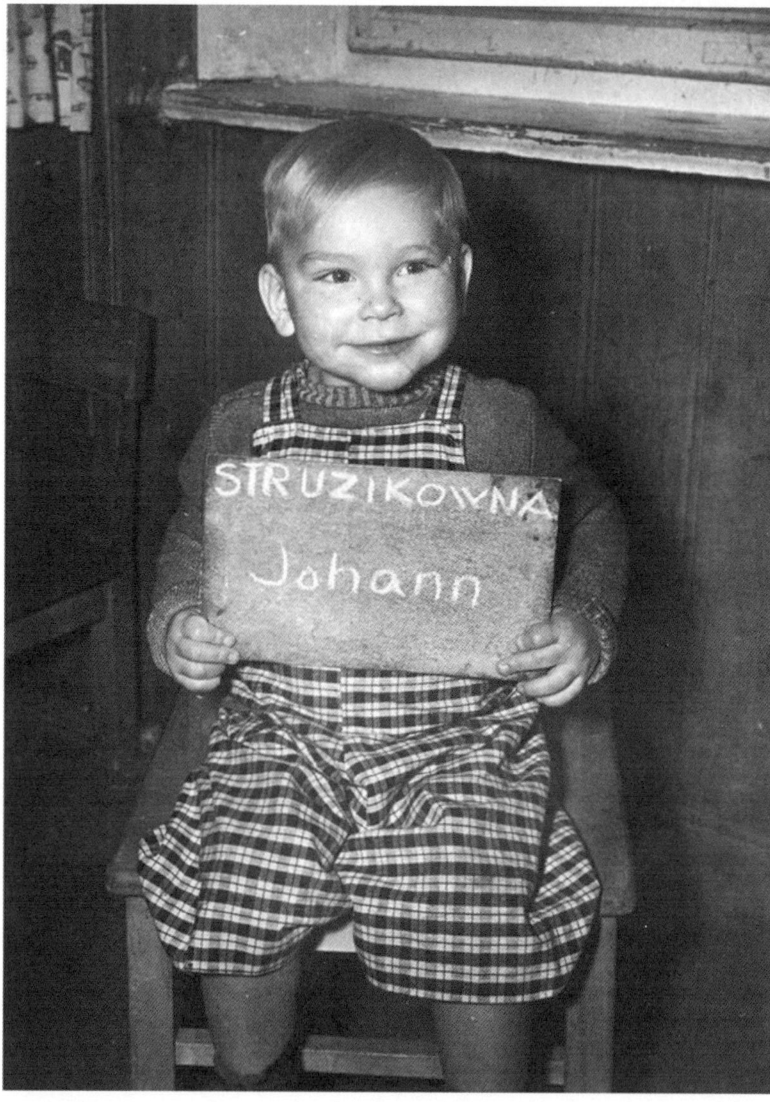

Johann Struzikowna smiles from the photograph at the United States Holocaust Memorial Museum. He's holding a placard with his first and last names. He's wearing plaid overalls with suspenders and a sweater, and he looks to be about two years old.

The boy is among the children placed at Markt Indersdorf. There, on the grounds of a former convent, U.S. forces set up on July 11, 1945 the first international processing center for the very youngest DPs – or "displaced persons", as the Allies call foreign nationals in Germany's zones of occupation.[1]

His last name seems familiar.

It turns out there are quite of few of these "poster children". Several hundred, in fact. I examine the expressions on their faces. Some are silly, others are frightened or glum. Their ages vary.

The Ukrainian twins Joseph and Alfred Lamzek are maybe two months old. Shortly after the pictures are taken, they die. First Joseph, then, several days later, Alfred.[2]

There are also older children. A group born in 1931 and 1932 stands out, mot of them from Chorzów. According to Captain Palaszewski, the U.S. Third Army's liaison officer for repatriation: "In Straubing, Bavaria, I found 60 Polish girls aged 10-15, all deported by the Germans on January 9, 1945 from Königshutte (Chorzów). They are heavily Germanized, disoriented and indoctrinated."[3]

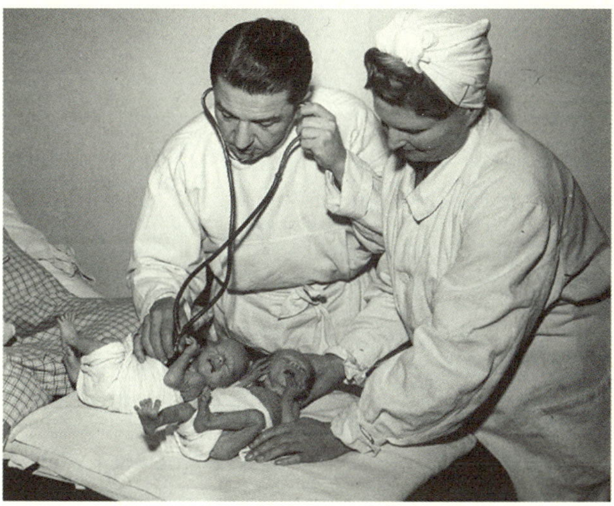

Medical personnel examine Joseph and Alfred Lamzek

[1] United States Holocaust Memorial Museum [hereafter: USHMM], https://collections.ushmm.org/se- arch/catalog/pa1043336

[2] USHMM, https://collections.ushmm.org/search/catalog/pa16650

[3] Letter from Capt. Pałaszewski, liaison officer to the Chorzów/Königshütte City Administration, AAN, zespół: Generalny Pełnomocnik Rządu RP ds. Repatriacji, sygn. 313, karty nr 12–15.

***

Markt Indersdorf is located about 14 kilometers north of Dachau and about 45 kilometers outside Munich. This is where they send children who survived the concentration camps or were born to slave workers.

Telegrams are sent out to locate their families. Their photographs are published in newspapers in hope someone will recognize them. Amid the chaos, little Johann's parents are being sought, too.

But nobody claims the child.

So how did Johann end up at Markt Indersdorf?

***

Before World War II, the convent was also the site of an orphanage. When the decision was made in 1945 to establish a center for underage DPs, the Sisters of Charity of St. Vincent de Paul helped U.S. GIs prepare the site.[4]

The children's caretakers are personnel from the United Nations Relief and Rehabilitation Administration (UNRRA). Among the volunteers is a woman named Greta Fischer.

The Markt Indersdorf facility ultimately takes about 350 children, of more than 20 nationalities. These include "racially valuable" children abducted by the Nazis for Germanization purposes or deported for slave labor to the Third Reich. Some have had their names changed and their former identities erased. Some of the older kids had served in the *Volkssturm* – a people's militia raised and deployed by Germany in the last stages of World War II.

UNRRA helps in establishing the children's true identities and arranging adoptions, repatriation or emigration to third countries.

The center remains active until late July and early August 1946, when its young wards are transferred to Prien am Chiemsee. Afterwards, the convent is used solely to care for orphaned Jewish children left without guardians after the war.

---

[4] Carrie Hagen, "This Orphanage Did More Than Find Homes for Children of the Holocaust. It Helped Them Reclaim Their Humanity", *Smithsonian.com*, March 14, 2017. https://www.smithsonianmag.com/history/orphanage-helped-them-reclaim-their-humanity-180962516/

***

At the Archiwum Akt Nowych [Central Archives of Modern Records, or AAN) in Warsaw, I pore over copies of repatriation lists, because I can't get Johann's last name – Struzikowna – out of my mind. On the website of the U.S. Holocaust Memorial Museum, I come across more pictures of the little boy. They aren't labelled, but there's no mistaking that it is him.

The AAN files mention a child called Jan Struzike or Struziki, who's on the list of children repatriated to Poland on June 5, 1946. A few rows down the list is another child with the same surname. This boy, Walter, is a year younger. Is this pure coincidence, or could they be brothers?

In many cases, the children's surnames in the repatriation files correspond with those photographed at Markt Indersdorf.

Slowly, a picture starts to emerge.

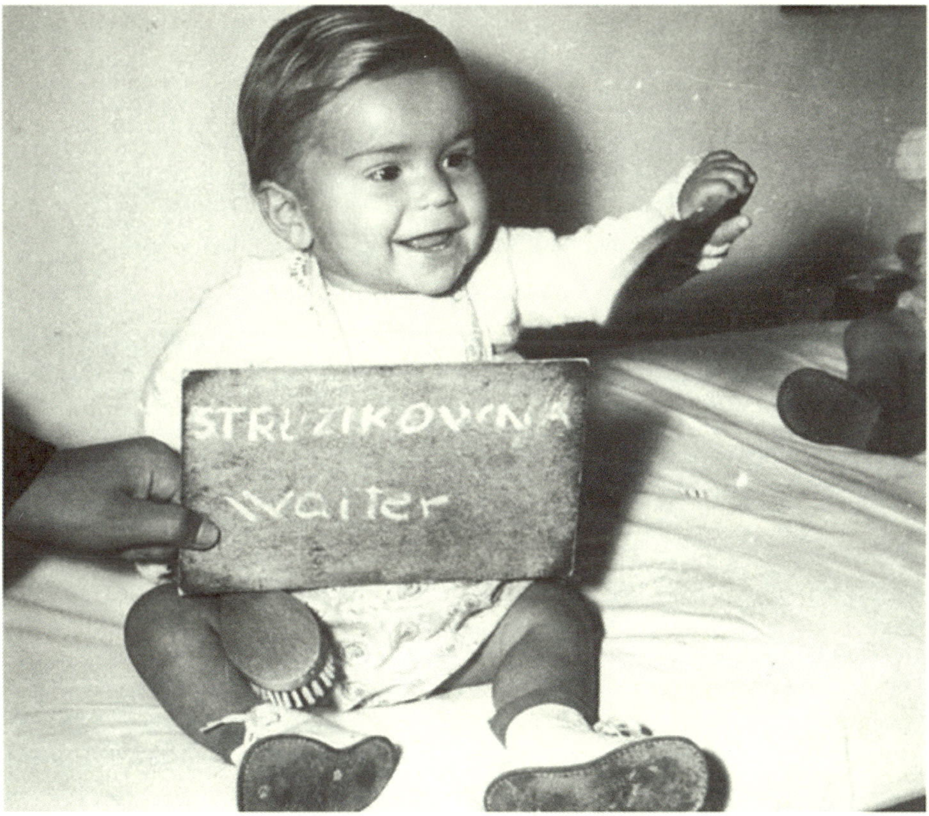

Walter Struzikowna

***

The repatriation train from Markt Indersdorf rolls into Koźle station with 116 children aboard. All of them are directed to temporary quarters at the distribution center. Almost half are going back to their families – parents, uncles, aunts, or other relatives. Most, however, are headed for Children's Homes in Szopienice, Katowice, Tarnowskie Gory, Mysłowice, Głąbczyce, Dziedzice and Nakło. To this last orphanage, five children registered as having been born in Munich or Dachau are sent. They include the two Struzik boys.[5]

For now, that's all I know.

***

And all this time, little Johann (Janek) keeps smiling at me from the photograph.

***

I look for clues in the archives and on Facebook. More than 20,000 people become interested in the story of the little boy in the photograph. One of them is Dominika Pawlina, who finds Walter's picture on the pages of the U.S. Holocaust Memorial Museum. She sends me the photo on Messenger. So now we have confirmation of a brother – provided it's not coincidental.

Walter is so little that someone else is holding his placard for him. He's playing with a hairbrush and a hand mirror, a mischievous smile on his face. He and Johann don't resemble each other. I now have dates and likely places of birth, along with various facilities where they were housed and processed. But once they get to the Nakło orphanage, the trail breaks off.

Several months pass. I get an email from the Institute of National Remembrance (IPN) with the results of a previous archival search.

***

These documents bring those boys in the black-and-white photographs to life.

What kind of boy was Janek?

[5] Repatriation of Polish children from Germany 1946–47 – manifests of transports arriving in Katowice and Koźle, 2/283/0 Education Ministry in Warsaw, AAN, jednostka 3675, sygn. 321/2.

"Quite normal, a little rowdy, cries frequently. He's developed quickly and seems much happier, better able to keep himself occupied. Extremely intelligent, speaks and understands a little Polish, understands and speaks good German. Has a healthy appetite."[6]

And Walter?

"Walter was in very poor condition, malnourished, little appetite, cried non-stop for many days. At the beginning we saw very slow progress, but during the past two months he has been developing rapidly. He appears very intelligent and has a good disposition. He eats and sleeps well, demands a lot of affection and mothering."[7]

On October 31, 1945, Greta Fischer prepares a report on children from the so-called "Swiss list". She evaluates each child's developmental progress. Her notes indicate that she knows these boys well.

Could it be that Janek and Walter were sent to a Swiss sanatorium, like several other children from Markt Indersdorf, on account of their delicate health?

I find the Struzik boys again on another list of "unattended" children appended to a 1948 letter from John S. Widdicombe, head of the Polish office for IRO's Preparatory Commission (PCIRO), to the ITS director at Bad Arolsen. This document indicates that of 729 children, nearly 200 have been returned to their parents, 225 to other relatives, 113 have been placed in orphanages, and 92 with foster or adoptive families. Of the remaining 104 children, 10 have died, six ran away, two were committed to psychiatric hospitals, three returned to Germany etc.[8]

[6] Document on children from the so-called Swiss list, Kloster Indersdorf, 31 October 1945, materials recovered by the IPN, nr 81998795#1.

[7] Document on children from the so-called Swiss list …

[8] Letter from John S. Widdicombe of the PCIRO Polish office do the director of ITS PCIRO-Arolsen on unattended Polish children, 22 June 1948, materials recovered by the IPN from ITS Arolsen, nr 87417761#1.

Children at Indersdorf convent.

Even more interesting, this list contains three children with very similar last names – Walter, Jan and Johann. It appears likely there has been a mix-up on their surnames. In various documents, a number of different versions appear: Struziko, Struzikowna, Struzikow, Struzik, Strucikowna. Erroneous dates of birth are also given.

Johann and Walter are also on a list of "closed cases" prepared by the ITS in 1948, with case numbers 900 and 901. The first 27 children on the list – for example, Kurti (born in 1942) from Poland and three-year-old Poldi from Czechoslovakia – have no surnames at all.

The ITS regards these cases as closed because the children were repatriated.[9]

[9] List of children repatriated to Poland 8/E/67, materials recovered by the IPN from ITS Arolsen, nr 87417763#1.

Mealtime at the Markt Indersdorf facility

***

Johann's birth certificate has survived. His middle name is given as Marion and his surname as Strucikowna. HIs mother is Maria Strucikowna (in all other documents, she appears as Maria Struzikowna), and his father is Jan Rack, from the village of Zabawa, near Kraków.[10]

Johann was born in Munich at Severinstrasse 2. I check the current appearance and occupants of this address. Google indicates that it is a welfare office, including a *Jugendamt*, family assistance, and other social services. It's also a place where adoptions can be arranged.

His mother worked as an assistant at the St. Joseph *Altersheim*, or old age home.

The documents contain numerous errors, giving Johann's and Walter's birth dates in several different variants. ITS list 009 states that Johann was born in 1933, while ITS 006 claims he's a girl.[11] Or perhaps there is no mistake after all? Perhaps Maria gave birth to twins in 1943 – a boy and a girl, followed a year later by Walter?

---

[10] Birth certificate of Johann Marion Strucikowna, 16 June 1950, and his baptismal certificate (issued on July 9, 1948 for baptism performed on July 31, 1943), materials recovered by the IPN.

[11] Document ITS 006, Munich, 10 September 1947, materials recovered by the IPN.

Later on in the files there is an annotation that Johann's birth date had been given incorrectly. But for me, the most important information is that the earlier date of birth, given as Sept. 25, 1944, is actually the birth date of Johann's brother – Walter. His brother![12]

***

I check the "tracing correspondence" records for Johann Struziko. It turns out someone was looking for him as recently as 1988.

***

The information I find in the IPN archive points to Ustroń, in southern Poland. I send out Facebook inquiries to Ustroń residents almost at random. From several dozen messages, I get replies from two people. One expresses a desire to help, while the other remembers Walter and gives me the telephone number of someone who knew him well. I set out for Ustroń.

At the picturesque mountain resort, I meet Walter's old buddies – "Flimon" and "Faja".

Both men are fond of saying that in their younger years, they were closer to street urchins than altar boys. They wore their hair in bowl cuts like the Beatles and had run-ins with the cops. For one stunt, when they marched in a May 1st parade with a sign reading "Ustroń Wankers' Union", the local militiamen worked them over with nightsticks. Now it's just another funny story. There's a place in it for Walter as well.

Roman Myrmus, aka "Faja", takes me to a few addresses where somebody should remember "Wally" [*in Polish, "Waldek"*] – as Walter was called by his friends. We go past a kayaking pond, which used to be a cooling basin for the old ironworks, now a scenic overlook for the Parkowa Restaurant. "Wally" used to work as a bouncer there, deciding who would get in and who didn't. Only about 200 customers could be seated. He used to let his buddy, Jerzy "Flimon" Bukowczan, in through the back door. You could make money as a bouncer, because there were always more people trying to get in than there were tables.

---

[12] Handwritten note, 10 October 1988, concerning the birth dates of the Struzik brothers, materials recovered by the IPN.

"Wally did alright. He could always grab a bite at the restaurant, the customers gave him tips, and he'd help people find rooms for after supper," his friends say.

"People used to ask Wally to send them overnight guests on dancing nights. He referred a few to us as well for single night stays. They'd be on their way the next day," says "Flimon".

Wally lived nearby, just a stone's throw away from work. But no current tenants in his building remember him. Residents from the neighborhood also draw a blank.

"To be honest, he didn't really hang out with anybody. You couldn't say he had a real friend," says "Faja".

Walter moved to Ustroń in the 1970s. According to "Faja", he didn't have any family. At first, he worked as a handyman at the local grocery. He rented a flat on Parkowa and then got a place by the "old oak" forge on Daszyńskiego Street. Local legend has it that the oak was planted in 1683, to honor King Jan III Sobieski before he marched off to defeat the Turks in Vienna.

***

Various clocks chime the hour at "Flimon's" apartment.

"I knew Wally pretty well. He liked to come to my mother Eufemia for dinner, because she'd make those home-cooked Silesian meals – roasts and potato dumplings. She knew all the specialties and was just a really good cook. So Walter used to buy the groceries on Saturdays and bring them to the house, and she'd cook."

"He was a well-known character in Ustroń. Everybody recognized him, but almost nobody knew anything about him. He wasn't a talker. Besides, he didn't trust people and people didn't trust him much, either."

In Ustroń, people used to refer to Walter as "the Auschwitz kid".

"He was really a loner, not very well-liked. If somebody had an issue with him, he was the kind of guy who'd just reflexively turn it into a fight, and he was a big, strapping fellow," says "Flimon".

He didn't say anything about his past, except that he was born in a camp. Everybody thought he was talking about Auschwitz. "Flimon" remembers Wally had a number tattooed on his arm.

But the documents say Walter was born in Dachau.

He used to play poker with "Faja". Evenings, he'd let people into the restaurant and find them a place to stay for the night.

"He'd work nights and sleep during the days. That was his whole life," says "Faja".

But what about his brother, smiling Janek from the photograph? Did they ever get back together?

"We never heard about any relatives or a brother visiting. We never even knew he had a brother!"

A letter from the Swiss Red Cross indicates that Johann's case was closed in 1948, since he had been repatriated to Poland from Switzerland on May 18, 1946. Which raises the question about whether he may have stopped over at Indersdorf on his way from Switzerland to Poland.

***

On Nov. 25, 1987, Walter writes to the International Red Cross requesting confirmation that he was born in the Dachau concentration camp on September 25, 1944. He appends a declaration of transfer from the camp to a children's home.[13]

This declaration was made in an October 1987 letter from the Caritas Social Welfare Home for Children, stating that "Walerian Struziko", as a small child, was transferred from Dachau and placed with "Caritas Katowice in the aforementioned facility."[14]

A handwritten note dated October 10, 1987 mentions that Walter was born at the *Altersheim*, where his mother Maria worked as an assistant. It says Maria was born on March 22, 1918. So the information is inconsistent.[15]

Walter keeps looking for his mother and his brother. He writes to various organizations, including the IRCC, which informs him in a 1988 letter that his inquiry has been referred to the ITS in Bad Arolsen. From now on, he should expect to get information from this source. Arolsen makes inquiries in France. The

---

[13] Letter from Walter Struzik do International Red Cross, materials recovered by the IPN from ITS Arolsen, nr 113534361#1.

[14] Certificated issued on October 30, 1987 by the Caritas Catholic Association, ITS Arolsen, materials recovered by the IPN.

[15] Handwritten note, 10 October 1988, ITS Arolsen, materials recovered by the IPN.

French Red Cross in 1991 responds "regretfully that we have been unable to locate this person" (and it is seeking a "Maria" or "Marla").

House by the "old oak" in Ustroń where Walter lived

Walter keeps writing. From the ITS correspondence it is clear that he doesn't believe the story the sisters told him about Johann's death at the children's home in Nakło Śląskie. The two brothers were together there. He emphasizes that there has been no official confirmation of this ostensible fact.

***

I read about Walter's death in the November 6, 2008 edition of *Gazeta Ustrońska*, the local newspaper.[16]

"The guys will know where he's buried, I think it's in the Municipal Cemetery," says "Faja".

We go to the funeral home. A dark-haired woman leafs through the register. She finds Walter's name, inscribed in ink in a graph paper notebook.

The employees think it strange that we're looking for Walter.

"Wally just had Bożena, who was a lot younger. First he died, and then she did, too, not long after," says the lady at the funeral home.

---

[16] *Gazeta Ustrońska*, 6 November 2008 (nr 45), http://archiwum.ustron.pl/me- dia/gazeta/2008/45.pdf

***

We go to the cemetery with “Faja”.

“Let’s find Zygmunt, he’s got a head like a computer,” he says.

“Who’s Zygmunt?”

“He’s the gravedigger.”

“I’m looking for Walter Struzik. Can you help me?” I ask the man “Faja” introduces me to.

The gravedigger squints and interrupts his work, then strides silently across the cemetery.

We’ve found Walter.

***

But what about that tow-haired, smiling boy in the photograph? Whatever happened to him?

Walter’s grave in Ustronie

“Like I was alone in the World”

March 1940. The Social Welfare has placed an eight-week-old infant from the Dachau hospital with Magdalena Mayr, who lives in nearby Deutenhofen. The woman mothers and takes care of the child for the next six years. Little Heinrich grows up with his “sister” Fini, who’s a few years older, not knowing that his parents were Polish.

Henryk Kowalczyk

Heinrich is just six years old when his well-ordered life changes in a single instant. He’s just started school, where he’s doing quite well. The war has been over for just a few months.

“One day a Red Cross car drove up to our farm. An American woman got out. And just as short time later, Fini and one of her cousins were getting me packed, and I was dressed in a sweater with a stag design embroidered on it. I remember it precisely, because later I lost it,” Henryk recalls today.

The arrival of the Red Cross representatives came as a surprise for little Henryk, or Heinrich as he thought of himself then. Just like the hurried packing. But looking back in hindsight, Henryk acknowledges that certain memories from his early childhood suggested that something about his past was amiss.

"I remember that my German mother used to send packages to my father – my Polish father. Chains of thick sausages – I can still picture them in my mind. One day the package was returned, which meant that the addressee had died. I imagined they had dumped father into a big hole in the ground and filled it in. That's when I understood that I had a father, and to this day I'm sure that was my reaction. But what I didn't realize is that this fact had anything to do with Poland."

Chocolate Negro

Six-year-old Heinrich is bundled with his suitcase into the automobile with the American woman. The sudden arrival of these guests made a big impression on the boy, especially because the social workers came with an escort of American soldiers.

"That was the first time I'd seen tanks. One of them literally rolled into our front yard. Another pointed its cannon at our window. Then one of the soldiers took me in his arms and literally showered me with chocolate. He was black, and it was the first time in my life I had seen a Negro. I kept eating chocolates the whole day," Henryk recalls today with laughter.

Henryk Kowalczyk – for that was the real name of the boy who had been taken in by Magdalena Mayr – didn't know where he was going, but he had a good idea that it would be a one-way trip. He remembers being taken all over Germany.

"I remembering being at the seaside. But why and from where? Dachau is in southern Germany, a long way from the sea," he wonders today.

Some of Henryk's strongest childhood memories date from this period.

"One day I'd come back from a trip and they'd put me to bed in my bunk, and it turns out my sweater with the stag was missing. I broke down in tears. That sweater had been knitted for me by my German mother."

While in the camp, the boy received a photograph inscribed with the word "*Mutter*".

For a long time, I thought she was my natural mother. It was only my wife who made me realise this was impossible, because the dates don't match."

Frankfurters on Christmas Eve

"I don't remember anything bad happening to me there. I was treated kindly."

Henryk, as Heinrich, spent six years with the Mayr family. He was especially close to Fini, Frau Mayr's daughter. Henryk pulls out snapshots from those early years. On one you can see a fair-haired boy with blue eyes, accompanied by a girl several years older. Both are sitting on the knees of a teenage girl.

Family photos from Henryk's stay with the Mayrs

"That's Fini, that's her cousin, and that's me," Henryk says. Those two girls were the playmates of little Heinrich's childhood.

"Apparently I didn't like a boy who lived upstairs," Henryk adds. The boy was probably the brother of the older cousin in the picture.

Henryk doesn't remember many other details of his early childhood, but he certainly had warm relations with his German mother.

"Everything was fine. My clearest memory is of a Christmas Eve when we had frankfurters for supper. I tell that story often in Poland and nobody believes me. [*Polish Catholics observe a strict fast on Christmas Eve, where the traditional meal always consists of several varieties of fish and meatless dishes–translator's note.*] But I remember it distinctly."

Little Heinrich's appearance meant that he was ideally suited to swell the ranks of German society. Nazi ideologists preferred such Aryan-looking children.

Convent discipline

"I remember the trip to Poland," Henryk says. "The train stopped for two or three hours. I clearly remember us stopping by a river. Long after the fact, I realised this must have been the Oder. We got off the train at Koźle and I remember that clearly as well. The nuns were waiting for us."

Children repatriated from Germany were placed in a children's home run by nuns in Czechowice. When they arrived at the home that night, the building seemed huge, even though it was only two stories tall. Next to the orphanage was the convent. None of the children spoke Polish, so learning the language was a priority.

"I remember one of the nuns, Sister Hyacinth, was very strict. From the beginning she said in a very sharp tone that we were forbidden to speak German. The only reason we understood was that she said that in German."

Six-year-old Henryk Kowalczyk picked up Polish quickly. He arrived at the children's home in November 1946, and by September 1947 he was attending school. He was a good pupil. The only problem were his classmates, who took to calling him a German whenever there was the smallest dispute. In retrospect, Henryk doesn't think the teasing bothered him very much, since he was so focused on schoolwork.

"They put me straight into the second grade. That year of German school really helped."

Among his classmates were two other repatriated boys from the Czechowice children's home.

The nuns kept a watchful eye on progress in school and were quick to punish any misdeeds.

"After the report cards came out, if anyone got bad grades, they pulled their pants down and got a spanking from Sister Amata."

Henryk was baptized just before his first communion and received his official birth certificate in 1953. He stayed in the Czechowice children's home until he graduated from high school and treated the place like home. To this day, he remembers the oranges they used to give out during the holidays and the nun who ignored her Mother Superior's orders and taught the boys how to dance.

His childhood and teenage years in Czechowice differed little from the lives of his classmates.

"I remember falling in love for the first time when I was 15 or 16 years old."

The sisters were rather strict, but his relationships with some lasted for many years. Later Henryk went to university, met his wife and got started on his grown-up life.

For many years, he forgot all about his German childhood and repatriation.

A Letter from Fini

In the late 1980s, Henryk is startled to receive a letter from Fini, or to use her proper name, Josephine. The now grown woman wants to renew contact with the man she knew as her brother. A regular correspondence develops. At the same time, Henryk Kowalczyk decides to start investigating his own roots. He knows how to go about it, because he is an archivist by profession.

He initiates an inquiry with the International Red Cross in Bad Arolsen. Unfortunately, the search results are meager. It was only possible to establish the identities of his mother and father, along with his place of birth. It turns out that Henryk is the son of a Polish prisoner of war working as a baker and a female farm worker, also of Polish nationality.

The Red Cross confirms that he was baptized in Dachau when he was only a few days old. The paper trail breaks off after 1941.

Josephine decided to get in touch with Henryk only after the death of her mother. Perhaps the older woman would have been able to say what happened to Henryk's mother. Today he just has a single photograph of himself and his natural mother. At most, little Henio would have been a few months old. Many years later, Josephine told Henryk that his mother probably died a few months after he was born. She likely visited the boy on several occasions after she had placed him with the Mayr family.

Henryk tried to pursue the matter in conversations with Fini, but she had no more information to give. It seems likely that the farmer who employed Henryk's mother treated her well, and that she probably died in a camp. After a few exchanges of letters, the contact with Fini broke off.

"Fini invited me to visit her home in Germany. I was very excited at the opportunity to meet again and bought myself a ticket. A few days before departure,

I got a letter from Fini saying that her son didn't want a Pole coming to visit. I felt hurt and returned the ticket," Henryk says bitterly.

Where is Home?

Not everyone who goes to war is a soldier. Many civilians disappear without a trace, families are broken up. During 'World War II, millions of people were deported as slave workers, prisoners of war were relocated, and racially desirable children were abducted and Germanized. Rarely do all of these things apply to one person. But that is what happened to Henryk Kowalczyk, now living in Kielce.

"One thing I wonder about is how my mother would have been deported from Poland in 1939," he says.

The date is indeed very early, since the initial decision to transport forced labor from Poland was not taken until November 25, 1939. Henryk's parents must have been on one of the very first deportation trains. At that stage, the slave worker system had not been properly organized.

What we do know is that Henryk Kowalczyk's mother, Anna Pawlak (born 1920), worked for a farmer named Hermann at Rudeshofen, in the Dachau district. Little Henryk was born at the Dachau hospital on January 19, 1940.

We also know that in December 1940, Henryk's mother fell ill and was hospitalized. This was possible due to a health insurance policy her employer had purchased. She was registered as living in the Dachau district until May 1941. Afterwards, according to documents prepared by the Polish Red Cross, Anna Pawlak was "sent home".

"What does that mean, 'sent home'? Where is home?" Henryk asks today.

Her mother came from a village called Podgórze. There are at least 20 villages of that name in various parts of Poland.

Another unsolved mystery concerns his father and those food parcels. That would indicate his German family knew something about the boy's background. All the evidence suggests that his father died. But surely he must have had relatives, so Henryk Kowalczyk could have cousins living today somewhere in Poland.

"My main concern is for my daughter. There's nobody on my side of the family – not one aunt or uncle. It's like I was alone in the world. That stings a bit and makes me angry about life. It makes me feel inferior somehow," Henryk admits.

“Remember that You’re Polish”

It’s late July 1942. Emilie Edelmann, the director of the Lebensborn’s “Main Department A”, has some good news for Wilhelm Rossmann. The Main Race and Resettlement Office (*Rasse- und Siedlungshauptamt*, or RuSHA) in Litzmannstadt, as the Polish city of Łódź was called under German occupation, is preparing a party of children for Lebensborn. Some are to be dispatched to the “Pommern” processing center at Bad Polzin (Połczyn-Zdrój).

“If one of those children is a girl meeting your specifications for age and appearance, I will be happy to pass her on to you. In the near future, I will be sending you a couple of snapshots to give you some idea of what the child is like.”

There is not a single word about the girl’s parents or background.

For months, Maria and Wilhem Rossmann have been in regular contact with Lebensborn. Wilhelm has been particularly insistent, renewing his “polite request that you expedite this matter as much as possible. We are very desirous of breathing new life into our presently very quiet home.” Clearly, Emilie Edelmann has taken the Rossmanns’ request very much to heart, writing back that she understands the situation and is anxious to be of assistance.

At roughly the same time, almost 500 miles to the east, the Łódż Youth Office (*Jugendamt*) is drawing up a list of “children suitable for Germanization” who are to be transported west to the Children’s Home in Bruckau (Bruczków) in Wartheland, as the Germans call the province of Greater Poland (Wielkopolska), newly annexed to the Reich. After processing at Bruckau, where they are to be issued new certificates with altered surnames and dates of birth, they are to be sent on to Lebensborn centers in Germany.

Before that happens, however, the children are to learn the German language and German discipline — both entirely new to them. At Bruckau, punishments for even the most minor infractions are severe. One of the gravest offences is speaking Polish. Older children who cannot be brainwashed into forgetting their native language or parents often whisper to the younger ones: “Don’t forget you are a Pole.”

We know from speeches by Reichsführer SS Heinrich Himmler himself about plans to "steal German blood" from the occupied countries of Europe. However, neither Wilhelm Rossmann, a simple schoolmaster at Lemgo, nor the bulk of German society had any idea just how brutal this Germanization process would be.

Barbara is Selected

Lebensborn correspondence with prospective adopted parents maintained the fiction that these children were orphans of German parents in Poland who had been murdered by Polish partisans. The term used for such children was *Ostkinder.*

In early September 1942, after months of being shuttled between orphanages and Germanization centers, a group of several dozen children arrives in Bad Polzin. Director Edelmann sends the promised snapshots to the Rossmanns. They show two sad-faced, disoriented little girls, both photographed at the Łódź Race and Resettlement Office.

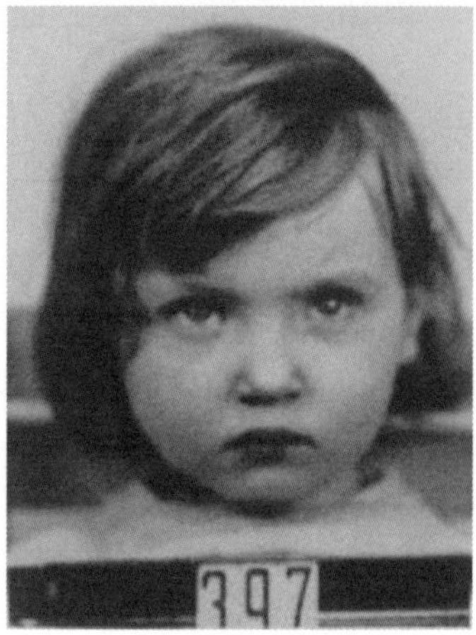

Bärbel in 1942, ID photo taken by the Reich Main Race and Resettlement Office

"How did I come to be chosen? I asked my parents about that when I came back as an adult to visit them in Germany. *Mutti* said they liked both little girls and couldn't decide. In the end, they placed both pictures face down on the table and picked one at random. It turned out to be me," says Barbara Paciorkiewicz, who was born in 1938 in the Polish port city of Gdynia as Barbara Gajzler.

Barbara keeps that same childhood snapshot among the many documents she has collected over the past several decades at her apartment in Łódż. Together, they portray Barbara's difficult years as a child and young adult, full of unexpected twists and turns.

A Child with Aryan Features

"In February 1942, my grandmother, who was my caregiver at the time, was summoned to bring me to the *Jugendamt.* I didn't come home from that meeting," says Barbara. The city of Łódż, where she was living, had been annexed to Germany and renamed Litzmannstadt in 1939. As in other occupied Polish cities, the Youth Office in Łódź had been instructed to seek children "suitable for

Germanization" in keeping with Hitler's racial prescription to infuse the German nation with "new blood". Children displaying "Aryan" features were sought. Four-year-old Barbara Gajzler, affectionately called "Basia" by her family, met the racial testing criteria with an appropriately shaped cranium, fair hair and blue eyes.

"Children found by racial and psychological testing to be capable of being Germanized are to be placed in educational homes from the ages of six to 12. Younger children from the age of two will be placed with Lebensborn registered families," wrote Ulrich Greifelt, an SS police general and right-hand man of Reichsführer Himmler in all racial policy matters, in Regulation 67/I from 1942.

"I remember a semicircular hall with big windows and broad windowsills. I'm sitting on one of those sills with the other children. We're not allowed to speak the only language we know on pain of punishment. We also get punished for wetting our beds, which almost all the kids do because they can't cope with their treatment over the past few months. The crying was contagious, so the children were given tranquilizer shots to calm them down. Maybe it was also supposed to dull memories of their previous lives."

Sometimes the facility was visited by grownups from outside. On such occasions, Basia always hid behind the other kids, but one day a man came specially to see her and took her for a walk to the park. Then he said they would be going home, to Lemgo. The little girl starts crying because she doesn't understand what is happening. On the train, the man covers her with his jacket and she falls asleep. When they get home, two women are waiting to bathe and feed the weeping child. Completely worn out, she dozes off.

Basia has Parents

Next day, the world looks different. She awakens to smiling faces peering down at her.

"From that moment onwards, I had parents. The first words they taught me were *Mutti*, *Vati* and *Oma* ("Mommy", "Daddy" and "Granny"). I forgot all about my previous life. Mommy told me many years later that I often said something that sounded like "Pole", but she couldn't catch my meaning and thought maybe I wanted to use the toilet. Maybe somewhere in the back of my head I could still hear the older kids telling the younger ones who had forgotten all their Polish to remember they were Poles."

At Lemgo Basia—now called Bärbel—makes a rapid recovery. She no longer gets punished for minor infractions, though Vati might sometimes spank her. The whole household is tidy and disciplined, but even so, her new parents thoroughly spoil Bärbel. The attention of three adults—her parents and grandmother—is completely focused on the little girl. She also has two older brothers, Wilhelm and Günther, but both are away serving in the *Wehrmacht*. In December 1944 Wilhelm comes home on a short furlough and gets married to a nurse he met in France. At the wedding, Bärbel scatters flowers at the feet of the bride and groom. It's only natural, since she's part of the family.

To this day she remembers first meeting her other brother, Günther, when he came home from the war in June 1945. "He walked in through the kitchen door as Grandmother was pitting cherries and I was trying to untangle some string. 'I'll help you,' he said. Nobody recognized him at first," Barbara recalls.

"It was uncanny. The son who was sent all the way to Africa came back safe and sound. And right before he left, his younger sister Ursel had died. Now he looked me over (I guess they had written about me) and said: "Now I have another little sister to love."

"I always say I was born under a lucky star because my life could have turned out completely differently. I was put through a brutal racial selection and ended up with a family who accepted me as their very own daughter."

Shadow of a Dead Daughter

In everything she did, Bärbel had a constant companion – the Rossmanns' dead daughter Ursel. "I quickly understood that the clothing I wore and the toys I played with had earlier belonged to Ursel," Barbara says. "Her portrait hung in my bedroom, and I often heard Mommy sighing: 'Ach, my dear Ursel!'"

Every morning, she looked at Ursel's picture on the wall. Ursel was present as Bärbel went about her day. Getting dressed, she would hear: "Be careful with that, it was one of Ursel's things." She was always there, at school or play. "When I got in trouble, I'd call myself 'bad Bärbel', and when things were going well, I was 'good Ursel'."

Now Barbara wonders whether this was the source of her lifelong inferiority complex.

"Nobody ever told me that I was the inferior child, but the constant presence of that better Ursel might have stirred such feelings in me. As I got older, those feelings got more pronounced. Someone was always better than me."

Under SS Scrutiny

Lebensborn kept a watchful eye on children assigned to foster homes and required regular reports about their condition. On November 6, 1942, six weeks after collecting Bärbel from the "Pommern" facility, Wilhelm Rossmann reports that he and his wife have not been disappointed . To the contrary, all of their hopes and desires have been fulfilled.

"Bärbel proved a very fast learner and quickly adapted to our family life. She is a child greedy for love and affection, but she is also capable of demonstrating love in return. Bärbel is very well-behaved and obedient, but also joyful and energetic. She's shown good physical development in a very short time and has already gained more than two pounds."

Again Rossman asks for Bärbel's birth documents and other personal information, and once more he is refused. Apparently, the files have not yet been forwarded from Litzmannstadt.

Eventually, Lebensborn decides simply to issue Bärbel a new birth certificate. On July 21, 1943, nearly a year after Basia arrived in Lemgo, Lebensborn's Adoption Placement Department writes to Wilhelm Rossmann:

> *The child Bärbel currently under your care, born on February 2, 1938, is to be issued a birth certification. Please consider which surname you prefer her to have in this document. You may choose to use the child's original surname, "Geisler", or your own. It is also permissible to give the child an entirely neutral last name to avoid reminding her of the past.*

Postwar Inquiries

If Katarzyna Kossak had not asked the Polish Red Cross in 1945 for help in recovering her grandchild, perhaps Barbara would never have discovered her identity. It was a time when millions of people in Poland were seeking their loved ones – chiefly by applying to the Red Cross. Little Basia's mother had died very early in the war, while her father had vanished without a trace in September 1939. That left her grandmother to take up the search.

The Polish Red Cross operated its own representative office in Germany, where together with the International Tracing Service (ITS) it collected information about Polish displaced persons (so-called DPs) in the country. This included stolen children, who by various estimates may have numbered between 50,000 and 200,000. In the case of Bärbel Rossmann, the ITS search didn't take long, because already in 1946 Lemgo's mayor was already passing information to the Allied Occupation Authorities about the presence of a Lebensborn child in his town.

Several years then pass before the respective institutions connect the dots. Finally, the ITS determines that Bärbel Rossmann and Barbara Gajzler are the same person.

Katarzyna Kossak then writes a letter to her granddaughter.

> *Dear little Basia, if you only knew how many sleepless nights your Granny went through after they took you away and said that you are a German child with a German last name. That doesn't mean anything, because your blood is Polish. That's the way it is, Basia, my precious little girl. Granny cried for you for so long, but now I have hope you will return and we'll be together again. I will work with all my might to make sure you are safe and happy with your Granny.*

Mrs. Kossak also had to sign a written pledge to "provide full care and material provision" for Basia upon her repatriation to Poland.

Just before Basia's departure, Wilhelm Rossman wrote Katarzyna Kossak a letter to which he never received a reply.

> *Dear Mrs. Kossak,*
>
> *Tomorrow our Bärbel sets forth on her journey back to you, her grandmother. This letter is to give you some basic information about your granddaughter's life until now.*
>
> *I collected her from the Polzin/Pommern orphanage in September 1942 and brought her to our home. The previous year, we had lost our daughter and dearly wanted new life in our empty house. About Bärbel we only knew that her surname was Geissler and that she was born in Gotenhafen (Gdynia) on Feb. 2, 1938. Despite numerous requests and inquiries, we were never able to obtain any more information about her relatives. We took her into our home as our own child, always treating her and bringing her up in that way. We also gave her our own name. She always felt good here. In 1943 she caught scarlet fever but was otherwise healthy and happy. For the past three years she has attended*

primary school. Bärbel is a talented child but lacks the stamina and willpower to do well at school. She is adept at drawing and painting, which she works at diligently.

(…) Parting with her is not easy for us. However, we do understand that a child should be with her relatives and that you have first claim. We send her back confident that we have done our best for your granddaughter. We wish you much joy with Bärbel and hope she will adapt quickly to her new home and stay healthy and happy. In the future, we would be grateful for information about her life and fate.

The Road Home

Of all this, 10-year-old Bärbel learns nothing. In May 1948 she steps into an automobile with a lady who drives up to the house in Lemgo and promises to take her on "an excursion". After six years of life in a loving, peaceful environment, Bärbel is a trusting child. Suspecting nothing, she says goodbye to her parents. She's not even surprised at spending the night away from home. After all, it's a sightseeing trip.

Her first stop is an UNRRA facility somewhere in southern Germany. UNRRA stands for the United Nations Relief and Rehabilitation Administration, which was the main conduit for humanitarian aid to refugees in the last years of World War II and its immediate aftermath. Children at the UNRRA center received clothing—the girls got to pick out pretty dresses and shiny new shoes. They were also given fresh fruit and plenty of chocolate to eat.

Bärbel in 1948, her final picture taken before she was repatriated from Germany

"They taught us English and talked about traveling across the ocean," Barbara recalls. "For years I couldn't understand why they made me study English when I was supposed to return home, where everyone spoke Polish. What I learned much later, after living in Poland, was that UNRRA was preparing us for possible adoption by American families. And in fact, some of the Polish children abducted by the Germans for Germanization ended up being transported to the U.S."

Basia's next stop was the town of Augustdorf, not far from her former home in Lemgo.

"This was a transit camp for displaced persons of various nationalities in the process of being repatriated," Barbara says. "They all spoke different languages and were waiting for transport home. While there I learned that Lemgo was nearby. Since the police station was located right across from the children's hut, I marched over there and called home to my parents, having remembered their phone number."

They came the very next Sunday, her foster mother in tears. "'Don't worry, *Mutti*, I'll come back and bring you sausages'," Barbara remembers saying while trying to cheer her up. "I think this was maybe because I was somehow associating my upcoming departure with the trips *Vati* used to take to the country during wartime, from which he came back loaded with delicacies for the table."

It was to be the last time they met for many years.

"Finally, they put together a train for us, with sleeping cars. My place was in the very top bunk. I remember the train halting for days at a time in open country before resuming its journey. All the time people kept repeating "Poland, Poland". I doubt I had the least idea what they were talking about. Was I supposed to be happy and laugh the way they did?"

Polish Home

The train trip terminates in Katowice. There, the children are remanded to a Red Cross center located right next to an orphanage. Bärbel, who has just learned that her real name is Barbara Gajzler, can peer through her window and see children at the orphanage peeling potatoes in gray-colored aprons. She doesn't want to end up there. In the meantime, relatives are arriving at the center to reclaim their children.

"And what about me? I cried and envied them," Barbara says. "Was I going to an orphanage like the one I could see from the window? Who's going to come for me? Could it be *Vati*?"

Finally someone calls out her name. She doesn't react to Gajzler, so they call out Rossmann, and only then does Basia understand that they're talking about her. Someone says "*Onkel*" and she wraps her arms around a stranger's neck.

"My uncle, startled by my reaction, reached into his bag and handed me a sausage roll," Barbara says. "That was the first time I ate a whole sausage with one hand and a roll with the other. That taste stuck in my mind for years. I was so happy I didn't even notice my entire baggage with the beautiful dresses and patent leather shoes was lost in storage."

That uncle is married to the sister of Basia's mother. She's supposed to stay with them, because her grandmother Katarzyna Kossak from Łódź decided they would have an easier time understanding Basia, since they had been on forced labor in Germany themselves.

"The problem was that I couldn't understand their German at all. I didn't understand what was happening or why I had to live there, and I missed my parents in Lemgo terribly," Barbara says. "I assumed it was all some colossal misunderstanding."

After a while, it became clear to Basia that she was expected to take care of her aunt's children. "But how was I supposed to babysit when I couldn't even speak Polish?" Her responsibilities also included fetching water, which involved long journeys through the rubble-strewn streets of Gdańsk.

Her uncle has nothing but the worst things to say about Germans. They take her to Stutthof to see what remained of the former concentration camp there.

In the autumn, she starts school. Even though she's 10 years old, Basia is relegated to first grade because of her horrible Polish. The kids are merciless, calling her "Hitlerette" and laughing at her harsh German accent.

"They signed the armistice in May 1945, but for me the war lasted much longer," Barbara Paciorkiewicz says now.

One day her grandmother Kossak comes to visit her in Gdańsk. Mrs. Kossak immediately collects her granddaughter from school and takes her back to Łódź. It's not clear whether she had been informed that the girl was being exploited as a nanny and housemaid or whether she just sensed something was wrong.

In Łódź

Mrs Kossak is tight-lipped and withdrawn, but at least Basia has fewer chores at Grandma's. However, the girl still can't quite figure out what has happened to her and why she was repatriated to Poland.

"Today such a child would be under psychiatric care, but then it was look out for yourself," Barbara says.

Basia practices her Polish incessantly. "Morrusek, Morrrrusek", she calls to the family dog, exaggeratedly rolling her r's. She does this even when Morusek is not around. Thanks to such persistence, Basia loses the guttural German "r" that sounds so alien to Polish ears.

But her grandmother has a hard time making ends meet. As a result, Basia is often shunted off to other relatives, where she is not always welcome. One drunken uncle decides he "won't bring up foreign brats" and sent Basia and her trunk straight back to Granny's.

When a social worker suggests Basia should be placed in a children's home, Mrs. Kossak doesn't resist. Neither does Basia, who may be only 12 years old but still has her pride, even if she vowed never in a million years to live in an orphanage. She ends up at the Girl's Home on Karolewska Street in Łódź, where every girl is coping with her own wartime trauma.

Barbara doesn't sound bitter when she speaks of her difficult childhood. Returning to Poland was hard, but her stay with the Rossmann family in Lemgo was one of the best times of her life.

Letters from Lemgo

During her eight years at the orphanage, Basia spends every Sunday at her grandmother's. She spends much of the time reading aloud, since Granny is going blind. One day her grandmother springs a shocking surprise, announcing that she's made a find in her daughter's wardrobe cabinet in Gdańsk – the place where Basia lived for her first two years back in Poland. Apparently, there were letters from her German family in Lemgo. And for five years, nobody had said anything about them!

Back in January 1949, ten months after Basia left Lemgo, her German parents write to their "dear little Bärbel" – "Surely it can't be you have forgotten about us?" They're worried that their letters are not getting through since they've heard nothing back. Obviously, this could not have been their first letter. Why has this correspondence been hidden from her all these years?

"We hope you are well and happy with your grandmother. We hope this letter reaches you and cheers you up. Please, write us back and let us know how you are. We yearn for news from you!"

She will read this letter over and over with tears in her eyes.

Finally, she feels up to writing a reply. In Polish, because she's already forgotten her German. So an exchange of letters begins. Wilhelm Rossmann sends an official invitation from Lemgo – at that time, this was required by the authorities in communist-ruled Poland from any citizen who wished to obtain a passport and travel to the West. Unfortunately, repeated applications from Basia are refused. Only in 1968 does she succeed. Basia's arrival in Lemgo comes exactly 20 years after she last left the home of Maria and Wilhelm Rossmann.

Family

The welcome in Lemgo is tinged by tears of happiness and regret. Little Bärbel's parents are shocked by her postwar experience of being shuttled between relatives before landing in an orphanage for eight years. They speak with a dictionary in hand until Basia starts to recover some German. After all, it was the first language she can remember speaking. Back in Lemgo, she becomes Bärbel again.

"There was lots of joy and affection from family, neighbors and friends who knew me as a child," Barbara says. "They kept saying 'Ah, our little Bärbel is back!' I constantly had tears in my eyes and was so choked up I could hardly speak. I was greeted like a queen coming back from a long trip."

The picturesque town she remembered as a child had grown even more beautiful. She arrived during Advent, so there was a Christmas market festooned with lights in the main square. It made quite a contrast with factory grime and grayness of Łódź.

Bärbel, who had worked in the textile industry sketching decorative designs for dresses, scarves and T-shirts, soon gets a couple of orders from the local printers in Lemgo. She sets to work with a will. The designs prove so popular that they go through several large print runs. *Mutti* is overjoyed. Basia sheds her Polish inferiority complex and starts to feel that she's equal to any Western designer.

Bärbel (L) scatters flowers at her brother Wilhelm's wedding

The family starts urging her to stay in West Germany, where she would have a good job.

"I was trying to decide whether to move into a brand-new luxury home or build my own life," Barbara says.

Even so, it seems to Basia that she has already put the worst behind her. Her life is now in Poland. By this time, she has her own flat, a job and friends. There is also an Antoni waiting at home, a friend since their time together in the Łódź children's home. For years he's been pestering her to start a family together. He calls her "Bajka", which means "fairy tale" in Polish. "Come on, Bajka, let's make a home like the one you had in Lemgo."

"Many times I swore I'd never marry, because it seemed to me that having a family was a sacred, special thing—something I never had growing up in an orphanage," Barbara says. "I didn't think I could create that kind of family. But maybe the trip back to Lemgo and the time spent with my family changed something in me. In Lemgo, I remembered what it's like to be with people who love and respect each other."

Barbara and Antoni get married and have first a son, Artur, then a daughter, Aneta.

The idyll doesn't last long. Just when Aneta turns two, and young Artur is starting school, Antoni is killed in an automobile accident.

"Suddenly we lost the one person in the world we needed most," Barbara says. "After eight years, I became a widow and my children semi-orphans, without a father. 'God, don't let them be orphans like me,' I used to cry. I worried about whether I could be a mother and father to them. How will I manage? Who is going to keep me going?"

Mutti and Vati

She could always count for support in Lemgo, where she spent many summer months with her children.

"I liked being alone with the kids and it was always fun travelling together. I would tell them stories and sing, that's how we entertained ourselves on trips.

"It's strange to think that the first time I drove there with the children, I'd just gotten my license and had less than a hundred km under my belt, and here I go off on a 1,200 kilometer jaunt to West Germany. On the autobahn, stuck between those huge tractor-trailers, I felt as tiny as an ant. In East Germany I got a speeding ticket, probably because I wanted to show that my little Fiat 126p wasn't any worse than those fancy Western cars," Barbara says with a laugh. She always seems full of energy and good humor. There's no trace of bitterness, even when she talks of the past.

Lemgo was a place to recharge her batteries. She felt grateful to her foster parents, which she tried to express many years later in a letter.

Dearest Mom and Dad,

Thanks to you I feel truly blessed.

You took a little girl from Lebensborn in Polzin [now Połczyn-Zdrój] and became parents to her. From the first day at your side in Lemgo, I felt safe (…)

Life, however, played a nasty trick on us and we had to part. I was only 10 years old and had no idea what was in store. Only much later did you find out what happened to me. But while a horrible war was going on, all of you – Mutti, Vati and Oma – gave me a home. Later I met my older brothers, who always treated me like their little sister. They still do, to this day. I never realized that this was a taste of the happiness that had been stolen from me. Afterwards, I tasted bitterness, too.

It was hard to go back to an unfamiliar Polish identity when I had lost my parents and was forced to go live in an orphanage. As an unwanted child, it was difficult for me to learn how to love others. I missed you terribly, and all the time you were trying to track me down through the Polish Red Cross. I didn't want to be Polish and spent a lot of time trying to find my place, without knowing who I was or who I belonged to. (…)

At difficult moments, after I started my own family and lost my loving husband and the father of my children, you were my pillars of support. (…)

I think that is the most important thing I learned during that brief period of living together in your home. It's what I try to pass on to my own children, who are my greatest joy.

Your Bärbel

Witness to History

Today, Barbara Paciorkiewicz is one of the most important surviving witnesses to the abduction and forced Germanization of Polish children. In 1994-2006, she chaired the Polish Association of Germanized Children, a Nazi victims' organization established in 1989.

She recalls how the Association came to be.

"Sometimes important events have incredibly trivial origins. In this case, it was an accidental meeting of two women on a street in Łódź in 1988. They looked at each other for a long time before asking: 'Where do I know you from?' Then they remembered. As small children, during World War II, they were both kept in German centers for "reprogramming" national identity – in other words, Germanization. Just think how strong those experiences and bonds must have been for those two to recognize each other after all those years on a city street. Their names were Alina Kubiak and Helena Orzechowska."

The two women started contacting others with similar experiences, which is how the Association was founded. From that moment on, these victims of an almost forgotten Nazi crime would have a voice and a chance to gain some public recognition. One of their first achievements was the installation in 2006 of a commemorative plaque at 113 Piotrowska Street in Łódź, the site of the *Jugendamt* where four-year-old Basia Gajzler was summoned with her mother in 1942.

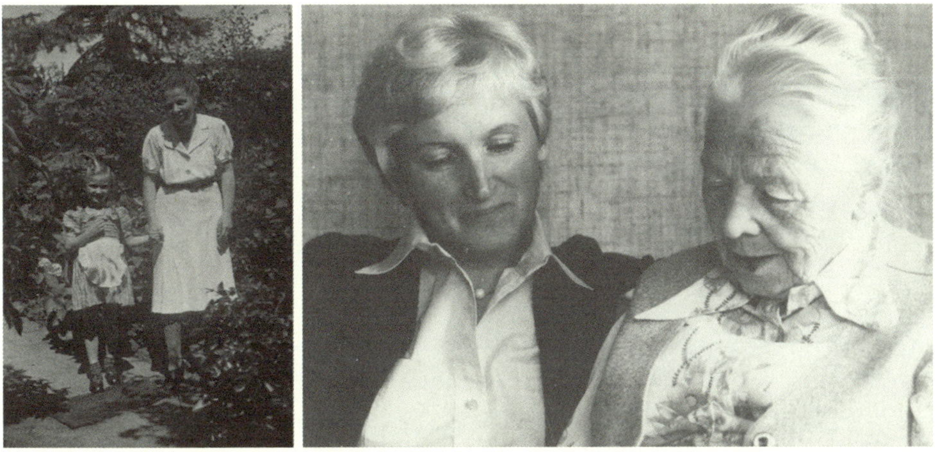

(L) Bärbel with her Mutti Maria Rossmann in Lemgo. (R) Barbara Paciorkiewicz with Maria Rossmann in Lemgo, 1970s.

These children never received reparations from Germany, since they didn't meet the legal criteria for victim status. Even so, the Association was able to persuade the Polish government to grant them veterans' benefits. This required collecting documentary proof that they had been subjected to forced Germanization.

"The early days were quite difficult," Barbara recalls. "People who signed up for the Association usually had no documents confirming their status. During the war, the Germans went to great lengths to conceal their abduction and Germanization operations, including destroying all written records. So our most important task was to find any traces of this criminal procedure by applying to various institutions, including the ITS in Bad Arolsen."

"Our Association also lobbied for financial aid to the neediest victims, whose pensions don't cover their most basic needs, such as medicine and other daily necessities."

Barbara first saw her own ITS file in 2001.

"Many times I asked myself where I belonged and whether I was Polish or German," Barbara says. But that was then. Now, she has no doubts about being Polish.

Same Place, 80 Years Later

Barbara Paciorkiewicz today

Połczyn-Zdrój is the place where Barbara was collected by her *Vati* in 1942. Today, the presence of children selected for Germanization is indicated by a plaque on the wall of a sanatorium housed in the same building.

Nearby is a small memorial by the local sculptor Michalina Wianecka, portraying a young girl with windblown hair and a wispy dress, clutching a suitcase. She gazes uncertainly into the future.

The inscription on the large boulder on which the statue is perched reads: "To the victims of Germanization in 1939-1945, from the citizens of Połczyń-Zdrój and the Institute of National Remembrance".

At the upper corner is another short text: "Remember that you're Polish – Barbara Paciorkiewicz".

"That's a phrase taken from one of my press interviews," Barbara says. "It's what the older kids used to say to the little ones who didn't know what was going on. They probably said it to me, too."

Across the way is a small chapel. Supposedly, it was built on the gravesite of children who died at the "Pommern" facility. Although this report has never been confirmed, someone from Połczyń-Zdrój is always lighting a votive candle and leaving flowers there.

Barbara says local residents also care for the statue of the little girl.

"The kids bring her flowers and brightly colored leaves, and one of the local ladies knitted her a woolen scarf," Barbara says. "Those wartime children didn't get that sort of care and attention, but perhaps at least they'll be remembered. Let's not forget about the children of today's wars, including those abducted Ukrainian kids. Let's hope they survive to return home and someday say they were truly blessed, like little Basia."

“Krampus will come and take your nipple”

Anna calls me up. “I just remembered something – Krampus. I remember they used him to scare us,” she says.

“Where?”

“I don’t remember exactly. Maybe in Austria...”

***

It’s not clear how Anna ended up in this picturesque little town in the Austrian state of Styria. “Willkommen in Öblarn” is written on the postcard she shows me.

Images from her childhood – a wooden hut, the long kitchen table at the Angerers’ farm, a doll, a brown dress with a detachable collar, holding hands with somebody called “brother”, beets julienned into little strips, *Mutti* waiting, bread smeared with molasses, soldiers, bundles on the train, UNRRA parcels. Perhaps nobody in Öblarn would believe Anna’s story that she’d been there. “But Mrs. Berezowska remembered specific details, and they matched up,” archivist Johann Madl tells me.

She remembers running downhill with her “brother” to the woods, where they could hide and watch tanks rolling through the village. And they’d been expressly forbidden to go into those woods.

***

Anna has fair hair and blue eyes.

***

“I’m sorry to be calling about such nonsense, but I found something called a “Krampus game” in a tourist brochure I got in Austria,” Anna says during our next phone conversation.

I visit Öblarn in July 2018, stopping with Irmina and Rudolf Lasser. In the corridor outside my attic room, there’s a picture of several Krampuses – horned imps who accompany St. Nicholas and hand out switches to naughty kids. The locals tell me all about how these little devils used to prance about during the traditional Advent masquerade processions. "For children, the whole thing was scary and unpleasant," says Adelheid Planitzer.

Anna mustn't be a naughty girl. If she is, Krampus will come and steal her *Nupel.* That's the German word for "nipple" or "pacifier".

Anna Berezowska (L) as a child; the boy and woman beside her are unidentified

In a 1981 letter from the Polish Red Cross, Anna Berezowska discovers that her name was found "on a list of Polish children located in Austria (sent by the Polish Repatriation Mission in Villach) and on a manifest of adults and children living in Austria sent by the Polish Red Cross in Katowice."[1]

They put Anna on a repatriation train to Katowice in 1948. But her name didn't appear on any passenger list.

---

[1] Personal collection of Anna Berezowska.

Anna Berezowska seeking her identity in Öblarn, 2009

***

"Were you in Öblarn after the war?"

"Yes. I even visited the place where that little wooden cottage once stood. I lived there with Rosa Stauder. As you entered, there was a kitchen with an open fireplace to the left, where a fire was always going. To the right was a bedroom with a great bed and feather comforter. Whenever they tucked me in, *Mutti* was sitting beside me and singing lullabies or telling me a story."

"In another building, there was an even bigger kitchen with a long wooden table and benches. That's where I was given slices of bread with molasses, washed down with milk."

"At some point – it must have been just after Christmas, because there was a tree with decorations and I remember getting a *Puppe* doll – *Mutti* woke me up in the middle of the night and said I should get dressed. Two soldiers picked me up, and I remember her standing there and crying."

"I never saw her again."

Anna pieces together these scattered images and tries to build a childhood from them.

If she were born in 1944, Anna would have returned to Poland as a four-year-old. How is it possible for her to remember anything?

And yet – there's Krampus, her *Nupel*, and the warm smile of *Mutti* Rosa.

***

What would a little girl from Poland be doing in rural Austria during and immediately after World War II? Why would she only have been taken in the evenings to see *Mutti* Rosa – a solitary woman who for reasons not yet apparent to me came here from the Naturns district in Italy's South Tyrol? Were the girl's natural parents deceased? Who were they? Slave workers? Did they have to hide the child? Or maybe Anna's delivery took place in a Lebensborn facility? Both she and Johann Madl refer to a maternity clinic. I meet Madl at Adleheid Planitzer's home. For years, he's been trying to help Anna in her search. Madl asks whether I have time to spare, and he arrives carrying a thick binder.

***

Austria was a good testing ground for Heinrich Himmler's Germanization scheme. Shortly after Germany annexed Austria in the 1938 *Anschluss*, Gregor Ebner, head of Lebensborn's health department, visited Austria to scout locations for future facilities. He concluded that in newly acquired *Ostmark* [the Nazi name for Austria], these centers should be built along the same lines of those existing in the "old Reich".[2]

Facilities for children fulfilling the necessary racial criteria were often located in picturesque tourist spas like Traunsee, a mountain-enfolded lake which also hosted the "Alpenland" children's home. At the lake's northern end was the town of Gmunden, and four kilometers from Gmunden lay the village of Oberweis. There, in 1938, the Gestapo requisitioned a castle for Lebensborn. The facility began to operate in 1943 under the supervision of Maria Knipp-Merkel, who had earlier worked for Lebensborn in Kraków. The facility was equipped with furniture

---

[2] Koop, *Organizacja Lebensborn*, p. 147.

confiscated from Jews – six freight cars delivered by the Gestapo, according to the historian Volker Koops.[3]

Oberweis was intended mainly for Polish children selected for Germanization.

On the southern shore of the lake is another place often mentioned in documents about the Germanization program – Ebensee.

In the book *Czas niewoli, czas śmierci* [A Time of Captivity, A Time of Death], there is a reference to 200 Polish children sent to Oberweis from the Germanization center at Kalisz. They had passed their racial examinations and already spoke German.

After the Oberweis facility was evacuated in March 1945, some 60 children were transferred to the Merie-Eich camp in Upper Austria.[4]

Thanks to the efforts of top management, another confiscated property was added to Lebensborn's portfolio – the "Wienerwald" sanatorium in Feuchtenwald, about 60 km from Vienna. This formerly Jewish-owned spa boasted its own forest, stables, greenhouses and sunbathing pavilions in a 34-hectare park.

These are just a few snapshots of what *Ostmark* had to offer for Germanization.

***

After the war, Austria became a place to look for lost Polish children. Engineer Landsberg wrote about this in a report dated October 13, 1945:

"In Germany as well as Austria, large numbers of children can be found who were deported from Poland for Germanization purposes and handed out to local farmers. Finding these children is difficult and time-consuming, especially since the smallholders have become attached to the children and don't want to give them up. Among these children, there is a large group of orphans, and in many cases it is impossible to even establish their family names."[5]

The Polish Red Cross was responsible for locating and caring for these children. More than 50 of them were being kept at an orphanage in Salzburg.

---

[3] Koop, *Organizacja Lebensborn*, p. 148.

[4] Jacek E. Wilczur, Roman Hrabar, Zofia Tokarz, *Czas niewoli, czas śmierci*, Wydaw- nictwo Interpress, 1979, p. 132.

[5] Koop, *Organizacja Lebensborn*, p. 147.

Lansberg urged that the American military government be made to issue a decree making it compulsory to report such children, with severe penalties for any attempt to hide them.[6]

***

In the ITS documents Anna Berezowska received from Bad Arolsen is the annotation: "taken by the Germans". We don't know when or from where. We don't even know if the reference is to her, because it could apply either to Anna or to the girl who thought she was Anna. Because in 2015, Anna discovers that Anna Berezowska, the daughter of Julian Berezowski and Mirosława Genyk Berezowska, is not at all who she thinks she is.

Lebensborn facilities at that time ran their own civil registry offices. Their purpose was to eradicate all evidence of a crime. Accordingly, the first and last names of stolen children were changed, along with their dates and places of birth. The usual practice was to add two years to their age. The point was to put off the scent any relatives who came looking for them later.

***

I review more files from the Central Archives of Modern Records (AAN) in Warsaw.

"The recovery of children in Austria is proceeding. Despite our lack of accreditation in the American sector and the liquidation of our facility there, we succeeded recently in freeing 15 children. This was thanks to cooperation from the IRO [International Refugee Organization–*translator's note*] and especially its Social Welfare Department and its director, Mrs. Brownlee. There has lately been a tendency, especially in the Austrian *Jugendamt*, to refuse to surrender Polish children for adoption in cases where the child is an orphan and has no Polish relatives. Our delegation has strongly opposed this tendency, stressing that even Polish orphans should be returned to their homeland, where they will certainly get better care from an orphanage or foster home than they would from Austrian family."[7]

---

[6] Excerpt from Engineer Landsberg's report, 13 October 1945, collection on the Polish Government Plenipotentiary for Repatriation, AAN, sygn. 313, karta nr 7.

[7] Document dated 15 March 1948, AAN, PCK Zarząd Główny, sygn. 101, karta nr 34.

"A certain problem is posed by children born to parents of the Greek Catholic faith in former areas of southeastern Poland that are now part of the USSR. We do not know whether we have a right to reclaim children whose parents were Polish citizens, but sometimes of Ukrainian nationality. Today it is often difficult to establish details of the parents' national identity. In most cases, these are children of forced laborers deported by the Germans from eastern Małopolska and Vohynia provinces."[8]

Other documents show some parents weren't informed that their children had been repatriated.

"Please bring to the attention of the Polish Red Cross district office in Katowice that transported children should be scrupulously and promptly returned to their parents or families. Recently there have been instances in which parents or families have written the IRO to express concern about the fate of their children, even though the child had been repatriated long before. These situations create an unfriendly attitude toward the PCK and the recovery program, while heightening uncertainty about the children and making it harder for us to work here."[9]

Öblarn

[8] Document dated 15 March 1948, AAN, PCK Zarząd Główny, sygn. 101, karta nr 34.

[9] Document dated 15 March 1948, AAN, PCK Zarząd Główny, sygn. 101, karta nr 35.

***

I look everywhere for a child named Anna Berezowska: on available repatriation lists, in documents I have access to, at the AAN in Warsaw. I call the children's home, which still operates at the same location. Everywhere, I draw a blank.

I send more than 100 emails to various institutions in Austria. A response comes back from Astrid Simmer of the Austrian Red Cross, who writes that all possibilities of obtaining further information have been exhausted.

Anna has been corresponding for years with ITS Bad Arolsen. According to the latter, citing information from the Austrian Red Cross, Anna's parents were Julian Berezowski and Mirosława Genyk Berezowska. Later, this turns out to be an impossibility. ITS Bad Arolsen notifies Anna of the mistake in a letter of January 21, 2015.

"We conducted a search whose results indicate that the child named Anna Berezowska emigrated with her parents (Julian and Mirosława Genyk von Berezowski) to Canada… We regret deeply that we cannot offer you any further assistance."[10]

After years of searching for her identity, Anna finds herself back where she started.

Surely a person can't simply vanish into thin air? There ought to be a few clues, witnesses, photographs, documents. Somebody must remember something.

***

What about *Mutti* Rosa? Who was this mysterious, solitary woman in the mountain cottage? I started by searching the obituaries. I check out every Rosa Stauder, comparing photographs, always seeking a woman who was born in 1899, in the Naturns district in Italy.

I get a response to one of my emails from Valentin Stocker at the Naturns district council. He promises to find someone to help in my search.

Two weeks later, the information comes back.

Rosa Stauder – Anna's beloved *Mutti* – was born on January 2, 1899 in the village of Staben, Naturns district, population 300. She was baptized the day she

[10] Personal collection of Anna Berezowska.

was born by Father Franz Gasser. Rosa's mother was Maria Platzer, and her father was Josef Platzer. Her godmother was listed as Rosa Platzer.

Rosa Stauder "mutti"

I still don't know why Rosa moved or perhaps fled to Öblarn in central Austria, more than 400 km northeast of her home. Or why she was given a little girl to care for. What I do know is that Rosa's younger sister, with her son, were also staying in the same place.

Could this be the "brother" whose hand Anna remembers holding?

Mutti Rosa remained alone until the end of her life. She practically had to be dragged by force from her cottage, which was about to collapse on top of her. She spent her final years at the Öblarn seniors home, where she died.

"Madl sent me pictures of *Mutti* Rosa's grave, so I'd see it's being tended for," Anna says.

***

"I woke up on the train. They must have given us sleeping pills or tranquilizers, because I don't remember much. What I do recall is them airing out the carriages and unloading some bundles. Later I learned they were children who didn't survive the journey."

"After we disembarked in Katowice, at the Polish Red Cross, after a while the children began to 'disappear'," Anna remembers. "They 'disappeared' because somebody came to collect them, someone waiting for them. I didn't 'disappear' and went to an orphanage instead."

***

I want to help and send a search inquiry to the PCK, but it doesn't work. Not even because I'm not related to Anna. Put simply, the questionnaire is so constructed that a person searching for their own identity will have no possibility of filling it out. You have to give a last name (Anna doesn't know whether her surname is Berezowska), your first name (is she really Anna?), a date of birth (Anna has two and isn't sure whether either one is correct), place of birth (there are at least three possibilities), the first names of her parents and the maiden name of her mother (if only she knew).

The only question she can confidently answer is her last place of residence.

***

Halina Świerczewska had written to the Polish Red Cross since 1947 about adopting a child. She lost her husband and children during the war.

"We are pleased to report that unless the parents of Anna Berezowska can be found, there is nothing in our opinion that stands in the way of entrusting the little girl to your care," we read in a reply from the PCK office in Villach, Austria.[11]

[11] Personal collection of Anna Berezowska.

Halina Świerczewska with her daughter (L) and Świerczewska's husband (R), both of whom died in the war.

It seemed that Anna's parents – if she is indeed Anna Berezowska – were never found, so Halina Świerczewska was cleared to adopt her.

The Central Archives of Modern Records contains hundreds of documents on Germanization, repatriation, and the activities of various institutions responsible for finding lost children.

Among the files are documents from the PCK Delegation in Villach, Austria. I scan right past the name Berezowska, then flip the page back.

It's a brief note, handwritten on a yellowed slip of paper.

"Professor Ludwik Berezowski, sought by Halina Świerczewska from Sosnowiec, the father of Anna Berezowska, is currently living with the child at Öblarn 27."[12]

In other words, right next door to the cottage where Anna lived with Rosa Stauder.

Ludwik?

[12] Document from April 1947, AAN, PCK Delegation in Austria, sygn. 11, karta nr 34.

***

I go to see Anna and show her a copy of the document. We meet at the headquarters of the My Wartime Childhood Foundation.

"Anna, have you ever heard anything about a Ludwik Berezowski?"

"No, never."

So it's time to look for Ludwik Berezowski.

I start with Jagiellonian University in Kraków, given the connection with Julian Genyk Berezowski.

The university replies that no one by the name of Ludwik Berezowski studied at UJ between 1850 and 1939.

"If you find any more detailed information – perhaps his middle name or any other evidence that such a person may have studied at Jagiellonian University – please write. In the course of our search we happened to discover on the website of the Polish Armed Forces Museum that a Ludwik Berezowski, DOB 31 May 1894, was a captain (munitions)."

Anna Berezowska examines documents in her Warsaw flat

I turn next to the Historical Office of the Central Military Archives. They have personnel records for a Ludwik Berezowski, son of Mikołaj, born 1894 in Latyczów.

Another clue points toward Breslau. I check with Wrocław University (which then was called *Schlesische Friedrich-Wilhelms-Universität*) whether a Ludwik Berezowski was enrolled as a student or employed as a teacher. The university conducts a search which comes back negative.

My next step is to ask the Wrocław District Court if they have records of any court cases from the 1960s involving Anna Berezowska, Ludwik Berezowski or Anna Świerczewska. This is because Halina repeatedly travelled to Wrocław, supposedly to visit a dentist. As it turns out, the trips were to deal with "wartime matters" related to Anna. At first the Court refused to disclose any information unless Anna came in person. But at that particular time, health problems absolutely precluded any possibility of travel. Later came the news that none of the regional courts under the Wrocław District Court's supervision were able to locate any case files.

The next clue leads to the Osobowice cemetery in Wrocław. The mother of a friend helps track down the grave of Karolina and Ludwik Berezowski. I learn that the grave is tended by a granddaughter and paid for through 2034. Ludwik Berezowski came from the southeastern borderlands of Poland, from a small town near the present-day Ukrainian city of Lviv. I write to the management board of the Wrocław Municipal Cemeteries, asking for contact information to the person paying for the Berezowski family grave.

"In response to your email, we wish to inform you that we passed on your request on 13 November 2017 to the person listed in our records as the custodian of the grave of the decedent Ludwik Berezowski. As of today we have not received an answer nor has the letter been returned."

Silence.

***

"Did Halina ever pass along any information?"

I ask because even though Anna was legally adopted by Halina Świerczewska, they only met many years later.

"No, we were never good about talking with each other. We had other things to worry about."

***

From the PCK notes on Austria I learn that in 1945, the biggest concentrations of Poles were in the vicinity of Salzburg, Linz and Villach. They were mostly forced laborers (on farms or in factories) or political prisoners. Many Poles ended up in the area after fleeing from Vienna, which near the end of the war endured a several-week siege by Soviet forces.[13]

Besides the Polish Red Cross, other groups involved in aiding or tracing deported Polish children included the Polish Committee in Gmunden and the Polish Center in Linz. Employees of these organizations sought out Polish kids in Oberweis, Salzburg, and at the UNRRA Children's Home at Ebensee.

At that time, Austria was in total chaos. Funds were lacking and documentation was incomplete.

***

How does it feel to be 70 years old and still wonder who you really are?

When we meet for the first time, the table in Anna's flat is spread with documents she received from the Red Cross and the Arolsen Archives, along with letters from Johann Madl.

Anna goes over all the places she's been since she arrived in Poland in 1948. She lists the various people who took care of her. There are a lot of names to remember, and Anna keeps correcting herself. Katowice, Wisła, Jastrzębie Górne, Międzyzdroje, Wisła – that's where she started elementary school, Rybnik, Kętrzyn.

"What a mix-up!" she says.

Later there was the Little Children's Home in Otwock, which she doesn't wish to discuss. She was a teenager by then. "German bastard" was something she heard frequently in those years.

And now Warsaw.

The information in all these documents doesn't add up to a logical whole. None of the pieces fit together.

But the details in Anna's memory ring true. There was a long table in the farmhouse. Rosa and the wooden cottage did exist. Krampus was also there, but he didn't take the nipple. Anna is 74 years old, probably....

[13] Notes from PCK Delegation in Austria, Vienna, 30 November 1948, AAN.

“I no longer wish to look for anybody”

The document from the Polish Red Cross was probably compiled in February 1947. It is list of “children currently in Italy whose families are requesting repatriation.” The entry for Teresa Lindner contains a short annotation: “Uncle Edward Kryjan, Łódź, Rolnicza Street, I wish to take in and raise the child.”

The problem is that Teresa, now nine years old, is in Barcelona, at a special hostel for Polish children victimized by the Germanization program. The facility was sponsored by the Polish government in exile and the Spanish authorities. Little Teresa arrived there in April 1946, in the first transport of Polish children from the resettlement camps near Salzburg.

Who knew that Teresa’s Uncle Edward was trying to find her? Did Wanda Tozer, employed by Poland’s Honorary Consul in Barcelona, who was responsible for liaison between the Polish and Spanish authorities? Or Stanisław Horoba, headmaster of the school operating at the hostel? Did others on the school faculty or staff know?

Teresa certainly didn’t. She only finds out about it from us, 70 years later.

Back then, in 1947, the young girl should have been repatriated to Poland, since her family were looking for her. From the surviving documents, it’s not clear why the system failed. Perhaps the blame could be attributed to tensions between the Polish Red Cross subordinated to the government in exile, in this case through General Władysław Anders’ II Corps, headquartered in Italy, and the Polish Red Cross delegation in Austria, which reported to the communist authorities in Warsaw. It was the II Corps PCK which organized the first transport in 1946 of about 100 Polish children from the Salzburg camps to Italy and, ultimately, Spain. While this was happening, the Red Cross delegation in Austria was sounding the alarm that “shuttling children around from Salzburg to Italy, ostensibly for health reasons, needlessly complicates their repatriation.”

In the end, Teresa remains in Barcelona – for 10 long years. In 1956, she departs for the United States, where she gets married. Her last name now is Gilbert. Teresa has children and grandkids now. She never went back to Poland.

Teresa Lindner and Maksymilian Jadoch, Barcelona, 1955

"What's the point, if I don't know where to look for my family," Teresa explains in 2008 to a curious Spanish journalist.

Would Teresa's history have been different had she known about her uncle's search?

***

Today, at 80 years of age, Teresa doesn't want to dredge up the past. We've gotten in touch by email. She prefers to communicate this way because she's become hard of hearing – telephone or Skype are non-starters. When I ask whether she'd like our help in tracking down her relatives through the "Stolen children" campaign, this is her response:

"Please don't go to any trouble – I no longer wish to look for anybody. I spent 10 years in Spain, and if my uncle really wanted to find me, he could have gone to the Spanish Embassy in Warsaw and asked for some information. After all, they broadcast stories about us on Radio Free Europe. Now I'm just too old – I want peace and quiet in the few years I've got left. I'm sorry, I know that sounds a little harsh."

***

We had encountered each other a few months earlier. I came across a report that in December 2008, there had been an unusual gathering in Barcelona. The Polish consulate and the Barcelona City Council had organized a reunion of about 20 of the 130 Polish children who had found shelter in Catalonia after the war. My search for the members of this reunion led me to Cristina Fuster, the daughter of Wanda Tozer.

"It's very moving that after all these years, people still remember the experience of those who suffered so much during the war," Cristina writes back from Madrid. In a subsequent email she passes along contact information to Teresa Lindner, who was one of those attending the reunion.

We make contact in January. Teresa is genuinely surprised by my interest. The whole "Stolen children" campaign intrigues her and she asks how she can help. I ask her if she'd agree to go back to her painful childhood and talk about what she remembers before the Germans tore her away from her family.

Christmas in Barcelona, 1949

Bishop Józef Gawlina visits the Barcelona hostel, 1953

It takes nearly a month before Teresa answers. "In the end I decided that I'd prefer not to talk about it. In June, I'll be turning 80. I think it's high time to leave the past behind me. I've already told my children and grandchildren about it. It made them sad to think that my life didn't turn out the way it should have, but they're also proud of having that kind of mother and grandmother. Wishing you good luck with your inquiries."

Despite this refusal, we continue to correspond by email. We exchange information about our families, the "Stolen children" campaign, her friends from the Barcelona days and modern life in general.

"I don't think people today would be interested in things that happened nearly 90 years ago. We're living in a completely different reality now. Everyone's more worried about what's going to happen tomorrow than with what happened way back when," she writes in one email.

Then, suddenly, a surprise. In the meantime, it turns out that Teresa had mentioned me to her friend Aleksandra Gruzińska, also a victim of Germanization who was sent to Spain after the war and later went to the U.S. Aleksandra didn't want to talk with me herself, but she persuaded Teresa to do so. "[Aleksandra] still thinks I should agree to this interview," Teresa writes. "I don't remember much, but if you want to ask about something, go ahead."

Do I want to ask? You betcha! I email about 20 questions and settle down to wait. After a month, Teresa sends the first part of her reminiscences. The next comes two months later.

***

"I had two sisters and a brother, along with a mother and father. I don't know where we lived."

"We were Catholics. Mother kept a little shrine to the Virgin Mary with two candles in a corner of the house. I remember because I had to dust it."

"I can't remember the first names of my parents. For little children, it's always "Mommy" and "Daddy", anyway. I do remember the names of my siblings. The oldest was Stefania, then Wanda, whom I always thought of as my twin sister, and Jerzy, the youngest."

"My father had a small shoe repair shop. I remember fetching him dinner from home."

"I remember when he died. I was too young to know what he died of. His death came as a shock to our relatives and a lot of people came to visit. Daddy was lying in a bed and people were kneeling around him, praying. I remember the day of his funeral, when they laid him in the casket and loaded it onto a black hearse hitched to a black horse. But we children weren't allowed to go to the cemetery."

"I don't know how I came to the orphanage or where it was. The name "Kalisz" sticks in my mind. I know that I went to the orphanage with one of my sisters. My mother visited a couple of times and promised to take us away. But she wasn't able to in time."

"They separated me from my sister and gave me to a German family. They were childless, and I don't think they liked me – maybe because I was Polish. I really don't know when they even took me. Maybe they were paid money for it?"

"I don't remember the name of that German family or where we lived. I think the man was a tailor, but I didn't have much to do with him. I spent more time with the woman. She used to beat me. I don't know how long I was with them."

"I remember sitting in a shelter while we were being bombed. Afterwards, when we climbed out, there was a big crater in the garden. The windows were also blown out, but the house was intact."

"One day my "*Mutter*" came to school and took me out of class. At home some people dressed in uniforms wanted to talk with me. The German woman kept telling me to repeat in German: 'I don't understand,' and that's what I did at first. But they found a way around that by offering me some chocolate. That won me over. So I went with them to the Salzburg camp. The German woman never once visited me – not that I wanted her to. Then I landed in Barcelona."

***

Waiting for the next instalment of Teresa's reminiscences, I send her an excerpt from a Polish Red Cross letter that we discovered during the "Stolen children" campaign. It's the note confirming that Uncle Edward wanted to find Teresa and raise her. I ask whether she remembers such a person and would wish to locate possible relatives.

Teresa refuses. She doesn't want to open old wounds. Besides, she doesn't remember any uncles. "Uncle Edward from Łódź" means nothing to her. She repeats that she wants peace and quiet and apologizes for remembering so little.

"The mind is a treacherous beast. It shoves something into the unconscious and later you can't retrieve it. There must be some sort of terrible mental block that I can't break through, no matter how hard I try. I never even have dreams about those times," she writes.

The email ends like this: "Thank you very much for your interest in our stories. But now I just need to say goodbye."

The last group of Polish children departs for the United States, Barcelona, 1956

“They made a German out of her”

“Janka, I’m your brother. We all survived the war – me, Irena, Piotr and Eugeniusz. We’ve found you. Come back to us in Poland.”

Józef Sowa wrote those words in 1965 to his sister in Germany, who had been deported during the war and Germanized. She wrote back six months later, in German.

“I don’t know about having any family in Poland. I’m from here, I’m a German.”

***

Janka was a quiet, modest girl. When they took her away, she was not quite nine years old. The family who adopted her had lost their own daughter in an accident and needed help in their business making boots for the army.

***

“In order to get permission to visit my sister in Germany, I had to apply to the secret police. And they turned me down. I’m sure they thought I wanted to emigrate. Me? To Germany? After everything that had happened to us? We had gone through all that and survived. I had no need to go to Germany – it was my sister I was after. And I guess in the end that argument convinced them.”

But Janka couldn’t believe that she had a family. Józef travelled to Germany, stepped out on the station platform in Hannover and had a good look around. Who was he even looking for? Almost 20 years had passed. Then he caught sight of her walking on the arm of some man. She was an attractive young woman. Rolf’s wife, Jörg’s mother.

“Right away, I realized that she couldn’t speak a word of Polish. Then I thought that things had returned more or less to normal in Poland, so we could bring her back. But how do you bring a German woman back to Poland? She was raised there – one school, then another, a job, different history, different culture… She’d had that German identity drummed into her head something awful.”

***

"Jasia, do you remember Momma? 'Jasia' is what I call Janka. In Germany she's known as Anita. I ask her in German. She doesn't remember any Polish, even though she was already seven years old when they took her away."

"Jasia, you ran away through the fields with Momma and Irena."

But Janka doesn't remember anything.

"How can she not remember?"

***

"After the war, they called us very lucky (lucky! – Józef pronounces the word with ironic emphasis) not to have been sent to the gas chambers. But they had no idea what it meant to be an orphan during the occupation, or what it was like in Germany, being beaten by strangers."

All five Sowa children were taken to Germany in 1943. This may have happened 10 or 15 days after the raid on the Sowa farm that saw the bodies of their parents and the Jews they were hiding dumped into a lime pit. What the exact dates were, Józef doesn't recall.

"Our oldest brother Gene, who was 15 then, was sent to do hard manual labor on the estate of a German count in Grottkau, or Grodków today. The workers were housed in barracks there. Gene worked very hard to earn extra rations for us. The Germans trained me as a stable hand – I curried the horses and shoveled manure. Piotrek used to ride with the overseer to watch the field hands work – Russians, Germans, Ukrainians, Czechs. The overseer took him along just for fun. The whole time, they made him speak German."

What happened to your sisters?

"After everything happened, we boys waited for Jasia and Irena to show up. We didn't know whether they were alive or not, but they survived."

Irena was taken by a German farm family in a different village. She cared for the small children, did the laundry and the cooking.

Meanwhile, Janka was turned into a German girl.

Józef Sowa (1933-2023)

"Just like little birds, they plucked us out of the nest one by one. Jasia was taken by Marianne Pilch, a German woman born in Upper Silesia. A real Nazi – both she and her husband! He made boots for the Wehrmacht, and she was a den mother for the Hitlerjugend. Jasia had to work hard – she stretched the shoe leather on wooden blocks and did the cooking. They didn't let her go to school at all. Frau Pich said she'd been given a child to do the work as a gift from the German government. They called my sister Anita Pich, not Janina Sowa."

***

"I sat down with my sister and her husband at their dining table and told them the whole family history. Rolf, a German, broke down in tears and left the room. And my sister told me she'd had enough of these stories and that I had insulted her husband. I ate dinner without much appetite and stayed until breakfast the next morning, when I packed up my things and got ready to leave, to go back to Poland. But they asked me to stay and then things calmed down a bit."

"I ended up sending 12 days with my sister. Two days less than my visa. They packed some of their old clothes for me to take back. The German passengers in my compartment later made humorous comments about how my family loaded me up with junk on the platform. They didn't realize that I understood and spoke German. So I explained to them that I'd listened to their story and now I would tell mine – about my family and what Germans had done to us. At first, they listened, but when I started telling them how my parents had been murdered, they got up and left."

***

"We invited Jasia to Poland. It took some arranging, because at that time you needed to get permission to have a foreign visitor. We organized a family celebration to welcome them."

The day after Janka's arrival, Józef took her to visit the family grave. Everyone else thought it was a bad idea. Too overwhelming. But Józef insisted.

So he showed her where the house stood, where they ran away with Mom, where the farmyard and the orchard were. He showed her the place where the lime pit was dug, which the Germans later used to dispose of the bodies of their mother and father. The place was later marked by a provisional grave, a little mound topped with turf. That's when it all came back to Janka and she started crying.

Janka appears to be German. She dresses and acts like a German. Even after all these years, she's been to Poland maybe only five times.

"This isn't her country, it's not her Poland. It's a continuing emotional conflict, but also a political one."

Józef Sowa can't bring himself to accept the fact that her sister was taken away and effectively Germanized.

"All of us see that they made a German out of her."

"Every time I tell her stories and try to teach her a little history. But one time she pushed back that everything wasn't like I said, that Poles had also invaded other countries and murdered people and that I was just dead set against Germans. She simply hadn't experienced the whole thing the way we had. She simply didn't want to believe it."

"And your sister's husband, Rolf?"

"He was a very good man, but he's no longer with us."

"Back then at the table, when you were telling your sister the family history and Rolf burst into tears, was that because he was offended, the way your sister said?"

"No, Rolf was genuinely moved."

"Are you in touch with Janka's son, Jörg?"

Yes, Jörg – we call him Grzegorz – has started coming to Poland. He's interested in the family history."

***

Józef steps out cautiously into the field.

First to where the farmyard used to be, then, slowly, he steps over the threshold of a vanished house, peers into his father's workshop, into the barn.

He points to the hideout entryway, to the ventilation duct.

He paces off the distances.

He talks about how they used to grow cotton.

How Momma used to spin and then weave the cloth for scratchy children's clothes.

Dad was a carriage maker and used to haul provisions to the ghetto.

Józef stops for a moment to touch the cross.

"Goodbye, Mom and Dad."

Józef Sowa at his parents' grave

In Lieu of an Epilogue: The Pain of being Uprooted

The trauma of stolen children played out on many levels in their postwar lives. Those who returned to Poland after undergoing Germanization in the Third Reich were forced to re-learn the language they had forgotten. Some, it turned out, had no one to return to as all of their relatives had been killed. What memories could a person like that use to build their identity? How easy is it to live without knowing where you came from or who were your family and relatives? In the context of specific personal histories, just posing these questions opens up limitless horizons of fear and pain. This is what stolen children had to deal with their entire lives, often without ever getting any answers.

Biologically and psychologically, human beings are constructed to seldom remember events and experiences from their early childhoods. If they do, these memories usually recur as fragments, or more often are passed down through stories told by our immediate family. Most of us, however, at various points in our lives, have direct contact with small children – either with our siblings, our own children, or later with grandchildren. Interacting with them gives us some idea of their way of perceiving the world, allowing us to recognize their fears and phobias and read their emotions.

This cognitive strategy can help us understand today, almost 80 years after the events described in these pages, the scale of the tragedy experienced by young people who were subjected to a monstrous Nazi experiment in social engineering.

Extermination, Deportation, Refugees

This kind of social engineering – underpinned by ideologies of nation, race and class and understood here as a methodology for managing societies that goes beyond manipulation and propaganda to encompass deportation and mass murder – was not something peculiar to Himmler and the Third Reich.

Similar projects could be found in Europe both before and after the Second World War. One could recall the Armenian massacre of 1915-1917, carried out by the Ottoman Turks and followed by a refugee wave in Europe estimated to have numbered 115,000. This was followed by the end of World War I and the collapse of the Ottoman Empire, which forced about 1.3 million Greeks to emigrate from Turkey and Bulgaria.

Russia's October Revolution also released an enormous mass of refugees, estimated in 1922 alone to number somewhere between 700,000 and 800,000. And let's not forget the mass executions of people and groups regarded as hostile by the Soviet regime, not to mention deportations of whole ethnic groups such as the Tatars and Chechens, the 1940 Katyń massacre of Polish officers, or the example of young Pavel Morozov, who denounced his own parents and was presented as a symbol of the USSR's success in creating a "new Soviet man."

These trends were amplified after World War II as political decisions about borders and spheres of influence triggered mass population movements. One example was the "repatriation" to areas newly acquired from Germany of millions of residents from the eastern parts of prewar Poland, which by decision of the Yalta and Potsdam conferences had been awarded to the Soviet Union. This, in turn, required the expulsion of the German population from these areas to be given to the Polish state. One of the aftershocks of this human cataclysm was "Operation Vistula", or the Polish communist regime's mass resettlement of the ethnic Ukrainian population of southeastern Poland in 1947-1950 to crush a nascent nationalist uprising.

Meanwhile, from Germany and liberated areas of Western Europe, millions of refugees, slave workers, deportees and other war victims waited for an opportunity to return to their homelands and their loved ones. Often this proved impossible due to changes in the political map and the emergence of an "Iron Curtain" cutting the European continent in two.

In September 1945, the United Nations Relief and Rehabilitation Administration (UNRRA) was caring for 6 million refugees, a figure that does not include 7 million refugees in the Soviet occupation zones of Germany and Austria and about 12-13 million Germans who voluntarily or involuntarily left their homes in East Prussia, Silesia and other formerly German territories.

Childhood Trauma

In comparison to the numbers given above, an estimate of 50,000 to 200,000 Polish children (and up to 300,000 in Europe as a whole) abducted by the

Germans from families and orphanages for Germanization may seem like a relatively small figure. As always, however, it should be remembered that the victims of these ideologically motivated procedures were human beings. And it was they, usually left alone to their own devices, who had to deal with the psychological trauma of their wartime experiences. This situation was especially damaging to children.

Realization of this fact began to dawn while World War II was still underway. In Great Britain, several studies were performed in 1941-1943 on the effects of aerial bombing on children. Intuition suggested to the researchers that repeated exposure to stress and danger should have a negative impact on children's psyches. As it turned out, however, these negative effects depended on two main variables: 1) the duration of these negative, stress-inducing stimuli and 2) the presence or absence of a child's parents or caregivers.

One study, *Infants Without Families* (1943) by Anna Freud and Dorothy Burlingham, found that if the bombing took place while small children were accompanied by their mothers or other caregivers, they did not seem especially affected. The event was treated simply as another childhood experience.[1] In other words, the short-term nature of these traumatic events and the durable bond with their caregivers allowed these children to place these events alongside many others forming their general outlook on life.

On the other hand, the researchers found that if the traumatic experiences were prolonged, or if no sources of emotional support – whether parents, caregivers or other community members – were available to help children work through the trauma, then deep-seated psychological changes could occur. These could manifest themselves as changes in personality, behavior or moral development, and could take the form of Posttraumatic Stress Disorder (PTSD), a weakened response to outside stimuli, or diminished future expectations.[2]

Scholars also debated the importance of a child's age when the trauma occurred during a separation from family, especially mothers. Observation of Jewish children placed with foster families in the Netherlands after the war showed that children between the ages of two and seven were most sensitive, since this is the time of greatest maternal attachment and dependence. Children aged seven to 12

[1] Neil Boothby, "Displaced Children: Psychological Theory and Practice from the Field, *Journal of Refugee Studies*, vol. 5, no. 2, 1992, p. 112.

[2] Boothby, "Displaced Children".

displayed much more emotional independence, in part because of the natural need at this age of belonging to and identifying with a peer group. In adolescence, sensitivity to negative factors associated with family separation again increased, accompanied by an acute lack of self-confidence. Afterwards, dependency on parents gradually diminishes as young adults become autonomous.[3]

Later studies involving Cambodian refugee children who suffered psychological and physical harm under the Khmer Rouge regime also appear to confirm these earlier findings. Four years after these children left Cambodia, half were still showing symptoms of PTSD. Moreover, these PTSD symptoms were more likely to be manifested by children who were not living with their immediate family.[4]

In 1946, UNESCO estimated that 8 million children in Germany were homeless, along with 6.5 million in the Soviet Union and 1.3 million in France. The death rate among French children in the summer of 1945 was twice the prewar level, while in Vienna it was four times higher. In 1947, 35% of Czechoslovakia's under-18 population were suffering from tuberculosis. And to complete these nightmarish picture, 13 million European children had lost one or both parents.[5]

Effective Treatment

In the early days of the postwar period, social workers, foster families and other institutions specializing in caring for child victims were often surprised at the incredible resilience and speed with which their wards adapted to new conditions. At the same time, most of these children remained withdrawn, silent, and either mistrustful of adults or too susceptible to their authority.

The children were observed having difficulty with spontaneous play and continuing to employ a whole series of survival tactics, including concealing their true age, hoarding food,[6] carefully guarding their few possessions against the widespread practice of theft,[7] and a high degree of mistrust toward their adult

[3] "The Psychological, Educational and Social Adjustment of Refugee and Displaced Children in Europe", *International Union for Child Welfare. A report prepared at the request of the United Nations Educational, Scientific and Cultural Organisation,* Geneva 1952, pp. 32–33.

[4] Boothby, "Displaced Children", pp. 112–113.

[5] Tara Zahra, "Lost Children: Displacement, Family and Nation in Postwar Europe", *The Journal of Modern History* vol. 81, no. 1 (March 2009), p. 46.

[6] Zahra, "Lost Children", pp. 51, 53.

[7] "The Psychological, Educational and Social Adjustment", p. 34.

caregivers, often displayed in aggressive behavior.[8] Later, the children gradually opened up and smiles returned to their faces. They gradually began to build healthy relations with their peers and the frequency of pathological behaviors began to diminish. When it appeared that the children were over the worst and had begun to develop positive attitudes, setbacks and regression often occurred. This forced social workers to develop detailed therapeutic strategies and adopt a more long-term approached.[9]

Once again, a close correlation was noted between the presence of close relatives, especially mothers, and a child's ability to make a smooth, rapid return to social and psychological stability. As Maria Pfister, who studied child refugees in Switzerland, wrote: "Children who were separated from their natural or foster mothers, and especially those who witnessed their mothers being killed or taken away, are most likely to suffer serious psychological consequences, especially neuroses, stubborn muteness or excessive shyness."[10]

No Memories of the Past

The stolen children in this book were subjected to similar psychological and social processes. Since they were part of an academic study, we can only extrapolate from observations made of children who went through similar experiences during the war. One interesting example that may help us understand the tragedy of children torn from a safe, emotionally supportive environment is the case of the Polish children who found themselves in Pestalozzi, a small Swiss village, after the war ended.

As one of the authors of this study noted: "When the war began, most of these children were in Upper Silesia with their families or in orphanages. After the Third Reich's annexation of this territory, they became Germans. Their education was conducted in German and the older children were inducted into the Hitlerjugend. With the approach of the Red Army in 1945, these children were supposed to be evacuated, but instead they escaped through Czechoslovakia and Austria, where they ended up in an area controlled by the Western allies. Some were put in refugee camps, while others chose life as vagabonds.... Over the span of a few years these children were forced to leave their homes and twice changed their language, environment, culture, religion, and sometimes nationality. They were also subject to

[8] Boothby, "Displaced Children", p. 108.

[9] "The Psychological, Educational and Social Adjustment", pp. 35–36.

[10] "The Psychological, Educational and Social Adjustment", p. 37.

traumatic wartime experiences.... What perhaps is most striking is that they had no memories of the past that could be used to build upon. In other words, they were completely uprooted, and this fact at least partly explains the enormous difficulty these children had in adjusting to new circumstances."[11]

It would appear that similar problems confronted stolen children, especially those who were voluntarily or involuntarily repatriated to Poland after the war. Even in cases where relations with their German guardians had been strained, upon return they had often had to overcome the barrier of relearning the native language they had forgotten. To make matters worse, they had to do this in a postwar Poland that had become much more ethnically and culturally homogenous, and in which an official anti-German campaign (stipulating, among other things, that "German" should not be capitalized in violation of conventional spelling) made it difficult for them to establish normal relations with their communities and peers.

To this must be added all the psychological baggage typical of people with wartime experiences. The situation becomes even more complicated – especially in light of the research observations on refugee children discussed above – when abducted children were unable to build a positive relationship with their German caregivers after being torn from their native environment, and then after being repatriated, discovered that their families and relatives were gone. What usable memories would such a person have to build their own identity? How do you live without knowing your background, parents or relatives? The question "Where do I come from?" might seem abstract or nonsensical to most of us. But in the context of these individual stories, it opens endless vistas of anxiety and pain that the victims had to cope with for the rest of their lives.

Identity – Being Oneself

Some of the sociological theories on identity formation stress that consciousness of oneself is unceasingly shaped in relation to others, who form a milieu that helps define the individual and his or her place in the community. In other words, imagining oneself requires the participation of separate others, who are in some sense different from ourselves. In this sense, for example, I understand that I am a man because I know what a woman looks like; I am a Pole because I have met or learned about other people who speak different languages, cultivate different traditions, and observe different value systems. Identity in this sense is the product of an

[11] "The Psychological, Educational and Social Adjustment", p. 39.

individual's "moral horizon", which is a collection of orientation points that allow individuals to locate their own place in society. According to Charles Taylor, identity "situates me in the moral world, assigning me one place among all the many theoretical possibilities. It places me somewhere, as opposed to leaving me in a disorienting and unbearable 'nowhere'."[12]

Identity can also be viewed through the prism of continuity and change. From this perspective, it is a question of what causes me to remain me despite all the changes that occur in my life. Changing your hairstyle or outfit does not usually cause a loss of identity. The same is true for collective or group identities. We are not in doubt about our families and who belongs to them. Sports fans do not question the national team, even though the composition of the squad changes over the years and players are substituted for during the games.

It seems that memory is the crucial factor here, of events and symbols from our individual lives and those of our communities, which together provide a sense of continuity. The philosopher Leszek Kołakowski stated explicitly that "there can be no personal identity without the memory which makes it conscious – in other words, without the consciousness of one's history."[13]

The role of memory in forming personal identity suggests the existence of some kind of core, which despite all the changes that occur in life, allows one to retain a coherent vision of oneself and one's role in society.

As the academic literature on identity indicates, the self is by no mean homogeneous. The philosophical school of American pragmatism and symbolic interactionism in sociology both held that social reality is formed by a constant process of interpreting and negotiating the meanings ascribed to symbols. It is composed of the subjective I – which has reflexive self-knowledge – and the objective me – the "social self", which G.H. Mead defined as "an organized collection of other individuals' attitudes taken in as one's own."[15] By this definition, identity depends enormously on the community a person belongs to and on the collective culture of our closest relations or the group that constitutes our point of reference.

---

[12] Charles Taylor, "Źródła współczesnej tożsamości", in K. Michalski, ed., *Tożsamość w czasach zmiany. Rozmowy z Castel Gandolfo*, Wydawnictwo Znak, Kraków 1995, p. 10.

[13] Leszek Kołakowski, "O tożsamości zbiorowej", in K. Michalski, ed., *Tożsamość w czasach*..., p. 46.

14 Zbigniew Bokszański, *Tożsamość, interakcja, grupa: tożsamość jednostki w perspektywie teorii socjologicznej*, Wydawnictwo UŁ, Łódź 1983, p. 64.

[15] Peter Berger, Thomas Luckmann, *Społeczne tworzenie rzeczywistości*, PIW, Warszawa 1983, pp. 249–250.

This happens because we wish to act in accordance with the expectations others have about us. Taking the argument a step further, it's worth noting that this understanding gives the community the power to delimit an individual's identity. Especially in societies with a relatively simple social structure, it is hard to escape these defined roles. Indeed, in these societies, the objective self largely corresponds with the self-reflective subjective self.

As Peter Berger and Thomas Luckmann aptly observed, "everybody knows who everybody else is and who he is himself. A knight is a knight and a peasant is a peasant, to others as well as to themselves."[16] The oppressive character of these interactions can be seen in people who for some reason or other are stigmatized by their communities. This could apply to individuals – such as the physically or psychologically disabled – who do not fit within the repertoire of objective identities accepted by the community. The identities of people stigmatized in this way will be entirely determined by socially imposed definitions, regardless of whether they coincide with that person's subjective identity. In general, identities can sometimes be defined by small and apparently insignificant divergences and symbols. These draw a clear distinction between those who are on "our" side from "theirs."

From the interactionist standpoint, forming an identity is a constant process of negotiating its scope between the individual and society. In such situations, it is only possible to change an imposed identity when an individual succeeds in creating a subjective identity capable of standing up to the objective one. When the construction of such a "counter identity" is successful, heretofore stigmatized individuals begin to escape the bonds of socially imposed definitions and identities. They stop being who they were, disrupting the prevailing system of identification.

Children with No Mirrors

This sociological argument allows us to view the tragedy of "stolen children" from a different angle. How could individuals who knew so little about themselves be expected to adjust to a new environment? In effect they were already Germans, often proficient in the language and versed in its distinct cultural code. In what sense were they still Poles? Once they were repatriated home, these young people discovered that it was forbidden and a curse to be German. At the same time, the concept of Polishness was difficult to grasp and often alien to them.

---

16 https://amstudugm.wordpress.com/wp-content/uploads/2011/04/social-construction-of-reality.pdf, p. 184.

One could say that a combination of extremely unfortunate circumstances – especially the lack of immediate family to provide emotional support and fertile soil for re-establishing roots – accorded these stolen children a status even worse than homeless refugees, of whom there were multitudes seeking a place for themselves in the first postwar years. Very few of these children had any of the cultural competencies needed to begin assembling a self-identity. Stolen children, in particular, usually had no memory, sense of continuity, knowledge of their origins, or even a native language. Their reflexive selves could only focus on what was self-evidently true: I come from nowhere, I am foreign, I don't know where I come from or who I am. On the other hand, their objective identities, imposed by society, could become oppressive and stigmatizing.

To a certain extent the situation of stolen children can be compared to local ethnic minorities on the "recovered territories" awarded and annexed to Poland from Germany after the war. For the Germans, groups like the ethnic Silesians or Kashubians were Poles. For the Poles, they were Germans. They were treated as foreign intruders in their own homes. Socially stigmatized, they had few opportunities to escape their inferior status or at least find out who they were and where they came from.

Lesson for the Future

Finally, the stories of these people have something to tell us about the origins of postwar Europe. To some extent we are all progeny of these "stolen children", child refugees and orphans. Uprooted several times and forced into premature adulthood, they had to grapple with problems their parents and children never encountered.

Learning about their history gives us an incredible opportunity to understand how we became what we are today and why Europe chose the path it did in the 1950s – toward peaceful unification instead of something else. The stories of these children help us feel what it must be like for the more than 10 million child refugees currently roaming the world in search of refuge from the famines, wars, and religious and ethnic conflicts of our 21st century. To ignore the lessons of these stolen children would be both short-sighted and a grave sin of moral omission.

Acknowledgements

This book could never have been written if a teacher from Freiburg, Christoph Schwarz, had not raised the subject of abducted and Germanized children. His interest resulted in an exhibition whose significance was recognized by Jaromir Jankowski from Deutsche Welle, the German international broadcaster, and Michał Drzonek from the Polish website Interia.pl. Thus was born the Polish-German "Stolen Children" campaign, which marked a first international attempt to establish the identities and contact these victims of Germanization, who revealed to us the terrible story of thousands of Polish children.

Describing this forgotten chapter of history would have been impossible without the people who agreed to talk with us about their painful childhood experiences. Therefore, our greatest thanks are reserved for the heroines and heroes of this story – Zyta Suś, Teresa Lindner, Anna Szafraniec, Józefa Posch-Kotyrba, Halina Skalbmierska, Anna Berezowska, Józef Sowa, Julian Grudzień, Hermann Lüdeking, Folker Heinecke, Janusz Bukorzycki, Maksymilian Jadoch, Jan Dopierała and Henryk Kowalczyk. To them we owe a debt of gratitude for their openness and honesty, along with apologies for the pain we inflicted by probing their memories for details of events they may have tried long and hard to forget.

Thanks are also due those who helped us locate other surviving witnesses to the Third Reich's criminal racial policies. In particular, we should mention Tomasz Grzybowski, Karina Noga, Cristinia Fuster, Piotr Janiak, Mirosława Sosna, Barbara Pastuszka and Anna's family.

We are also grateful to archives and institutions whose employees assisted our research and helped us use their collections. They include: Joanna Lubecka (IPN Kraków), Artur Ossowski (IPN Łódź), Agnieszka Jaczyńska (IPN Lublin), Magdalena Sierocińska (IPN Poznań), Mariusz Olczak and Katarzyna Wysoczyńska (Archiwum Akt Nowych, Warsaw), Grażyna Schlender (State Archives in Kalisz), Sister Ruth Kawa (Sisters of the Holy Family of Nazareth convent in Kalisz), Dariusz Pawłoś and Agnieszka Dzierżanowska (Foundation for Polish-German Reconciliation), Andrea Rumpf (Achern-Illenau Archive), Corinne Schulze (Kohren-Sahlis Museum), Eulalia Rudak (My Wartime Childhood Foundation), Verena

Neusüss (ITS Arolsen), Jacek E. Wilczur, Andrzej Pozorski (Chief Commission for Prosecution of Crimes Against the Polish Nation), and the State Archives in Opole. We also wish to thank everyone who helped us to reconstruct the histories of particular individuals and places, including Teresa Szymczak, Andrzej Kaszubkiewicz, Dorothee Schmitz-Köster, Johann Madl, Roman Myrmus, Jerzy Bukowczan, Adelheid Planitzer, Rudolf and Irmine Lasser, Grażyna Wira, Leszek Chałupniczak, Maria Nowakowska, Janina Janicka, Lucyna Nowicka, Maria Jańczak, Stanisława Grzeszczak, Elżbieta Guszczak, Urszula and Hieronim Michalak, Anna Marcinkowska, Valentin Stocker and Edward Haduch.

We would also like to acknowledge the video operators, film editors and photographers from Interia.pl who helped document our research trips: Krzysztof Zając, Marcin Rapacz, Paweł Krawczyk, Agnieszka Skierczyńska, Kamil Langie and Dominik Langie.

Credit is also due to our bosses, who simply decided that this story was worth chasing. From Deutsche Welle, we wish to thank Rozalia Romaniec and Bartosz Dudek, and from Interia.pl, Krzysztof Fijalek as well as the late Zygmunt Moszkowicz, who passed away while the campaign was being prepared and especially, Wojciech Olszówka, for his efforts in editing and preparing for publication a book co-written by six authors. As long as a single victim remains alive and troubled by thoughts of his or her lost identity, the story of these stolen children will not be over.

Photograph and Illustration Sources

Agnieszka Waś-Turecka

Ewelina Karpińska-Morek

Monika Sieradzka

Tomasz Majta

Interia (video stills – Krzysztof Zając, Marcin Rapacz)

Paweł Krawczyk

Private collection of Anna Berezowska

Private collection of Barbara Pastuszka/Mirosława Sosna

Private collection of Folker Heinecke

Private collection of Halina Skalbmierska

Private collection of Henryk Kowalczyk

Private collection of Hermann Lüdeking

Private collection of Janusz Bukorzycki

Private collection of Józef Sowa

Private collection of Jan Dopierała

Private collection of Maksymilian Jadoch

Private collection of Piotr Janiak

Private collection of Zyta Suś

Archiwum Akt Nowych

United States Holocaust Memorial Museum, courtesy of Lydia Chagoll

United States Holocaust Memorial Museum, courtesy of G. Howard Tellier

United States Holocaust Memorial Museum, courtesy of James Blevins

United States Holocaust Memorial Museum, courtesy of Lilo, Jack and Micha Plaschkes

United States Holocaust Memorial Musuem, courtesy of Robert Marx, Yaffa Eliach Collection, Center for Holocaust Studies, Museum of Jewish Heritage, NY

Sisters of Nazareth Archive

Illenau Arkaden Museum

Polish National Digital Archive (NAC

Institute of National Remembrance (IPN)

ITS Arolsen

Wikimedia Commons (Mathiasrex), (Aleksander Bartel)

The views or opinions expressed in this book, and the context in which the images are used, do not necessarily reflect the views or policy of, nor imply approval or endorsement by the United States Holocaust Memorial Museum

Sources

I. ARCHIVAL COLLECTIONS

Archiwum Akt Nowych [Central Archive of Modern Records, Warsaw]

Documents on the search for Polish children in Germany and Austria after World War II, including activities of the Polish Red Cross (PCK), foreign delegations of the PCK, the Polish government representative for restitution, the International Refugee Organization (IRO), and the State Repatriation Office.

Archiwum Instytutu Pamięci Narodowej [Institute of National Remembrance Archive, Warsaw]

Files concerning the Germanization of Polish children, the RuSHA (Race and Settlement Main Office) trial, and the fate of slave workers in the Third Reich.

IPN investigation files on murders committed by Nazi German officials in 1943-1945 of Polish children born to forced workers in the Third Reich.

IPN investigation files on the extermination activities of German staff at the children's facility in Wąsocz, near Rawicz, in the years 1943-1945.

Archive of the International Tracing Service (ITS), Bad Arolsen

Documents on Lebensborn activities and the fates of Germanized children.

State Archives, Kalisz

Tadeusz Martyn collection.

Kalisz municipal records

Gostyń Museum Archive

Edmund Nowak, lecture given on the unveiling of a memorial plaque to the victims of Germanization at the palace in Bruczków, Sept. 1, 1971.

Sisters of Nazareth Archive, Kalisz

Documents and photographs on the Kalisz *Gaukinderheim*.

II. DOCUMENTARY COLLECTIONS AND MONOGRAPHS

Adamczyk, Wiesław, *Kiedy Bóg odwrócił wzrok. Odyseja wojenna, wygnanie i wybawienie* (wstęp Norman Davies), Poznań 2011.

Berger,Peter, Luckmann,Thomas, *Społeczne tworzenie rzeczywistości*, PIW, Warszawa 1983 [Polish translation of Berger and Luckmann, *The Social Construction of Reality: A Treatise in the Sociology of Knowledge*, Garden City, NY 1966].

Bokszański, Zbigniew, Tożsamość, interakcja, grupa: tożsamość jednostki w perspektywie teorii socjologicznej, Wydawnictwo UŁ, Łódź 1983.

Fedorowicz,Agnieszka, *Skutki eksperymentów medycznych przeprowadzanych na kobietach i dzieciach w niemieckich obozach koncentracyjnych*, Lublin 2010.

Haduch, Edward, "Niemieckie zakłady paliwowe w rejencji opolskiej", Stowarzyszenie Blechhammer1944, http://www.blechhammer1944.pl/artykuly/34/Nie-mieckie-zaklady-paliwowe-w-rejencji-opolskiej

Hagen, Carrie, "This Orphanage Did More Than Find Homes for Children of the Holocaust. It Helped Them Reclaim Their Humanity", *Smithsonian*.com, March 14, 2017, https://www.smithsonianmag.com/history/orphanage-helped-them-recla- im-their-humanity-180962516/

Herrmann, Theo, *Hildegard Hetzer in Polen*, Mannheim 2012.

Hopfer-Pfister, Ines, *Geraubte Identität*, Böhlau Verlag, Wien, Köln, Weimar 2010.

Hrabar, Roman, *Skazane na zagładę*, Wydawnictwo „Śląsk", Katowice 1989.

Hrabar, Roman, *Hitlerowski rabunek dzieci polskich (1939–1945),* Wydawnictwo „Śląsk", Katowice 1960.

Hrabar, Roman, *Polenlager,* Wydawnictwo „Śląsk", Katowice 1972.

International Union for Child Welfare. The Psychological, Educational and Social Adjustment of Refugee and Displaced Children in Europe, Geneva 1952.

Jaczyńska, Agnieszka, *Sonderlaboratorium SS. Zamojszczyzna – Pierwszy obszar osiedleńczy w Generalnym Gubernatorstwie 1942–1943*, Lublin 2012.

Kawa, Ruth Jadwiga CSFN, Congregation of Sisters of the Holy Family of Nazareth, *Czas wielkich spraw. Wojenne losy kaliskich nazaretanek, Zgromadzenie Sióstr Najświętszej* Rodziny z Nazaretu, Kalisz 2018.

Kołakowski, Leszek, *O tożsamości zbiorowej, Tożsamość w czasach zmiany. Rozmowy z Castel Gandolfo*, K. Michalski (red.), [w:] Wydawnictwo Znak, Kraków 1995.

Koop, Volker, Organizacja Lebensborn. Rozrodcze stajnie Himmlera, Wydawnictwo Bellona, 2014.

Kubica, Helena, Zagłada w KL Auschwitz Polaków wysiedlonych z Zamojszczyzny w latach 1942–1943, Warszawa 2004.

Kuligowski, Wiesław, *Ja – Claus Kugler*, Fundacja „Moje Wojenne Dzieciństwo".

Malinowska, Anna, *Brunatna kołysanka. Historie uprowadzonych dzieci*, Wydawnictwo Agora, Warszawa 2017.

Pod okupacją niemiecką, Fundacja Polsko-Niemieckie Pojednanie, Warszawa 2016.

Polacy w Barcelonie. *Album historii. Polskie dzieci ukradzione przez nazistów pod opieką miasta (1946–1956)*, Konsulat Generalny RP w Barcelonie we współpracy z Ajuntament Barcelony, 2008.

Represje niemieckie wobec obywateli II Rzeczypospolitej w okresie drugiej wojny światowej, Fundacja Polsko-Niemieckie Pojednanie.

Schmitz-Köster, Dorothee, Deutsche Mutter bist du bereit – Alltag im Lebensborn, Aufbau Taschenbuch 2010.

Sierpowski, Stanisław ed., *Dzieje ziemi gostyńskiej*, Wydawnictwo Naukowe UAM, Poznań 1979.

Sługocka, Ludmiła, Bruczków. Tajna szkoła polska i dom dziecka w byłym zaborze pruskim, Poznań, Bogucki Wydawnictwo Naukowe, 2015.

Spodzieja, Ryszard, *Moim domem był Gaukinderheim. Historia ofiar Lebensbornu*, Black Unicorn, Jastrzębie-Zdrój 2012.

Staszyński, Ludwik, *Przemoc, poniżenie, poniewierka. Wspomnienia z przymusowych robót rolnych 1939-1945*, Warszawa 1967.

Taylor, Charles, Źródła współczesnej tożsamości, [w:] Tożsamość w czasach zmiany. Rozmowy z Castel Gandolfo, K. Michalski (red.), Wydawnictwo Znak, Kraków 1995.

United States Holocaust Memorial Museum, Greta Fischer papers, id 1993.23.553

Uzarczyk, Kamila, *Podstawy ideologiczne higieny ras i ich realizacja na przykładzie Śląska w latach 1924–1944*, Toruń 2003.

Wilczur, E. Jacek, Hrabar, Roman, Tokarz Zofia, *Czas niewoli, czas śmierci*, Wydawnictwo Interpress, 1979.

III. PERIODICALS

Boothby, Neil, "Displaced Children: Psychological Theory and Practice from the Field", *Journal of Refugee Studies*, vol. 5, no. 2, 1992, pp. 106-122.

Bosacki, Zenon, Siejak Maciej, "Tajemnica pałacu w Bruczkowie", *Gazeta Poznańska*, January 1967.

"European Childhood in the twentieth century", special issue of *The Journal of Modern History*, vol. 81, no. 1, March 2009.

Figielek, Jan, "Wieczornica poświęcona Marianowi Pogaszowi", *Ziemia Borecka*, nr 3(13), March 2000.

Gruzińska, "Aleksandra. "Children Remember The War: Polish Children In Barcelona (1946-1956)," *The Polish Review*, Vol. 55, No. 1 (2010), pp. 111-122

MAZ, "Marian Pogasz – Stary Marych," *Gazeta Poznaska*, May 23, 1997.

"Ośrodek germanizacji polskich dzieci", *Słowo Powszechne*, nr 203, 1991.

"Prawdziwej zasłudze cześć", *Przewodnik Katolicki*, January 23, 1927.

Rudzińska, Anna, "Losy gostyńskich dzieci w okresie okupacji niemieckiej", *Nowa Gazeta Gostyńska*, nr 38 (281), September 21, 2008, and nr 39 (282), September 28, 2008.

Smoluchowski, Zdzisław, "Pani na Bruczkowie", *Panorama Leszczyńska*, nr 17, April 24, 1988.

Zahra, Tara, "Lost Children: Displacement, Family and Nation in Postwar Europe", *The Journal of Modern History* vol. 81, no. 1 (March 2009), pp. 45-86.

Zduńczyk, Jacek, "Skazani na wynarodowienie", *Kalisia*, nr 11 (42) November 1997.

Zielonka, Jerzy, "Tajemnice pałacu w Bruczkowie", *Gazeta Zachodnia*.

IV. FILMS

Dobrowolski, Ireneusz, *Portrecista*, documentary film about the work of Auschwitz camp photographer Wilhelm Brasse, 2005.

Lehmann, Elisabeth and Sieradzka, Monika, *Stolen Children. The kidnapping campaign of Nazi-Germany,* documentary film about the abducted children of Poland, DW/MDR 2020.

V. OTHER

Personal interviews and private collections of the subjects of this book and their families: Anna Berezowska, Janusz Bukorzycki, Halina Bukowiecka, Jan Dopierała, Folker Heinecke, Julian Grudzień, Maksymilian Jadoch, Piotr Janiak, Henryk Kowalczyk, Teresa Lindner, Hermann Lüdeking, Józefa Posch-Kotyrba, Halina Skalbmierska, Mirosława Sosna, Józef Sowa, Anna Szafraniec, Zyta Suś, and Ilona-Helena Wielganowicz.

POLNISCHEN
MÄDCHEN
STRUZIKOWNA
Walter
POLEN—
JUGENDVERWAHRLAGER
14 IX
Nr. 356